KT-442-823

ELEVEN MINUTES LATE

A Train Journey to the Soul of Britain

Britain gave railways to the world, yet its own network is the dearest (definitely) and the worst (probably) in Western Europe. To Matthew Engel the railway system is the ultimate expression of Britishness. In his quest to uncover its mysteries he travels the system from Penzance to Thurso, exploring its history and talking to politicians and station staff. Engel (half-John Betjeman, half-Victor Meldrew) finds the most charmingly bizarre train in Britain, the most beautiful branch line, the rudest railwayman, and after a quest lasting decades, an Individual Pot of Strawberry Jam. A polemic and a paean ... it is also very funny.

ELEVEN MINUTES LATE

ELEVEN MINUTES LATE

by

Matthew Engel

Magna Large Print Books
Long Preston, North Yorkshire,
BD23 4ND, England.

British Library Cataloguing in Publication Data.

Engel, Matthew
    Eleven minutes late.

    A catalogue record of this book is
    available from the British Library

    ISBN   978-0-7505-3199-3

First published in Great Britain in 2009 by Macmillan
an imprint of Pan Macmillan Ltd.

Copyright © Matthew Engel 2009

Cover illustration © Neil Gower

The right of Matthew Engel to be identified as the author of this work
has been asserted by him in accordance with the Copyright, Designs
and Patents Act, 1988

Published in Large Print 2010 by arrangement with
Pan Macmillan General Books

All Rights reserved. No part of this publication may be reproduced,
stored in a retrieval system, or transmitted in any form or by any
means, electronic, mechanical, photocopying, recording or otherwise
without the prior permission of the Copyright owner.

385. 0942

Magna Large Print is an imprint of Library Magna Books Ltd.

Printed and bound in Great Britain by
T.J. (International) Ltd., Cornwall, PL28 8RW

To Geoffrey Moorhouse

friend, mentor, uncomplaining traveller

CONTENTS

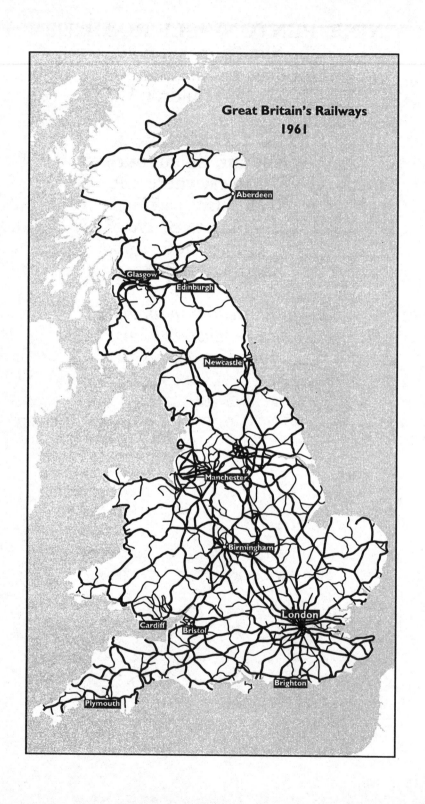

Great Britain's Railways
1961

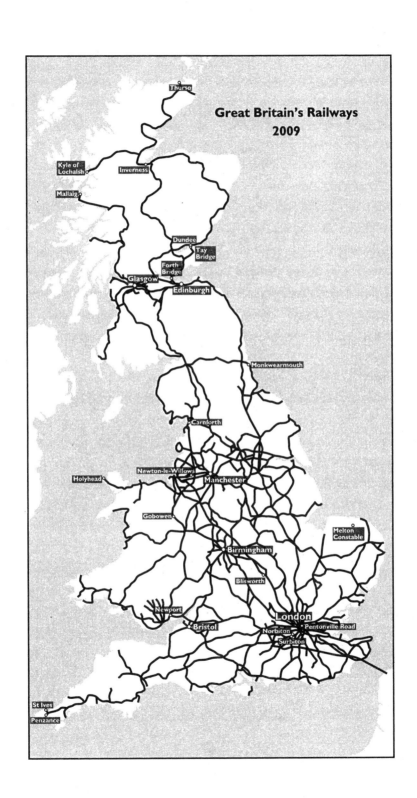

Great Britain's Railways
2009

PROLOGUE

GOBOWEN

Like so many of its nineteenth-century counterparts, the old railway town of Oswestry, on the Shropshire-Welsh border, no longer has a railway.

Since 1966 the stopping-off place has been the little village station of Gobowen, about three miles away, conveniently placed mainly for an indifferent-looking pub called the Hart and Trumpet, whose local nickname is easy enough to guess. If your mind works that way.

The station at Oswestry was and still is, in its sad, redundant way, rather grand. Along with many others, it is described in Gordon Biddle's guide, *Britain's Historic Railway Buildings*, as 'Italianate'; in most cases the Italian influence must have been clearer to the architect than to the average passenger. Gobowen is different. 'Incomparable,' Biddle calls it. 'A delightfully detailed Florentine villa.'

The buildings are in white stucco, very nicely restored. On a spring morning it is easy to imagine the *signora* emerging on to the platform into the strengthening Tuscan sun, perhaps to pluck a lemon to pep up her husband's evening *scallopine*. She is played – in my fancy – by Juliette Binoche: raven-haired, sleepy-eyed, an unpretentious floral print dress drawn tight at the bodice in a manner that would also enliven his dinner.

Gobowen acquired its own modest celebrity in railway circles because, in the 1990s, a group of girls from nearby Moreton Hall School took over the ticket office under the aegis of their geography teacher, David Lloyd, and yanked the place out of its decaying torpor. David Lloyd is dead now; the schoolgirls have dispersed where schoolgirls go; and there is no sign of Juliette Binoche either. Instead, a slightly disdainful-looking woman presides over the ticket office, which would have the atmosphere of a public library were it not for the presence of what must be the loudest digital clock in Shropshire, clunking away the seconds until the arrival of the 0744 to Marylebone.

But what an arrival! For this is no ordinary train. It is a new enterprise, as striking as the revival of the station, operated not by schoolgirls but by the Wrexham, Shropshire and Marylebone Railway. This splendid Victorian-sounding name disguises what should be the height of modernity, a train that specifically owes its existence to the privatization of the railways, a process completed by John Major's Conservative government in 1997, months before the voters ejected it from office with overwhelming force.

So, there we were in 2008, a mere eleven years later, awaiting one of the fruits of that most contentious legislation: an 'open access' train, one that neither British Rail, in its dying fall, nor its successor franchisees could or would contemplate – a direct link from Wrexham, through Gobowen and the Marches, to London, something that had

16

not existed for more than forty years.

The train has been provided not by the official franchisees but by outside entrepreneurs, who had negotiated the thorn-plagued thickets that constitute the privatized British railway business and gained permission to run up to five trains a day in each direction. Here was capitalism at its most beautiful. Anyone can run their own train: I can do it, you can do it. In this case, Deutsche Bahn, the nationalized German railway, was at the head of the consortium doing it.

This was only the third example of open access to emerge since 1997. One of the others, Hull Trains, was run by the ubiquitous First Group; the other, Grand Central, operating out of Sunderland, already looked troubled. But still it was a fine notion. Open access!

There was perhaps a good reason why the organizations that already had access had not thought of putting on such a train. This was because it was taking four and a half hours from Wrexham to London. Even if you spent the night alongside Juliette Binoche amid the lemon groves of Gobowen, it would still be quicker to get to London by driving to Liverpool and catching the Virgin train from there. Deutsche Bahn, which is not entirely stupid, was said to be interested in 'positioning'.

So not many people were waiting for the 0744. But what a treat everyone else missed. It came out of Wrexham General, the last station in the country still to be known as 'General', which makes it sound more bustling than it actually is and gives it a hint of the 1950s. Like the train itself.

The engine was a Class 67 diesel, the loco-motive entrusted with those other survivors, the Royal Train and the Fort William sleeper. It was pulling old inter-city stock, slightly shop-soiled, offering a sense of spaciousness in an era filled with hurry and rush. It felt too as though we were traversing a more spacious railway network through a more spacious country. I waited for wisps of smoke to pass the window, and a shrill steam-engine whistle. All the carriages were inviting but I sat in first-class to relish all the possibilities. *The Times* and the *Guardian* were both offered free. It should have been the *Manchester Guardian*. Perhaps they had news of Sputnik? Had there been a good hanging lately? That Gilbert Harding's not been getting himself in trouble again, has he?

And there was food, something regarded as an absurd frippery by most modern railway com-panies. 'Our menus are especially designed to bring you the finest fresh produce, all sourced from the Wrexham and Shropshire route,' said the blurb. I chose the Arbroath lemon kipper, in Ms Binoche's honour. It was a bit soapy but, one way and another, I was too enchanted to care.

Our course was so circuitous that it's entirely possible that Arbroath really was on the Wrexham and Shropshire route. We certainly stopped at Tame Bridge Parkway, though it wasn't clear to me whether we were crossing the Tame near Birm-ingham, the one in Manchester or the one that flows into the Tees. Or maybe it was the Tamar? We could rule out the Thames: we were still a heck of a way from London.

18

The company had not got permission to pick up passengers at Wolverhampton, or even to stop officially at Birmingham New Street or Birmingham International, the most substantial stations on the way. To avoid temptation at New Street, we took a most extraordinary set of back-doubles round the city, the sort of passage you might expect from an expert taxi driver rather than a railway train. These lines must previously have been known only unto God and the most zealous of experts. We saw Birmingham's limited supply of great tourist attractions, passing both football grounds: Villa Park and St Andrews. Gosh, is that Spaghetti Junction over there? Oh, look, there's an old fridge by the track. Shall I nip off, pick it up and clamber back aboard? There was time enough at this pace.

We did stop at Birmingham International, though the doors remained shut. Bewildered passengers on the platform asked who and what we were, as they do when the *Orient Express* or a steam special comes through. At Banbury we stopped but again could not pick up, merely put down anyone who chose this method of getting from Wrexham and Shropshire to Banbury, instead of using a cock horse. Hereabouts we picked up a little speed and, if I hadn't been paying attention, I might easily have missed the graffiti just south of Haddenham and Thame Parkway (which I don't think is the same as Tame Bridge Parkway): BRING BACK STEAM, it said.

I almost thought we had.

It was only the WS&M's fourth week of operation, and it was just getting started. By now the staff should be putting less soap in the kippers. The 2009 timetable was somewhat more urgent. (Half an hour has been knocked off the official journey time. However, Virgin Trains have retaliated by introducing a direct service from Wrexham via Crewe.) Wi-fi was said to be imminent, though I still think a telex machine might have been more appropriate; maybe some facility for the guard to telegraph ahead. This was the kind of train Prince Albert could have appreciated. As he said, after one of his earliest journeys on the Great Western, barrelling through the Berkshire countryside at more than 40mph: 'Not so fast next time, Mr Conductor, please.' This company does have a genuine sense of history too: it has named an engine after David Lloyd.

It was the sort of journey John Major ought to have been envisaging when he dickered with bringing back some version of the 'Big Four', the pre-war regionally based companies that he felt constituted the apogee of the British railway experience. Do I mock? Yes, but I feel very very mean about it. On its home ground Deutsche Bahn is, in my experience, magnificent. Its British subsidiary, Chiltern Railways, through whose territory we were now passing, has shown ever since privatization a remarkable, indeed matchless, commitment to making its train service better for its passengers. And in truth I cannot remember when I felt quite as relaxed and contented on a British train. I didn't want the journey to end. All my life I have loved travelling on trains, at least in theory. I was never a trainspotter (good heavens, no, not me, the very idea), and later on I'll prove it. But I have always been with Edna St Vincent Millay on this:

My heart is warm with friends I make,
And better friends I'll not be knowing;
Yet there isn't a train I'd rather take,
No matter where it's going.

She was a woman and an American, and could get away with sentiments like that. It's harder when you're a British male and have to deal with the psychological baggage connected with trains that has been lurking in the national subconscious ever since the railway was invented. I think I'll prove that later too.

But whenever I have had the chance or the choice I have taken the train. Lucky enough to have found newspapers daft enough to employ me and send me round the world, I have always quietly sneaked away on days off and found the railway station. I have even occasionally persuaded employers to send me abroad to take trains. I rode one of the last regular Canadian Pacific trains from Montreal over the Rockies to Vancouver before they closed the route: three days of pure bliss in a womb-like compartment amid the most extraordinary company, all lovely, all a little batty.

Later, the photographer Sean Smith and I became the first people, I'm convinced of it, to go from London to Berlin entirely by train: the Channel Tunnel was not open officially and everyone else being offered freebies was just going to Paris, having a long lunch and wandering round the shops. We went via Berlin to Hel (in Poland). And back, for the hel of it. (The old Night Ferry across the Channel (1936–1980) carried railway carriages on board ship. But that was a boat ride, not a train ride).

Sitting in quiet, comfortable railway carriages I have felt the cares of the world melt away in the most careworn places – in the Karoo Desert of South Africa in the 1970s, with the smuts from the funnel of a great Garratt loco snowing through the open window (the past lingered there, with a steam engine at the front and non-whites confined to the back).

In Cairo I remember being overwhelmed by black-clad Moslem women so desperate to grab a seat that they ignored the doors and swallow-dived through the windows. In total contrast, I rode another segregated train in a country with the initials SA – from Riyadh to Dammam, on the eve of the first Gulf War, with unaccompanied women barred, and accompanied women confined to special compartments. Husbands, brothers, fathers and sons were their only acceptable companions under Rule 1 of the Saudi Government Railroad Organization. This rule was in place, my neighbour explained, not because the Saudis did not respect women. 'Maybe we respect them too much,' he said.

I did meet a girl on the little diesel that winds its way from the Indian plains up to the cool of Simla. And I spent a most blissful day on the toy train that used to jog amiably through the achingly beautiful Jamaican hills from the slums of Kingston to the lapping waters of Montego Bay, picking up hawkers and trying to avoid goats, until too much of it was washed away by Hurricane Gilbert in 1988, and the line was abandoned for ever.

The ride doesn't even have to be scenically spectacular. All I have ever wanted has been calm, outer and inner. My happiest journey of all was a Sunday morning ride from Amsterdam to Paris. Six hours, I think. Damn-all to see, unless you count Belgium. An empty compartment; a guard occasionally offering coffee; an engaging novel. But one country always seemed to be absent from the list of happy journeys. In Britain I'm usually rushing to get somewhere. That didn't apply that springtime morning in Gobowen. All I was doing was writing a book.

I decided to write it one frosty morning in early 2007. I was travelling, as I often do, from Newport to Paddington – an hour earlier than strictly necessary because defensive travel has become an important shield against the vagaries of Britain's railways. That day, a prime spot on the Radio 4 *Today* programme, the first prize in the lottery of British lobbying, had been given over to a man with the unmemorable name of Anthony Smith, the chief executive of something called Passenger Focus, which purports to represent railway passengers.

Smith is appointed by the board of Passenger Focus which in turn is appointed by the government. This book will look in some detail at the role of successive British governments in the history of rail travel. At this stage, let's just say this puts Smith roughly in the position of a court-appointed defence lawyer in a Soviet show trial. He is allowed to put in the odd word on behalf of his clients – and indeed is frequently quoted in the news media – provided he does not do so too vigorously. In the Soviet Union that would have got him shot. This being Britain, it would merely endanger his OBE. Smith means well and is a cogent analyst of railway problems. But he is not exactly Mr Forceful and, on this occasion, he seemed to have forgotten which side he was on, and spent one of the most coveted slots in British broadcasting criticizing the train operators for not collecting fares with sufficient vigour.

Now one should always be mindful of the fate of the philosopher Professor C.E.M. Joad, the star of the 1940s radio programme *The Brains Trust*. Joad fell from grace for what was described in court as 'a common ticket fraud'. Travelling from Waterloo to Exeter, he told the ticket collector he had got on at Salisbury. He was fined £2 with 25 guineas costs, was sacked by the BBC and died in disgrace. Apparently, he did this all the time; it may even have been part of his philosophy. Against that, there is the more recent case of Tony Blair who, shortly after ceasing to be prime minister, was discovered on the Heathrow Express, ticketless, cashless, cardless. The conductor was so starstruck that he rejected offers of payment from the entourage and let Blair ride free.

The less bold among us generally pay our way, and have not considered a reluctance to rake in money as a major fault on the part of modern train operators. Rather the reverse: with them, corporate avarice generally seems more obvious than commitment to service, hence all the mousetrap-style automatic ticket barriers, an innovation neighbouring countries have managed to avoid, and one which slows up further the process of getting on a train. As in other countries, the companies have now provided ticket machines. However, thanks to the combination of Britain's ticketing regime and a mindset towards passengers that did not appear to bother Anthony Smith, these are often laid out so the unwary can easily be trapped into buying the most expensive fare imaginable.

That was not a problem in Newport that morning: the barriers were functioning but the ticket machines were not. 'The machines are bust,' I said to the vaguely uniformed figure patrolling the barriers. 'Would you tell me if the toilet was broken?' he asked. 'Why, are you in charge of the toilets then?' 'No. I'm not in charge of the machines either.'

The ticket clerk, his job presumably threatened by the march of technology, was certainly uninterested in the problem. As things stood, he was greatly in demand. And by the time I'd queued to see him, I had to race over the footbridge to catch the 0739. It could have been late; it could have been cancelled; it could have been packed owing to the cancellation of the previous train; it could have been on time and then stopped dead owing to a points failure at Didcot or the breakdown of a freight train at Swindon or a landslide near Bristol Parkway or a fault in the wiring in the Chipping Sodbury tunnel; six women in the quiet carriage might have been screaming into their mobile phones or – as happened one bleak morning – someone from the Environment Agency Wales might have chosen that very spot to give a full-throated, hour-long lecture to his colleagues, with everything short of a PowerPoint demonstration. And First Great Western might have forgotten to put on the dining car, as happened frequently around this time.

None of these things happened. Instead, they were serving breakfast. Yes, I do have a thing about breakfast. And the full First Great Western breakfast is one of the hidden delights of British life, an astonishing survival. It exists on only two trains – one from Plymouth and one from Swansea. It can even be listed with the Gobowen to Marylebone service as one of the few things that improved after privatization because, after British Rail was abolished, baked beans were added to the bacon, sausage, egg, tomato and everything. The breakfast is not advertised, it is not marketed, sometimes it is barely even announced. It is expensive but worth it, unquestionably the best breakfast on the network; I expect its abolition any minute.

I can't remember whether I had the full English that day or the kippers, which are never soapy on this service. But somewhere around the second helping of toast I took the decision to write this book. I wanted to explore the disasters and delights of Britain's railways, their geography, their history and their mystery – not just for what they are and what they were, but for what they say about the very strange country that they serve.

I love trains. I hate trains. This is a book about

trains. This is not a book about trains. It is a little about me. It may be a lot about you. This is a book about the British.

CHAPTER ONE

NEWTON-LE-WILLOWS

The train that now runs between Liverpool Lime Street and Manchester Victoria, currently operated by a company called Northern Rail, is unprepossessing even by the standards that the British have come to expect.

A two-car diesel Class 150 is scheduled to do the thirty-one-mile journey in sixty-four minutes, which is faster than the two hours achieved in 1830, but somewhat slower than you would expect between two great cities whose conurbations merge into each other. Especially these two. (Slightly faster trains go from Manchester Piccadilly.)

For it was on this route, only slightly modified by the passing years, that it all began. And I do mean *all*. It is reasonable to argue that what happened here in 1830 marked the beginning of not just the railway age but of the modern world as we have come to know it. None of the inventions and developments in communication since then has transformed the way of life that existed beforehand as completely as this one did. Not the telegraph, not the telephone, not the motor car, not the

27

aeroplane, not the internet.

There had been means of transport that might have been called railways for centuries before the Liverpool & Manchester. The Babylonians had roads with smooth stone blocks to ease the passage of vehicles; the Syracusans had roads with grooved tracks; copper miners in Cumberland were pushing wagons between rails in the 1560s. Probably some American intelligent-design theorist has concluded that Cain was run out of Eden on the morning express.

Dozens of experiments created the conditions that made the Liverpool & Manchester Railway possible; 375 miles of track were already open in Britain using a mixture of horsepower, manpower, gravity and a little steam. The most notable was the Stockton & Darlington, opened five years earlier by the chief begetter of this railway, George Stephenson. But even that was substantially dependent on horses. On 15 September 1830 Stephenson showed the world that it was possible to produce locomotives that could convey passengers and goods at speeds which even winged horses could never contemplate.

All this is recorded in (truly) thousands of other books. This is not a formal history of the railways. The outline of the story is here, but it is the footnotes of history that I find most fascinating and which seem to me to teach us something remarkable not just about the railways, but about Britain, about the world, about the way we are governed and where we might be going. Or, since we are talking about transport, not going.

And 15 September has an extraordinary

footnote: a tragic one, yet also bathetic; from this distance, it has to be said, the story usually makes people chuckle rather than cry.

The Death of a Dithering Politician...

Close to Newton-le-Willows station, south of the tracks and just on the Manchester side of a road bridge, there is a memorial. There was once a station here too, Parkside, but now the memorial is ludicrously placed since it is virtually impossible for the unprepared traveller even to glimpse it unless the train stops unwontedly. And the drivers – having moved lethargically through the Manchester suburbs – seem to take particular pleasure at speeding up round here.

The writer Simon Garfield thought the memorial looked like a railwayman's rain shelter. He studied it more closely than I did, but I thought it was instantly recognizable as a memorial: perhaps the local squirearch's family sarcophagus in a country churchyard. The only reliable way to get a better look is to approach it from the road and trespass onto the tracks. And the subtext of the inscription is that you really shouldn't do that.

The memorial commemorates 'THE RIGHT HON. WILLIAM HUSKISSON M.P.' who, on the opening day of this railway, was knocked over by an oncoming train as he tried to hold a particularly ill-timed conversation with the prime minister, the Duke of Wellington.

The accident 'deprived England of an illustrious

29

Statesman and Liverpool of its honoured Representative', according to the inscription, which is indeed true. Huskisson was a figure of considerable significance in the development of nineteenth-century economic policy who pursued notably advanced free-trade policies as President of the Board of Trade. They were certainly too advanced for Wellington, who happily took advantage of a threat of resignation that was not actually intended and, in 1828, got rid of him.

As part of Huskisson's general philosophy in favour of international trade and industrialization, he was an early enthusiast for the development of the Liverpool & Manchester, at a time when there was a great deal of scepticism about the whole notion of railways. Unfortunately, Huskisson is one of those historical figures – like the archduke Franz Ferdinand – whose entire life has been eclipsed by the nature of his death. He is now remembered primarily as the first person to be killed by a train, although this is not exactly true. Indeed, there is a record of two boys being 'slain with a wagon' on one of the wooden pit railways in County Durham in 1650. An experimental locomotive blew up, also in Durham, in 1815, killing sixteen, and there are reports of pre-1830 fatalities on the Stockton & Darlington.

The inscription also says that Huskisson was 'singled out by an inscrutable Providence from the midst of the distinguished multitude that surrounded him'. This is not true either. He was singled out for being a bloody fool.

Huskisson, Wellington, three future prime ministers in Grey, Melbourne and Peel, and a

30

whole host of other celebrities of the time were travelling in the first train to leave Liverpool, pulled by the engine *Northumbrian*, driven by Stephenson himself. Seven other locomotives also made the journey, on the parallel track.

Huskisson was no longer in the government; indeed he and Wellington were barely on speaking terms, and he evidently saw the day as a chance to patch up relations. The north-west was Huskisson territory. The previous night he had spoken to a huge crowd in Liverpool, telling them what prosperity the railway would bring, and had been rapturously received. He had marked the success by drinking a fair quantity of wine and was now evidently rather hung over.

When the train stopped at Parkside to take on water he got out and walked towards the duke's private carriage, 'dripping with gilt and crimson drapes'. Some of the trappings of stagecoach travel would remain part of the railways for years to come, likewise the etiquette and habits. It seemed quite normal for the guests to take a stroll on the road – even this new iron road – when the opportunity arose. Huskisson may have been emboldened by the success of the previous night; the duke, however, was very much off his normal territory. He was famously wary of modern innovations, and was also on difficult political ground: with the pressure for electoral reform growing, Manchester, a city without an MP of its own, was expected to give him a mixed welcome.

Huskisson clambered up to the carriage, and Wellington greeted him cordially enough. At that moment the shout went up: 'An engine is approaching. Take care, gentlemen.' (Even at moments of alarm, nineteenth-century man seemed to find the time to be long-winded.) Nearly all the guests on the track either got back into their carriages or took refuge on the embankment. Two did not.

The engine was the *Rocket*, driven by Stephenson's associate Joseph Locke, later to become a famous engineer in his own right. Locke responded by using the only means of braking available to him: throwing the gear lever into reverse. Huskisson, along with his companion William Holmes, was left clinging to the side of the duke's carriage. Had he stayed completely still, as Holmes did, he would have been safe – just.

Huskisson was always considered a bit sickly and accident-prone, with one foot permanently damaged after an unfortunate accident in the Duke of Atholl's moat. And that morning at Parkside, he was suffering from an unpleasant inflammation of the kidneys and bladder, compounded by the ancient curse of gout. The hangover might not have helped either. According to Garfield, who has provided the most complete modern description:

Huskisson doubted his judgment and began to move about. He manoeuvred his good leg over the side of the carriage, but those inside failed to pull him in. Holmes cried to him by his side, 'For God's sake, Mr Huskisson, be firm!' at which point Huskisson grabbed the door of the carriage. Unable to bear his weight, the door swung wide open, suspending him directly into the path of the engine. The Rocket *hit the door, and*

Huskisson was flung beneath its wheels.

In my fancy, the explanation is slightly different. Confronted by the need to take a decision involving transport, Huskisson suffered precisely the same mental block that was to afflict just about every British politician from that day to this. He dithered, he panicked, he got it spectacularly wrong. The death of William Huskisson was to be a motif for nearly two centuries of British policy-making, which has left the country with a staggeringly inadequate system of transportation.

Huskisson did not die instantly. The *Northumbrian* rushed him towards Manchester, past oblivious, cheering crowds. He was taken off the train at Eccles, still conscious, and carried to the vicarage. There he was placed on a sofa, given brandy, laudanum and the best available medical attention. The wound to his leg was beyond the resources available in Eccles in 1830. He died at 9pm, the very moment when guests were sitting down in Liverpool to begin the kind of banquet (turtle, Dee salmon, stewed partridges, roast black game; the works) that would be a regular feature of railway opening days across the world for the next seventy years and more.

The inscription is right on another point. The tragedy 'changed a moment of noblest exultation and triumph ... into one of desolation and mourning'. Indeed, the day was pretty dire even for those who yet knew nothing of Huskisson's fate. Wellington quickly decided he did not care for the mood of the Manchester crowds and ordered that he be returned to Liverpool as fast as possible. It was a grim journey back, though. Among the spectators, the disgruntled now outnumbered the excited: one train hit a wheelbarrow, apparently placed on the line deliberately; some were pelted with missiles thrown from bridges; the locomotives were starting to fail. Wellington had had enough and got out short of Liverpool, staging a strategic retreat to the Marquis of Salisbury's house at Childwall.

Only twenty guests sat down, two hours late, for the turtle, Dee salmon and all. Most of the others were still stuck on the railway, unable even to yell 'Nightmare!' down their mobiles to their loved ones, as their descendants would do after far less nightmarish journeys on Northern Rail or Virgin. And yet, before there was time to bury Huskisson, the success of the railway became an established fact. Anyone who read the story understood that the tragedy was not the railway's fault. All the fears that had assailed the public while railways were being discussed in the 1820s now melted away. The locomotives did not explode. The noise did not stop nearby hens laying or send cattle insane. The speeds did not send the passengers into paroxysms of shock.

Even at the conservative official speed limit of 17mph (though the train carrying the stricken Huskisson had touched 35mph), the railway was almost twice as fast as the quickest stagecoach. Within weeks the coaches were being forced to slash their fares. On 5 October the *Liverpool Times* carried five adverts promoting further railway companies. By the end of the year the railway was carrying the mail and running excursions. Other parts of the kingdom, the Continent and the world rapidly took an interest. Railways 'burst rather than stole or crept upon the world,' said the American writer C.F. Adams.

The Liverpool & Manchester was a stunning success, and a British success. Throughout the nineteenth century, and into the twentieth, British engineers and British capital crossed the planet to hand this great boon to the world. It *was* a boon too. Railways gave markets to farmers and traders who previously had none. They brought fresh food to cities that had previously known none. They brought knowledge where there had been ignorance. Public enthusiasm for the railways as a means of transport would not be in any doubt for nearly a century until the private car came along to issue a challenge as devastating – and as unexpected – as the challenge that the railways, in their turn, had delivered to the poor old stagecoaches and canals. All that was as true in Britain as anywhere else.

And the Birth of a Very Strange Relationship

Yet from the start there was always something odd about Britain's welcome for the railways. It was as though the bizarre dichotomy of that opening day – the triumph and the tragedy, and indeed the rather ludicrous nature of that tragedy – had left an indelible mark.

Commercially, no one had any doubt whatever.

35

Railways were seen as the transport of the future, which they undoubtedly were – and therefore a surefire means of making money, which they undoubtedly were not. This attitude survived the collapse of the 'railway mania' of the 1840s, one of the great boom and busts of history. After a short period of recovery, investors piled back into railway shares. And towards the end of the century – by which time every route that could conceivably be profitable had long since been built – local businessmen continued to put money into schemes to link remote locations to the national network. By then they were largely motivated less by greed than by pride, optimism and a powerful belief that their trade and their community could not thrive if they remained isolated.

Among intellectuals, the attitude was decidedly different. The response in both art and literature was far more muted and wary in Britain than in other countries, a point I will come to later.

And among politicians, confusion reigned from the start. Huskisson's indecision – do I climb aboard or run away? – produced immediate echoes. By the time the young Victoria came to the throne in 1837, it was clear that the infant industry was about to become a dominant force in the life of the nation. Yet parliament could not form a coherent view about its own duties. It had to balance the prevailing philosophy of laissez-faire against the case for regulating such an extraordinarily powerful industry.

Until the closing years of the century, it opted almost invariably for non-intervention except when public pressure became irresistible. Parliamentarians had their own angles too. By the 1860s more than a hundred MPs were directors of railway companies, and the 'railway interest' was very adept at steering governments away from interference. Trailing behind the British gave other European governments a chance to learn from the pioneers' mistakes. And each of them, to a greater or lesser extent, rejected the British model and opted for a system of government control.

The attitude of Victorian passengers was ambivalent too. As the railway ceased to be a novelty, their own lives changed and became increasingly dependent on the railway and the companies that ran it. Public attitude soon assumed a very British hue: tolerance, patience, exasperation, good humour, even affection. This was shown in the way the companies' names would be unofficially translated:

S&D   Somerset & Dorset
        Slow & Dirty

M&GN   Midland & Great Northern
        Muddle & Go Nowhere

S&MJ   Stratford & Midland Junction
        Slow, Mouldy & Jolting

L&B   Lynton & Barnstaple
        Lumpy & Bumpy

LC&D   London Chatham & Dover
        Lose 'em, Smash 'em & Turn over

MS&L   Manchester, Sheffield & Lincolnshire
       Money Sunk & Lost
(which became the)

GC   Great Central
       Gone Completely

All these were very apposite. I suspect the alleged nickname of the Great Western Railway – God's Wonderful Railway – was the creation of the company's highly effective public relations machine rather than a popular witticism. (The GWR's early routes to Wales and the south-west were circuitous, and Great Way Round seems to have been the popular choice). The GWR's twenty-first-century successor, First Great Western, became known as Worst Late Western, without any affection whatever. There were other nicknames too, like the Scratter in Northamptonshire (local slang: scratting about, which is self-explanatory really); the Tiddlydike (origin unknown) from Cheltenham to Andover; and the Crab and Winkle (two of them, one in Kent, one in Essex).

These days train travel has a different, greatly reduced, role in the daily life of the nation. And yet the British still maintain their unique, and uniquely perverse, relationship with the industry they invented. We find the railways a kind of exquisite torment.

The idea of trains as an enthusiasm and a hobby began in Victorian Britain, reaching its peak in the years after the Second World War. But at that time the appeal lay with the main lines

38

and the throbbing power of the great loco-motives. By the early 1960s, however, railways were going out of fashion, both as a means of transport and as a hobby. Politicians were anxious to annexe the word 'modernization'. It was a word that meant whatever the speaker wanted it to mean, like 'revolution' in the mouths of student activists later in the decade. But in utter contrast to the 1830s when railways were the epitome of modernity, they were seen now to be its very antithesis.

It was against this background that Dr Richard Beeching, the chairman of the British Railways Board, was able to carry through his programme of line closures with no coherent national oppo-sition and often very little at local level either. This period was very brief. The bulk of the clos-ures had been effected by 1967 and steam trains vanished from the British rail network the following year. Very quickly after that, the mood changed.

The 1970s saw a swing back to more traditional British values, i.e. a misty-eyed nostalgia. Coun-try cottages, which previously could hardly be given away, became more desirable than new homes. The modern British Arcadian dream took shape: living in a cottage (always 'with roses round the door') close to an oak-beamed pub serving real ale, and cricket on the green. And the vanished branch lines and steam trains became an important part of that make-believe idyll. The railways as such were no more popular than they had ever been, but they now had a fixed place in the landscape of the imagination.

Further closures became politically impossible, and if the railway line no longer existed, people would do everything possible to recreate it. By 2008, the European Federation of Museum and Tourist Railways (Fedecrail) included 102 passenger-carrying preserved railways in Britain and Ireland among its members. In the rest of Europe combined, there were 117. Its meetings were said to be totally dominated by the British.

Britain became dotted with heritage railways, from Keith & Dufftown in the Highlands to the Lappa Valley in Cornwall. On a summer's day in some parts of the country (e.g. rural Norfolk) it might be easier to catch a steam train than a bus, let alone a train on the former network. This attitude exasperated Edward Heath, prime minister from 1970 to 1974, who was what you might call an old-fashioned modernizer. He referred disparagingly to those who believed there was an alternative to expansion: 'an England of quiet market towns linked only by steam trains puffing slowly and peacefully through green meadows'. But that was *precisely* the England which many of those who could afford it did now want, provided their own train was somewhat faster, if still peaceful.

In 2007 the magazine *Country Life* judged Kingham in Oxfordshire to be 'England's Favourite Village'. The concept was of course absurd – if it was England's favourite, it would be overrun and thus unliveable. Never mind. What distinguished Kingham above hundreds of other contenders (and raised its property prices as well) was that it still had its own railway station, making it a suitable place from which to commute to London.

The *Thomas the Tank Engine* books were modestly popular in my childhood in the 1950s, rather went out of fashion during the Beeching era in the 1960s before returning with a vengeance to become a publishing and marketing phenomenon. And the media remained fascinated by trains, on the public's behalf. In the nature of things, this manifested itself most obviously whenever anything went wrong. From the start rail travel proved itself remarkably safe (astonishingly so, given how rudimentary the procedures were in the early days, and how reluctant boards of directors were to invest in improvements). There have been horrible disasters, of course, but Huskisson was emphatically not the harbinger: indeed no one quite as famous has been killed on a British railway in nearly two centuries since then.

Since the end of the Second World War about 9,000 people have been killed on Britain's railways, less than a third of them passengers. The comparable figure for roads is above 340,000. Roads now account for about twenty times as many passenger miles as the railways, which still makes railways, by my reckoning, about twice as safe. Yet the media attention and fearfulness generated by each of those accidents is entirely out of proportion to the risk involved. At Grayrigg in Cumbria, on the West Coast Main Line, a Virgin train with 111 passengers derailed in February 2007, causing the death of an 84-year-old woman. Contrast the headline news caused by that incident and what would have occurred had she died in a car crash. This is not a new phenomenon, as we shall see. It is one that will require some explanation.

A prurient fascination with train crashes is considered normal; yet it is considered strange to be fascinated by trains themselves. In 1955 the chairman of East London juvenile court, Sir Basil Henriques, told a 15-year-old boy – accused of stealing to fund a trainspotting trip to Harrogate – not merely that it was 'abominable' to steal but that he should have grown out of such a 'babyish' hobby.

Later, the word 'trainspotter' became (along with 'anorak') a generic term of abuse for anyone seen as over-interested in any subject, instead of following the more socially acceptable national trait of languid apathy. This has frightened many insecure people – young men, especially – away from pursuing what interests them, for fear of seeming uncool. Particularly if that interest really is trainspotting.

The journalist Jonathan Glancey, in an introduction to a recent volume about John Betjeman on trains, said that a colleague had warned him he should steer clear of writing about railways. It smacked of childhood, he implied. 'Do your career no good, old chap.' (One has to take a deep breath and remember that it worked well for Betjeman.) Nonetheless, the media remain – on behalf of the public – fixated with trains. Above all, railways remain, as they have been from the start, an ever-reliable source of wry, bleak humour. A cartoonist's delight. A national joke.

But the railways are not a national joke. They

42

are a national disaster.

Creating a viable transport network in the twenty-first century is one of the most complex responsibilities of a modern government. It requires long-term planning and financial commitment. There is political risk because projects go wrong (remarkably often in the case of Britain). And the reward may be so far in the future as to be invisible to politicians concerned with tomorrow's headlines, next week's polls and next year's election.

The British response has always been to let events take care of themselves. Alone in Europe, Victorian governments stayed aloof from planning the railway system. Though Hitler was building *Autobahnen* in the 1930s, the British failed to begin to accommodate the desire for inter-city travel on fast roads for another twenty-five years. Aviation policy has been a mishmash of confused responses, characterized most spectacularly by the saga of the Third London Airport that, after a search for an acceptable alternative lasting decades, finally ended up on the site (Stansted) where Whitehall intended to plonk it in the first place.

There are reasons for this, some of them good ones. This is an overcrowded property-owning democracy, full of fractious, private people guarding their lives against intrusions of all kinds. No one wants roses round the door *and* a motorway at the bottom of the garden. (A railway might be slightly different, but only if it was there in the first place.)

Transport minister has always been a job for

ambitious politicians to avoid. 'It's the most miserable job in government,' said Sir Malcolm Rifkind, a former incumbent. 'Anything you do right, no one's going to know for fifteen years. Anything you do wrong, they know immediately.' Since the election of the Thatcher government thirty years ago, twenty different politicians have held the job. Even before that, the only politician who actually used the post to enhance her reputation was Barbara Castle (1965–68) although Ernest Marples (1959–64), of whom more anon, certainly enhanced his visibility. One transport minister, Alistair Darling (2002–06) is believed to have been specifically told to keep his department out of the headlines. A grey man to whom dullness came instinctively, Darling followed his instructions admirably.

The problem with this as a strategy is that the consequences do mount up over a couple of centuries. It might be possible to argue that every single major decision or indecision taken by British ministers since the railways began turned out to be wrong. Huskisson's mistake was merely the first. That would be stretching the truth a little too far, but the general principle holds good. And it has never been more true than now. For the moment, let's take one incredible example.

In 2007 a transport white paper was very sceptical about the benefits of railway electrification, which currently covers around 40 per cent of the British network, far lower than in comparable countries. In 2008, as oil prices shot through the roof, the then transport minister, Ruth Kelly, began to show some tentative enthusiasm for the

44

idea. 'I can see great potential for a rolling programme of electrification,' she said. However, she added that this could not start to happen before 2015. That will be 158 years after George Stephenson reportedly predicted that electric power would supersede the steam engine. ('I tell you, young man, I shall not live to see it, but you may, when electricity will be the great motive power of the world.') It will be 131 years since the emergence of electric traction as a viable means of powering trains. It will be 84 years since a government-appointed body, the Weir Committee, recommended a comprehensive programme of electrification. And that assumes the projects actually got under way in 2015, which experience suggests is implausible.

Britain continued to build steam locomotives until 1960. Meantime, a third of the British route miles that are electrified use the third-rail system, first described as obsolete in 1904.

Two of the main lines from London, those out of St Pancras and Paddington (God's Wonderful Railway), are by some distance the most important non-electrified railways in Western Europe. It will be difficult and expensive to upgrade these routes as they stand because other countries abandoned diesel high-speed trains long ago, and Britain would have to bear all the costs of developing a new version.

We don't yet know how Britain will be able to generate electricity, if at all, by the second half of the twenty-first century, though it seems safe to rule out diesel fuel as an option. We don't even know how we might be able to get around. It is, however, very likely that in a densely packed area like Europe, the most effective and sustainable method of inter-city travel will be something that looks very like a train.

In a country as small and crowded as Britain that is doubly true. By 2050 the automobile industry may well have refined the technology to produce a motor car that neither depletes the planet's resources nor pollutes its atmosphere. Non-polluting cars cannot, however, solve the problem of congestion. Despite the plodding progress of the railways and the artificially low fares offered by budget airlines, internal air travel within England has become an absurdity. And that is increasingly becoming true of travel between London and Lowland Scotland.

It would be hard to design a nation better suited to modern rail travel than Britain: it is a natural hub-and-spoke country. London is an overwhelmingly dominant power in the land. The trunk lines radiate out from there; so do the major suburban lines; the need for complicated cross-country journeys is much less urgent than in, say, Germany, where as in the US, there are plenty of cities contending for influence.

Yet a high-speed railway map of Europe is already taking shape. Britain is represented by one remote spur, the line optimistically known as High Speed 1, connecting London to the Channel Tunnel. This was finally completed in 2007, a mere 205 years after the idea of a tunnel was first mooted. By early 2009, the government had experts researching the idea of High Speed 2 from London to the North. There was no prospect of it happening in anything other than an unimaginably distant future: 2027, according to the Conservative Party even from the comfort of opposition.

One must allow for three factors: the difficulties of building through the British countryside; the weary fearfulness that afflicts a governing class with a long record of disastrous management of major public projects; and the temptations of short-termism that inevitably afflict here-today gone-tomorrow politicians whose main aim is not to be gone until the day after tomorrow at least.

Britain has never been able to reconcile the past and the future. That's the disaster.

CHAPTER TWO

PENZANCE

And so, to explore the subject, I started wandering, and a strange thing happened.

I arrived at Abergavenny, the nearest station to my home and a place I try to avoid. Going from there to the junction at Newport and then from Newport to London increases the possibility of being late exponentially. *Both* the half-hearted little two-to-three coachers that arrive here *and* the high-speed train to London then have to be on time. And of course, one of the wonders of the privatized railway is that the one no longer waits for the other.

But here was the strange thing: I didn't care any

more. I wasn't going anywhere – the idea was simply to move. I had the freedom of the railways – a two-week Rover ticket – valid everywhere on National Rail services except the Heathrow Express, and the Heathrow Connect service between Hayes and Harlington and Heathrow. (I loved that Hayes and Harlington bit; it made the place sound so enticing.) First-class, second-class, whatever. Eight hundred and sixty quid, a bargain. All I had to do was to make two rush-hour return journeys from London to Glasgow, making sure I had the free first-class Virgin breakfast, and I was practically in profit.

As it was, I made seventy-seven separate journeys. Long ones, short ones, lovely ones, vile ones, packed in sardine cans, sprawled out in luxury. And was I late? Not once, not within the railway industry's definition that doesn't count delays of less than ten minutes (five on short trips). And certainly never eleven minutes late. Not in seventy-seven train journeys. The perversity was unspeakable.

Because I was free: free from schedules and deadlines and meetings and pressure. If I couldn't catch one train, I'd get another somewhere else. The very notion of punctuality became an ethereal kind of concept. So I was always punctual.

This new self looked at Abergavenny station through new eyes. In the days when the town had three stations, this one – the old Great Western Railway station at Monmouth Road – was 'much the most handsome', according to Biddle. Another Italian villa, he says, though in this case there was no sign of Ms Binoche even in my imagination. But that didn't matter. It was a perfect spring morning. The sun was poking through the young ash leaves; the potentilla and periwinkle were in bloom on Platform Two; and the Blorenge, the mountain to the south-west, was standing sentinel over us as the mist slowly cleared. It was lovely.

And the Arriva Trains Wales service to Cardiff Central was on time, or to put it another way – as they are obliged to do on Welsh stations – the train to *Caerdydd Canalog* was officially *Ar Amser*. In reality, it was three minutes late, but who was counting? This was a four-carriage train, different types of carriages – leased under the bizarre system that was another creation of privatization – hastily spatchcocked together, presumably in anticipation of a large turnout. For once, it was almost empty.

A recorded message enjoined us to 'familiarize yourself with the safety notices in the passenger saloons'. In my lightheaded mood, with few people around, I was unperturbed by the funny looks I was getting by wandering around. Also, I loved the idea that we were in a *saloon*. So I obeyed the instruction. My saloon had fifteen different safety notices, some bilingual, some not.

(1) IN CASE OF EMERGENCY...
(Melin Argyfwng)

(2) CAUTION: KEEP CLEAR OF THE DOORS
(Rhybudd: cadwch yn glir o'r drysau)

49

(3) EMERGENCY DOOR RELEASE
(I Agor y Drws Mewn Argyfwng)

(4) EMERGENCY ALARM
[not available to monoglot Welsh-speakers]

(5) FIRE EQUIPMENT

(6) EMERGENCY EQUIPMENT AND FIRST AID BOX

(7) SMILE! YOU'RE ON CAMERA

(8) INCONSIDERATE BEHAVIOUR CAN GET PEOPLE HURT

(9) CAUTION. PULL DOWN

(10) DO NOT OBSTRUCT THIS DOOR

(11) NO LUGGAGE TO BE LEFT IN THIS AREA

(12) IF YOU DON'T TALK TO YOUR KIDS ABOUT DRUGS, WHO WILL?

(13) NO SMOKING

(14) LIGHT LUGGAGE ONLY ON OVERHEAD RACK

This clearly had not covered all the possibilities: there was no mention of what to do if we made an emergency landing over water, and how to attract attention while on the life raft. Still, the familiar voice repeated a few of them, for the benefit of those passengers who had not been wandering the saloon taking notes, and added just one more:

(15) PLEASE MIND THE GAP BETWEEN THE TRAIN AND THE PLATFORM

She didn't do this in Welsh, creating the possibility of a fearful death for any Welsh-language monoglots in Newport. This is a city where the residents are known to have difficulties with English, as shown by an infamous incident during one of the great British sexual-deviant panics a few years back when a mob vandalized a doctor's house, having become understandably muddled between the words 'paedophile' and 'paediatrician'.

Then, just as we came out of Caerleon, we crossed what I now know to be St Julian's Bridge over the Usk, glinting in the sunshine as it swerved its way down to the Severn. There was a view to the west, looking towards a wooded cliff above the river that might have been painted by a seventeenth-century master. I had never noticed this view before.

Then we stopped dead twice on the way into Newport station, and all of us had to run like hell to get our connections. Including, in my case, a last-minute shift over the bridge from Platform 3 to 4.

First-class, Second-class, 143rd class

I did have a plan, of sorts. The aim was to go down to Penzance, the southern and western extremity of the system, and then to Thurso, the northern extremity, as fast as possible, and after that come back at leisure. So the immediate task was to get on to a First Great Western commuter train to catch a connection to Penzance. But I was content, enthused, suddenly wide-eyed about what I normally took for granted.

Maybe my mood was infectious. More likely it was the glorious May morning, with the young women all in skimpy dresses. Yet somehow the crowd on the 0815 into Bristol Temple Meads seemed equally light-headed. By 2008 commuters on the very wispy network of lines into Bristol had become the most put-upon in the country, but the springtime had got to them.

The train was a Class 143 Pacer, the second most notorious type of train currently used in Britain. The Pacers are all to a greater or lesser degree buses, adapted for use on rails. Only one of the originals, the Class 140, was ever built: it was last heard of in the Scottish Highlands, awaiting restoration, possibly for use as a poultry shed. The Class 141s were sold to Iran, a little-known instance of the lengths to which Britain was willing to go to support George W. Bush and undermine the Iranian government. The 142s still lurk, ready to pounce, in remote corners of the system.

The 0815 was jammed-full at the start, though it became much fuller once we had gone through the Severn Tunnel and back into England. The windows were filthy, not in the normal way, but streaked, as though they had been cleaned with a rag specially greased for the purpose. The supports for standing passengers to hold looked new, painted bright green and hastily drilled into the ceiling, which was then never properly made good. The cowboys had ridden this range. When another train went by, the doors rattled alarmingly and the air whooshed from underneath, which on such a morning was rather welcome.

As more people joined, at Patchway and Filton Abbey Wood, the conductor asked us to move further down the car (no saloons now); my scalp began to itch, unaccountably. 'Is it always like this?' I asked a woman who had stood with me since Newport. 'Oh, no,' she replied. 'It's usually *much* worse.' 'What's a bad day, then?' 'When it doesn't turn up and you have to wait an hour for the next one.' 'Or when the previous one hasn't turned up and two lots have to pile on yours,' someone chipped in.

'You're all lucky,' said the conductor. 'You should see the trains they have down at Exeter on the Exmouth line. These are Pacers built by British Rail. Those are the Pacers built by British Leyland on a bus body...' Aha, the notorious 142s. 'They don't trust them to get this far. They have to take them to the depot and fix them every night.' And so a cheery general conversation began. 'Public transport is not run for the convenience of the public,' said a jolly man with a beard. And we all ruminated on that for a moment. Then a man in a check suit said suddenly: 'Something's going to go wrong in a minute.' And sure enough we squealed to a halt outside Temple Meads, and spent five minutes waiting for a platform.

There had been the promise of a 'brasserie', First Great Western's second-division form of catering, on the 0913 down to Penzance. 'Regret no brasserie service,' said the indicator board tersely. 'Buffet only.' The chef was on holiday, I was told. Who could plan for such an emergency?

First Great Western trains are often characterized by this curious air of panic. It's a combination of the company's attempts to repair its dreadful reputation for punctuality, and the 1970s slam-door carriages. Staff fuss around as though the departure of the 0913 was like the lift-off of the space shuttle. The guards press the button to alert the driver with a huge effort, as if desperate to make a deaf man hear. (I have of late noticed a slightly calmer mood, following a change of management. Slightly calmer, I said).

But we were heading for what has long been regarded as the most relaxed part of Britain – an image that First Great Western's predecessor, the Great Western Railway, itself propagated more than a century ago. And after we had left Bristol with the customary FGW sound effects of squawks, rattles, clanks, rumbles and hisses (plus a strange buzzing, as from a swarm of bees) we settled into a gentle West Country kind of rhythm. And I got a 'breakfast bap' from the buffet: 'Lincolnshire sausage with sweetcure bacon, boiled egg and tomato in a white bap.' I don't know what sweetcure is, but closer examination showed that the whole product had forty-seven different ingredients including E numbers 472(e), 471, 300, 450, 451, 300, 330, 331, 250, 415, 407, 202 and 160. Perhaps there was even a soupçon of Iranian Class 141.

And the miles went by, until we reached the most spectacular stretch of main-line railway in Britain, from Exeter to Newton Abbot – first along the Exe estuary and then, thrillingly, along the sea wall at Dawlish before returning to the calm of the Teign estuary.

Isambard Kingdom Brunel chose to build this southward extension of the Great Western hugging the sea, though it is not at all clear why. He was by temperament a showman and a gambler, and no doubt the route appealed to his sense of drama. It appeals to *anyone* with a sense of drama: YouTube has a selection of clips showing the waves crashing over the tracks.

It took only five months from the line's opening in 1846 for it to be severed by a storm. But at the time far more controversy attached to Brunel's scheme of running it as an atmospheric railway, using a pneumatic tube to provide air pressure for power instead of locomotives. This enabled trains to touch 70mph, twice the speed at which Huskisson was rushed to Eccles. But the weather perished the leather flaps sealing the pipes and the leather had to be greased with tallow, which encouraged the rats, who then ate what was left. And it was unreliable and expensive. The experiment lasted less than a year.

Still, the trains have run for more than 160 years, minus interruptions for inundations. The other two rail links connecting Plymouth to the east were closed in the 1960s. Network Rail spends £400,000 a year to maintain the cliffs, the track and the sea wall. The government, in keeping with its general policy on climate change, hopes that rising sea levels are just a nasty rumour.

The tide was high when we passed, and there was a serious hint of chop in the Channel. The spray leapt upwards and hurled itself towards the windows. I was enthralled. The man opposite me just kept doing his Sudoku puzzle.

Then it was on to the South Hams and towards Cornwall. The train seemed happier down here, and the sound effects became less alarming. The slower pace of life seems to suit First Great Western, especially in Cornwall where the curves and gradients mean their trains don't have to cope with the endless pressure of trying to be high-speed ones. The timetable allows more than two hours for the trains to do the eighty miles from Plymouth to Penzance. Even the noxious taste of the breakfast bap had begun to fade. But you couldn't forget Brunel.

There are moments to be really grateful that these ancient High-Speed Trains are not wholly enclosed like the new Virgin ones. It is still possible to disobey the traditional injunction of railway companies and lean out of the window to get the perfect view as you approach the Royal Albert Bridge that links Devon and Cornwall. Recent restoration works to coincide with Brunel's bicentenary cleared the view of the entrance to the bridge. And the words I.K. BRUNEL, ENGIN-EER, 1859 shine out in white above the iron-grey arch. Just in case you didn't know.

The Slow Train North

In Cornwall the fine weather had been and gone. Penzance is a grey, granite town which would not look out of place in the north of Scotland, and that evening we could have been there already.

In 1898 there was a serious plan to run light railways further west both to Sennen, just short of Lands End, and to St Just. The commissioners who adjudicated on these matters approved the ideas in theory but rejected the particular schemes on offer. By the time the Great Western had instituted new fast trains from Paddington to Penzance in 1904 (seven hours then, just over five now), there were motor buses to meet them. And the light railways were never required.

There is something about this notion of the end of the line that set my mind racing. The train stops in a large but rather gloomy trainshed before a very solid set of buffers, an information board, a prefabricated buffet (which looked as though it served prefabricated food) and an even more solid granite wall. What if the railway had gone on? Bursting through all that, and then through Branwell's Mill family restaurant, the 2K Nite Club, the Ultimate Goals Fitness Centre, the Baltic Deli and DV8 Body Piercing, some of which might not have been there in quite that form in 1898.

The 1A bus to Land's End leaves from over the road. So does the National Express bus to Edinburgh (dep. 1300, arr. 0730, £93 return). I was terrified of forgetting myself and somehow ending up inside DV8 Body Piercing, so I stayed sober and had an early night.

What was then the longest daytime train journey in Britain began in Penzance at 0830 the next day. The scheduled run for the 680-odd miles to Dundee was 11 hours and 55 minutes. But I was getting off lightly. Between the wars there was a direct Aberdeen to Penzance service that took 22 hours. It still ran, a touch more speedily, in the early 1990s, when Paul Bigland of *Rail* magazine discovered a couple of scallop fishermen who lived north of Aberdeen, worked two-weeks-on, two-weeks-off a boat in Penzance, and really did use this train to commute. This service was restored, but only going south, in December 2008, presumably to cater for the growing total-madman market. It takes 13 hours and 44 minutes, though you can arrive in Penzance at the same time if you leave Aberdeen 22 minutes later and change three times. There are actually quicker trains if you change four times. Dundee in one dollop was far enough for me, thank you.

In any other country, they would make a fuss of such a train. But this is Britain, and the Penzance to Dundee is now run by a company called Arriva, which specializes in buses but, under the mysterious processes which now govern the railway, had recently gained the contract for Cross Country Trains from Virgin. The 0830 is not called the *Granite Express*, or *Palm and Pine*, the *Cornish Scot*, the *Pasty'n'Haggis*, nor even the *Cattle Truck Special*. After more than a decade of privatized trains, these companies can't be bothered to make even the most basic gesture towards making passengers feel special. It is called XC3170, although the numbering of trains for public consumption is an alien concept in Britain.

The train was a Voyager: the seats are hard; the luggage space is niggardly; and the toilets are notoriously unreliable and smelly. It was also grotesquely inadequate. That was not immediately obvious leaving Penzance, but there were another thirty-four stations to go before Dundee. And even then we whistled contemptuously without stopping through boroughs as substantial as Gloucester, Burton, Chesterfield and Berwick. Apparently, the Voyager is better at the stop-start stuff than the diesel high-speed trains because it has decent acceleration.

'This isn't a long-distance train, it's a commuter train,' said the first conductor. We had many miles to go before I would grasp the reality of what he said. He had never previously met anyone doing the whole journey and looked at me with an awestruck expression, as if he had suddenly just recognized a celebrity. Preening myself rather, I wandered down to what was described in the timetable as a buffet, but was still billed here – in Virginspeak – as The Shop.

The staff said Arriva was planning to remove this, and replace it with a bike rack. It was already a dark and dingy affair, like a corner store in a demolition area: it had cans of lager, Cup-a-Soup and Kitkat. There were six sandwiches to feed the entire train. Virgin used to sell headphones and a pointlessly abbreviated range of paperbacks – even less choice than for the sandwiches – aimed at people who wanted to read not just something but *anything*. Already the staff were staring at a blank wall where the paperbacks used to be, and contemplating the notion of being relegated to pushing a trolley round the curves of the disabled toilets and through the piled-up bodies and luggage, which they assured me would be there soon enough. 'They haven't made much difference yet, Arriva,' said one of them. 'But you were proud to work for Virgin. They've got a reputation. But *Arriva?*' He almost spat. 'Morale's very low.'

Elsewhere, the mood was still very jolly as we trundled through Cornwall. A group of lads were on their way to a stag party: six of them already laying into industrial quantities of Stella and Strongbow. 'We're all going to Bristol,' said one of them cheerily. 'Except for the stag,' he said, pointing to a bulky bloke with a copy of the *Daily Star*. 'He's going to Dundee. He just doesn't know it yet.'

It took us two hours and eight stops to get out of Cornwall, and I began to be rather grateful we weren't starting from Land's End. The Cornish main line is characterized by a huge number of viaducts, which are more easily appreciated from off the train than on it; it hardly touches the coast until Plymouth, and the countryside is rather bland. By St Austell I fancied a drink myself, which was possible but did not seem, at 0922, very sensible. At Bodmin Parkway I felt an overwhelming urge for a smoke, which was at least ten and a half hours away.

But out there was Britain, and soon enough it looked amazing. Going east, you approach

Brunel's bridge at right angles, so you can see it clearly without leaning out of the window, which is lucky because the Voyagers are sealed boxes. You can't miss the inscription, and down below you can clearly see The Union Pub, which has its front painted up as a Union Jack and its side turned into a Belfast-style mural. The sun peeked through the cloud and danced on the Tamar.

After a while, the whole journey began to seem like a sampler of the best of Britain, like a tourist board video or the latest gimmick from the BBC presentation department: we passed almost everything except London. The great Dawlish stretch was a disappointment compared to the previous day: the tide was out, and the sea had gone back to sleep. This may have been lucky: one of the Voyager's original quirks was that the computer wiring was in the roof and malfunctioned if it was pummelled by salt spray, which made it a great choice for this stretch of line. By Taunton the train was filling, and there were bodies and bags all over the vestibules as the buffet attendant had predicted. One toilet now stank and the next had a pool of liquid heading steadily towards the door like a trail of blood.

At Bristol, we got a fresh crew, and I regarded them the way an old lag looks at a new screw. I'd been going for four hours now, a third of the way. Who did they think they were, coming in and taking charge? I'm a lifer, me. This is also the way railway staff regard each new franchisee. One guard I met in the north, who had been in the same job for twenty-five years, tried to list all the different companies that had ordered him around, and the different-coloured uniforms he had worn. He gave up in despair.

I resented each new passenger even more. At Cheltenham, a man of about eighty plonked himself opposite me: he had an East Midlands accent and a ticket for Derby, and a large computer on which he began playing muzak. 'I hope you're not going to be playing *that* all the way to Derby,' I said.

'No,' he said firmly. 'I'm going to play a DVD.'

'With headphones, I trust.'

'No, I didn't bring them.'

Under Virgin I could have sent him down to The Shop to buy some. Instead, I crumpled, and moved to the far end of the carriage where there was a solitary seat which, according to the electronic display, was available until Leeds, and it didn't actually say it was booked from there. Anyway, the dipsticks who reserve seats never turn up; it's a well-known fact.

The age-profile of the travellers was odd, I began to notice. The average was about the same as you would expect but it was made up of the very old and the very young. There was a high percentage of puzzlers, readers – *Daily Telegraph* readers in particular – and the deaf. The last two categories tended to overlap. One woman was reading out news items to her very hard-of-hearing and very elderly white-haired companion.

'Solicitor who spent victims' £220,000 on strippers is struck off!' she said, very slowly and distinctly, for the whole carriage to hear.

'*Struck off!*' repeated the old lady, as though this seemed unduly harsh.

There was also the news of the funeral of Gwynneth Dunwoody, the Labour MP. 'It's Mrs Dunwoody's funeral. You know, the wife of the doctor in Totnes.'

'She wasn't very well-liked in Totnes,' the old lady said.

'Oh, I think she was a very staunch MP.'

This cut no ice whatever. 'Not very well liked *at all.*'

(I almost rushed over to defend the reputation of the deceased. Mrs Dunwoody, the outspoken chair of the Commons transport select committee, had kindly agreed to be interviewed for this book but died before the date we had scheduled. In a parliament of munchkins, she was indeed a staunch MP.)

We progressed through the broad country of Gloucestershire and Worcestershire. This looked achingly beautiful, flecked with buttercups and may blossom, sometimes with an old orchard in full bloom. Spring lambs skittered away from the passing monster, perhaps terrified by the whiff from the toilets. The old lady was unimpressed. 'It's not going very fast,' she said.

'It's been going at quite a rate,' said her companion defensively. 'It's been going *along.* But I don't think it's been making much of an *effort.*'

She was quite right. Privatized trains are not meant to make an effort. They have to be on time to avoid a fine, and the timetable is designed to ensure that it's difficult for them not to be on time.

We reached the once-famous Lickey Incline, the steepest sustained gradient on the network:

63

two miles at 1 in 37 north of Bromsgrove Station. It used to pose terrible problems for steam locomotives, and special engines ('Lickey Bankers') were kept on hand to give them an extra shove. These days, it is barely noticeable, and the train hardly slows.

It slowed down on the flat instead. We crawled the last few miles into Birmingham, stuck behind a goods train, only just managing to overtake a narrowboat on the Worcester & Birmingham canal. There were quite a few railwaymen standing around now, heading for New Street and the start of their shift. Some were discussing their new bosses. 'What you're trying to tell me, Dave, is that apart from being a load of penny-pinching bastards, Arriva are all right?'

I got talking to an old hand about the privatized railway in general. 'It's the little things that have changed,' he mused, 'The things that don't get done. The piles of rubbish by the line. Cleaning the weeds. No one's in charge.' There is also the strange fact that, even when a train fails to make an effort, as the old lady said, and then gets stranded, it remains notionally punctual.

The character of the train changed at New Street. It was Friday afternoon, and people were starting to leave their offices for the weekend, so a more businesslike, more middle-aged crowd joined the throng. And it *was* a throng now; they were standing even in first-class. Further down the train, Chris from Lincoln had been sitting on his kitbag since Exeter St Davids.

'I've slept in worst places than this,' he said cheerfully.

'Such as?'

'A snowy field for three nights with people shooting at you.'

He had just come back from Lympstone, where he had passed the famously vicious three-day test for the Royal Marines. 'I can't get up anyway,' he said. 'I'm completely knackered.'

Others were less content. 'It's always a nightmare on a Friday,' said one regular, standing till Sheffield. 'It's no good them apologizing. They know it's Friday. They should put an extra carriage on.' He must spend the rest of his week in a logical world, where common sense can apply. But this is the railway, and we are on a train set. It's not a sensible train set, like my old Tri-ang, for which Auntie Maisie could buy an extra carriage on my birthday. The Voyagers come in sets of four or five; so to add to this five-car set, they would have to add at least another four carriages. And the process of doing that is far too complicated for a Friday afternoon; suffice to say it involves the siphoning off of the taxpayers' and passengers' money in another direction entirely.

Anyway, I didn't feel much sympathy for him. My niece Jenny, who uses this line regularly between Sheffield and her in-laws in Cheltenham, has often had to spend the journey sitting on her luggage even when heavily pregnant. And, the hell with them, I still had my seat, covered with the detritus of the long-term inmate. I was thinking of applying for permission to stick pin-ups on the wall and maybe get a vase of flowers to make it more homely. I hadn't seen anyone standing who was old, lame or pregnant enough to make me feel uncomfortable about sitting. Compared to me, they were all just passing through.

However, I was starting to feel uncomfortable in another way. A third toilet was out of action now and I had needs. It was not an enticing prospect. This was British train travel at its most disgusting. It was often like this for the 118 years when the railways were initially private; and then for the 49 years when they were nationalized; and it's the same again now that they are re-privatized. Bad seats, bad toilets, bad food. Slow, grubby, inadequate. But it wasn't really a 'nightmare' (that all-purpose Britishism), not for me. I was still enraptured by the sight of England, even while we passed through the less obviously lovely bits of it. Sheffield station was a particularly pleasant surprise: it looked light, airy and rather welcoming: the awnings have been painted up in a fresh silvery-grey with a white rose motif that may have been intended to designate Yorkshire, but actually gave the whole thing the pleasing air of an upmarket tart's boudoir. And then Leeds.

Leeds!

I'd forgotten all about the reservation notice. Nemesis arrived in the shape of a young man called Angus who had two mobile phones, a pinstripe suit and an earnest expression. 'I think this is my seat,' he said, with some degree of confidence.

So I wandered along to The Shop, which still had six sandwiches, possibly the same ones. My new host was as baffled by his employers as his predecessors. 'If you've got a businessman going from Edinburgh to Bristol, he wants a bit of

66

comfort, decent catering,' he mused. 'Why not serve him breakfast? Wouldn't that help attract him? But when have you ever known the railways take a long-term view?' At Darlington, the coffee machine bust. The good news was that Angus vanished at Newcastle, and I got my seat back. Shortly afterwards, the train manager said two of the four toilets were now working; he was inclined to blame us, and said we should not put nappies or sanitary towels down them. It was not clear where else on this train you might put a nappy or sanitary towel, but that was not my problem.

Indeed (having found a functioning toilet), I was having some trouble remembering what problems I did have: what my life had been like before I joined this train. At Alnmouth we caught the sea again; the sun came out, and so did the evening golfers. I finally struck up a conversation with a passenger I had spotted on my regular patrols who had been there almost as long as I had: he was doing Truro to Inverkeithing, the whole thing bar half an hour at the start and an hour at the end. 'I've never done it before and I won't do it again,' he said. 'It's very full and very slow.'

In fact we could have both sliced about twelve minutes off the journey time by catching the slightly later train from Cornwall to London, going by tube from Paddington to King's Cross, taking a fast train to York and then getting this one – a more elaborate version of the game the adventurous can play on the little steam train that loops up to Darjeeling: jumping out, and then catching it up again.

Edinburgh came and went. It was misty now,

and the Forth Bridge was visible only faintly if you looked back from the Fife beaches, where the sea was rippling gently, providing an illusion of the Caribbean. We fell behind schedule in Fife, and at Cupar I began to get quite excited by the possibility that we would be eleven minutes late, justifying the title of this book, and ensuring that Arriva would be fined.

We were seven minutes *early* into Dundee. They do it by magic, or sleight of hand at any rate.

The Even Slower Train Further North

But the day's travel was still not over. To get to Thurso the next afternoon, I had to position myself in Perth for an early start, which meant a sixteen-minute trip on First Scotrail (First Great Western's more reliable brother). It notionally takes up to twenty-five minutes if the train has come from Aberdeen or somewhere, and they have to play the same kind of silly buggers over the scheduling.

The trick is to make the timing between the last two stations ludicrously long so that in almost every case it is possible to make up the time lost. It is a fraud on the public that makes train travel unnecessarily slow, but it is good enough for the government, the regulators and the passengers' feeble representatives.

We followed the banks of the Tay which, as night fell, looked very unsilvery. And the surrounding fields were full of polytunnels and rape, making it slightly less attractive than the stretch north of Birmingham New Street. At Perth station there was a large advert:

NEW ROUTE!
Dundee to Birmingham
From £34.99 on Flybe!

Next morning, there were David and Pru Jeffrey, two Edinburgh doctors who were walking from John o'Groats to Land's End on behalf of the Mercy Corps, raising money to improve the lives of people in villages round Darjeeling. They were waiting for the Inverness train on Platform 7: Perth has a surprisingly expansive station, and reaching Platform 7 is a serious hike in itself. Rather improbably, Pru was carrying a copy of the *Financial Times.*

'Only for the crossword,' she said, hastily, and added just as quickly: 'We're just going to the start, and then we begin walking. People think we're cheating, going by train.' Cheating? Lord, no. I thought they were doing it the hard way. Loads of people walk from one end of Britain to the other. Four thousand people a year are said to cycle it. There was a bloke who did it naked. Who does it my way? Shouldn't I have touted for sponsorship?

The stretch north of Perth is where travellers on the Inverness sleeper are woken by the attendant with a nasty cup of tea and even nastier bread roll. Then they open their eyes and the window blind and – wow! – they're in the Highlands. At Dunkeld we had to wait for a southbound coming out of the single-track section and had the chance to get out, a tricky operation since Dunkeld has eccentrically low platforms.

But this was a welcome opportunity. There is no chance of God's fresh air on these air-conditioned so-called Turbostars, and Scotland smelt tingling-fresh that morning, even above the mild whiff of diesel. George the conductor was not a fan of the Turbostars. 'I think they should bring a proper engine instead of these things,' he said. 'The heating goes hot-cold, hot-cold. And they're nowhere near big enough. This summer they'll be absolutely packed. Aye. Absolutely packed, it'll be. Well, we're doing our best to stop people going on trains, and they just keep on coming. They got nae consideration.'

At Pitlochry there was a wonderfully mad station building with what Biddle calls rusticated quoins, and completely pointless ornamentation on top. Everywhere there was spring green, silver birches and dancing rills. And north of Blair Atholl we were confronted by Beinn A'Ghlo, a long sinuous mountain, still snow-flecked in May, a combination that made it look like a spume-topped breaker about to crash down on the glen.

At Aviemore we passed a train hired by a railtour company in the nostalgia business. It comprised turgid old coaches with vile red seats pulled by a couple of foul old diesels. I remember those trains well, relics of the Darkest Ages of the railways. The tables were laid not just for lunch but for lunch-eon: crisp white linen, cut flowers, and a beautifully printed menu which we couldn't quite read although someone thought they had spotted the

70

word 'chicken'. And everyone went 'Oooh', as though the train itself were special.

Ridiculous.

David, Pru and I only had a few minutes to catch one of the three trains a day leaving Inverness for the far north, which was a frantic pace for a very unfrantic line. For a fit crow with a good sense of direction and rations for the journey, it is barely seventy-eight miles from Inverness to the end of the line in Wick. By road it is 106 miles and takes about two hours with a good run. By rail it is 175 miles and takes nearly four and a half hours.

Wick is not the northern extremity of the line, though it is now the terminus. Traditionally, the train always ambled as far as Georgemas Junction, the most northerly junction on Britain's railways and undoubtedly the most placid. Then it would split into two, half heading south to Wick and the other half north to Thurso. Now it takes a cheaper, more long-winded option, turning first to Thurso before returning down to Georgemas (...so good it calls there twice!), and thence to Wick before coming back to Georgemas and Thurso again.

I made a unilateral decision that Thurso was really the end of the line because (a) it made geographical sense; (b) I had someone to see there; and (c) enough was enough.

This distant limb of the British railway system has been a candidate for amputation since at least the 1930s, when the War Office intervened to save it. And many of the smallest stations and the various branches – twigs, more like – had

71

gone even before Dr Beeching could have the pleasure of picking them off in the 1960s. These included the old single-track line that trudged through the Black Isle to Fortrose, and gave rise to an old Highland joke: 'Aye,' said the traveller as the train finally pulled into Inverness. 'Well, that's the worst o' the journey over, noo.' 'How much further do you have to go then?' he was asked. 'China.'

Beeching did include the main line, if you can call it that, on his list of closures. But there was a certain worrying symbolism in cutting the railway from such a vast tract of country, especially as it happened to include three marginal seats. The government held off and, with a minimalist approach to staffing and signalling costs, the Far North line and its western sideshoot to Kyle of Lochalsh have clung on.

But, golly, it's one for the connoisseurs. From Inverness we crept round the south side of the Beauly Firth at a pace that would not have taxed David and Pru on foot. We passed wee Beauly, recently re-opened and arguably the tiniest of the 2,500-odd stations on the network (the platforms at Betjeman's favourite, Dilton Marsh Halt in Wiltshire, are even shorter, but Beauly only has the one). Then we headed north, skirting the Black Isle, to Dingwall.

About half the seats in the two carriages had been reserved for a party travelling from Dingwall to Ardgay. They proved to be passengers on a coach trip, mostly elderly ladies from Dunfermline, heading for the Falls of Shin, which turns out – and I am not making this up – to be a Harrods outlet store in the middle of nowhere ('See Mr Al Fayed for yourself as he graces the entrance courtesy of a genuine Madame Tussaud's waxwork.') The idea was to give the coach travellers a little taste of the train to break up their journey.

'We're going to see a waterfall,' said one old lady.

'Nooo, I don't think so,' said her companion. 'Shopping.'

'I don't mind, as long as they tell us when to get off.'

'TIME TO GET OFF!' bawled Dennis the conductor obligingly as soon as we got to Ardgay.

I did my best to help David and Pru with the FT crossword, and at the little request stop of Rogart was joined by Frank Roach who had agreed to spend an hour with me to chat about the route. Frank works, as development manager for the Highland Rail Partnership, in the station house at Lairg, the next stop back down the line, and actually lives in the station house at Rogart. He walked onto the train straight from his own kitchen clutching his own mug of tea.

Frank was not terribly impressed that I had come up from Penzance: he was brought up there and is clearly the world's leading expert on train travel from Penzance to Thurso. He says you can get as far as Tain, about a quarter of the way north of Inverness, in a single day – provided you don't mess about with diversions to Dundee. One senses that some people are attracted to geographical extremes the way others are attracted to political extremes. All the ex-communists in New Labour gleefully turned into right-wing authoritarians when given a hint of power, without ever pausing for breath in the middle ground. Frank no doubt would be very unhappy living in Warwickshire.

For anyone connected with rail in the Highlands, the bridge over the Dornoch Firth is the Holy Grail, which would knock about forty minutes off the journey to Thurso. A road bridge over the firth opened in 1991, but the Conservative government, for a piffling saving, kept trains off it. 'The Scottish Office thought that would ensure the railway would wither away,' says Frank.

Now, with devolution, the Far North Line is probably further away from closure than at any time since the First World War, especially with the impending decommissioning of the Dounreay nuclear power station, which will necessitate the secure transport of all kinds of nasty stuff. But the bridge seems to have receded towards the realms of impossibility, and the railway lurches off for miles into Sutherland before remembering where it's going and spending another stretch eccentrically heading south-east.

We stopped at Golspie, said to be the first town that a motorist, driving to Thurso from London or Exeter, cannot realistically avoid. Above it is the huge and controversial statue of the First Duke of Sutherland, mastermind of the Highland clearances. Then came the old private station for the ducal castle, Dunrobin (or, bearing in mind the family origins, Done Robbin'). The fourth duke, a gentler soul who loved railways, helped finance the line and in return was allowed to run his own locomotives and rolling stock, a privilege that lasted until nationalization. The station building is a half-timbered pavilion, now a museum.

For a while we hugged the coast. Near Brora three seals were sufficiently alarmed by our approach to bodysurf off a rock into the frigid North Sea. Then came Helmsdale where Charles and Diana spent a holiday just before their marriage and where, it is said, she first began to get the idea that she might actually be in love. Such a small mistake, so many tears.

The line cuts inland here, to avoid the impossibly high ground of the Ord of Caithness, so there is another huge meander, past the ruined crofts of Kildonan and the mist-shrouded hills of Kinbrace. Very little of this line is what you might call pretty in the Highland chocolate box sense, but almost everything about it is numinous, brooding, with a sense of life on the edge.

At Kinbrace Frank got out, knowing the southbound would soon be there to take him home again because Forsinard, the next stop along, is the only available passing place. I was impressed by his organizational skills. Then I noticed he had left his empty mug behind.

The line grew ever wilder as we approached the mysterious Flow Country. The old snow fences that the linemen used to maintain are now in ruins, which is an impressive gesture of faith in global warming. In the old days trains were regularly detained for long periods on these exposed moors by snowdrifts. As recently as 1978, seventy passengers had to be airlifted out in a blizzard by an RAF helicopter.

The Flow Country does not fit the popular taste for Scottish scenery at all, being bleached of colour and seemingly devoid of life. In the 1980s it was considered so useless that substantial tax concessions were offered to anyone sticking conifer plantations up here, with mild damage to the reputation of Terry Wogan, Cliff Richard and Phil Collins, once their investments became known, and rather more disastrous effects on the ecology of the peat bogs.

At Georgemas Junction Dennis the conductor began fiddling with a complex digital radio contraption. 'Is that something to do with the signalling?' I asked. 'No,' he said. 'I'm trying to get the Rangers score.'

We were bang on time at Thurso, which meant I had completed the journey from Penzance in 29 hours and 57 minutes, including a very pleasant Thai meal and reasonable night's sleep in Perth.

In Breach of Regulations

On the way back south, I requested a stop at Rogart in order to give Frank his mug back.

CHAPTER THREE

BLISWORTH

In the 1950s and 1960s, Andy Newbery and I grew up in adjoining villages just south of Northampton. He was in Blisworth and I was a mile away in Milton, which has now been poshed up and renamed Milton Malsor.

Milton was enveloped by a triangle of historic railway lines: there was what is now called the West Coast Main Line, passing over a massive arch built by Robert Stephenson between the two villages; there was the original branch line to Northampton and Peterborough, in a cutting just beyond the gravel pits; and on the far side of the village, towards Collingtree, was the much later loop line that finally linked Northampton directly, if never conveniently, to London in the 1870s.

That was the route which Stephenson – son of George and chief engineer of the London & Birmingham Railway – would have taken into Northampton if the stupid townspeople hadn't refused to allow the railway into town. Or so the story goes. Instead, the main line trains went close to our house and through the station at Blisworth, bypassing the town, as they still do. In the last days of steam, there could have been no better time or place for a railway childhood.

77

Except that I didn't have one. In fact, despite being a rather insomniac child, I don't even have a clear memory of ever *hearing* the trains. We could see them all right. I remember walking a couple of miles up Barn Lane (more than once but not much more) to the farm crossing over the tracks in the last days of steam. One day I saw the *Royal Scot* power awesomely north. Mum would take me to London from Northampton station to see my grandmother and the aunties. I can just recall the wonderful old Great Hall at Euston. Far more vividly, I remember the sit-down tea served on the 4.30 back home, with little individual glass pots of jam.

On a whim, I did take the train from Castle Station in Northampton to Peterborough one afternoon because I'd read that the line was closing. I must have been twelve, I now discover from looking at the closure date. That was not untypical in a sense: we were a self-reliant, unsupervised generation. It was untypical in suggesting I cared. Shortly afterwards, I swapped my Tri-ang train set for a Dansette transistor radio.

Andy Newbery spent his days off from school at Blisworth station with his friend Wilf. 'Apart from Camden Bank and a bit of a climb up to Tring,' Andy explained, 'Stephenson built the line very level, so by the time they got to Blisworth, through trains would thunder through at 80–90mph. Big exciting expresses through these narrow platforms. Enthusiasts would come from miles around.

'Time used to stand still. I used to leave home at eight in the morning and take my sandwiches.

78

We never got up to any mischief.' I can't vouch for this: I never joined them, I didn't know them. It was 2008 before I met Andy Newbery. I suppose I would have thought him uncool. I regret the half-century delay.

Andy heard the trains all the time: 'I remember lying awake on a winter's night and hearing all those iron-ore trains going clang-clang-clang-clang-clang. And the tank engines chuffing in and out of the quarry. You could recognize an engine by the exhaust note, especially if it was coming up the hill from Northampton. Those big goods engines, the 8Fs and 9Fs, they would almost be going walking pace by the time they came up from Milton.' He was warming to his theme now, was Andy. 'You'd hear the Jubilee engines with a three-cylinder beat. One of those would be like a rocket roar. And the Staniers had a hooter instead of a whistle. And oh, the beautiful smells. Hot oil, steam and smoke, that's the mixture, isn't it?'

Is it?

'That smell would permeate the air. You ask any steam fan, it's the smell that hooks you. You'd look at the drivers, they were like fighter pilots.'

Andy's dad worked on the railway: I don't think time stood still for him. 'My father was a permanent way man, a lengthsman. One of his jobs was fog duty. Ted Monk would come round at about 3am on a freezing January morning and throw something at the window. Dad had to do two things. He'd have to check the signal poles to make sure the lamps were clean. And he'd sit in the fog box, like an old portable toilet, and as the train went past, double-check for the signalman that he'd seen the tail-lamp and that the train hadn't split. He might also have to climb and check the Long Tom signal.'

We were standing by what was Blisworth station, closed in 1960. There is nothing left now, just a nasty metal fence between the road and the rails. I have the vaguest recollection of the old place, its signs painted in London Midland maroon and its awnings painted in London Midland dirt 'n' cream. Andy remembers it all: 'There was a mysterious opening in the ticket hall, and you'd go into this sulphurous-smelling subway only just about wide enough to walk through, and you'd hear the trains rushing overhead.' Then he took me to what was once the start of the Stratford & Midland Junction, the Slow, Mouldy and Jolting. I had never even heard of it when I was a child. My dad was a solicitor. I didn't go into his office and watch the writs and conveyances thundering through either. I wish I'd seen the Jubilees and Staniers with Andy and Wilf.

But I went away to boarding school, and enthusiasm about anything got you teased. When I was teased, though, it was for supporting Northamptonshire cricket and Northampton Town Football Club (The Cobblers) instead of predictable teams like Middlesex and Arsenal. No one teased me because the people of Northampton were so stupid that they stopped the railway coming in.

Spoiling the Shires, Ruining the Squires

In any case, they weren't that stupid. This calumny has been repeated in countless railway histories and the 1931 report of the Railway Commission on Transport and was recounted to me by several interviewees while researching this book. Critics have referred to Northampton's 'idiocy' and 'barbarous fury'.

It is apparently true that the townspeople now have more bling per head than anywhere else in Britain. That may be a sign that it is not these days the most over-intellectual municipality in the kingdom. It is not true that Northampton was daft enough to try to keep out the railway.

The myth persists despite being convincingly despatched by the local historian Joan Wake in 1935. It is correct that there was some opposition from the unelected corporation, which was then on the brink of abolition, but the townspeople as a whole pressed Stephenson unsuccessfully to bring the line through the town.

On 17 September 1830, just two days after the triumphant (begging Mr Huskisson's pardon) opening of the Liverpool & Manchester, the London & Birmingham Company was formed from two rival groupings to link the capital with what was fast becoming the country's second city. Urban Britain grasped the significance of events very quickly. And so did the countryside.

Such a line could not possibly avoid Northamptonshire (no one ever goes there, but everyone passes through) and, before the year was out, a protest meeting of county landowners was held in the White Horse, Towcester, presided over by Sir William Wake of Courteenhall. It voted unanimously that the railway would do 'great injury', adding: 'There is already conveyance for travellers between London and Birmingham every day at the rate of ten miles an hour, and water carriages for heavy goods, to a greater extent than has ever been required ... no necessity has been shewn for accelerated communication.'

The railway, someone said at the meeting, 'would spoil our Shires and ruin our Squires'. And indeed Stephenson eventually did put massive earthworks through the Wake estates, which may have rather spoiled things – though Courteenhall was not rendered intolerable until the arrival of the M1 130 years later. Presumably Sir William was bought off, as were all the other magnates whose land was vital to the project except Mr Thornton of Brockhall, who was so implacable that Stephenson had to avoid him and face instead the Kilsby Ridge, where, as Joan Wake put it, 'millions of tons of Northampton-shire clay proved less impervious than the stubborn opposition of Squire Thornton.'

There is no record of the Stephensons trying to deflect Northampton Corporation's opposition. Robert and his father George were now not without influence. If they had wanted to go through Northampton, they would surely have made their feelings known: they never did. It seems overwhelmingly likely that the 120ft difference in gradient in the four miles between Blisworth and Northampton, on the valley floor, put the Stephensons off from the start, given the primitive locomotives of the time. It was estimated in 1833 that even a gradient of 1 in 300, an incline imperceptible to the naked eye, required nearly twice as much pulling power as a level railway, and Robert Stephenson reputedly said that he could easily get the trains into the town, but couldn't get them out again. And, as Andy Newbery said, he constructed the entire line with the overriding aim of keeping it as level as possible, having learned that lesson from the crawl uphill on the Liverpool & Manchester near Rainhill. So that surely has to be true.

Northampton undoubtedly lost out as a centre of commerce in the nineteenth century because of its poor transport links. It was increasingly overtaken as a boot and shoe centre by Leicester, and its situation may not have been helped by the people's railway-derived reputation as clod-hoppers as well as cobblers. For places that actually resisted the railway, look at 'vehement' Maidstone or Windsor or Oxford, which tried to keep this intrusion as far as possible from the colleges. To this day, they all – like Northampton – have inferior train services, and Oxford is perhaps the only city where the coach to London is competitive on convenience as well as price.

The other great rail route of the late 1830s, the Grand Junction north from Birmingham to link up with the Liverpool & Manchester, was built through the plains of Staffordshire and Cheshire with a minimum of fuss. For the first six years the London & Birmingham had to get its trains up the hill out of Euston by cable, like a tugboat pulling an ocean liner. Stephenson had enough problems without worrying about Northampton. So lay off my home town please. It's bad enough when you make sniggering remarks about a load of cobblers.

The Great Wall of China? A Doddle!

The construction of the London & Birmingham line was one of the great adventures of the nineteenth century. Peter Lecount, one of Stephenson's assistants, called it the greatest public work ever executed. He dismissed the claims of the Great Wall of China, as requiring less capital and engineering skill, and thought only the Great Pyramid might compare. And it was on this line that the traditions of railway building took shape that spread across the century and throughout the world: the traditions of hard slog, abandon, riot and callousness.

However intrusive the railways proved to be, the arrival of the trains came as a blessed relief to much of rural England compared to having the company of the men who built them. Around Blisworth, three thousand navvies worked on a five-mile stretch of line, according to Terry Coleman's classic history, *The Railway Navvies:*

They lodged, when they could, in the villages, and when there were no villages they herded into turf shanties thrown up by the contractors. A few brought their wives. Others lived, nineteen to a hut, with one shared woman. They were paid once a month – sometimes not so frequently – and usually in a public house,

84

and then for days after, they drank their pay, sold their shovels for beer, rioted and went on a randy... The Irish marched to fight the Scots, the English fought among themselves, and no work was done until all the money was gone.

They were entitled to let their hair down a little. The railways were built with 'picks, shovels and gunpowder', by men not machines. And the men, in huge numbers, died in the attempt. No record was kept of the number of fatalities or injuries on the London & Birmingham, and Stephenson was not unusually inhumane. Most were killed by the arduousness of the task. Shown a list of 131 workers taken to Bath Hospital alone (minor injuries excluded) in less than two years during the construction of the Great Western, Brunel responded: 'I think it is a small list, considering the very heavy works, and the immense amount of powder used.' Some died by their own mad folly. Just north of Blisworth, in the Kilsby Tunnel, three men were killed 'as they tried to jump, one after the other over the mouth of a shaft in a game of follow my leader'.

Everywhere the navvies struck terror into the hearts of respectable Englishmen and, of course, Englishwomen. *The Times* reported in 1836:

Great alarm has existed in the neighbourhood of Acton, Ealing, Hanwell, Southall, &c., in consequence of the outrageous conduct of the labourers employed on the works of the Great Western Railways ... burglaries, highway robberies, and depredations of every description, have become so much on the increase, that it has become dangerous for individuals to be out alone after dark.

But even the navvies moved on eventually. By 1859 George Measom, the author of a succession of Victorian railway guides, was able to refer quite matter-of-factly to what was achieved at Blisworth. 'The Blisworth excavation contains 1,200,000 cubic yards, averaging 50 feet deep for 2 miles in length.' This was 'by far the most expensive and arduous work' on the entire line.

I feel ashamed: had I grown up a mile from the Great Wall of China, I expect I would have had some consciousness of what had been achieved. I lived a mile away from Blisworth, and never knew. And now, when I travel out of Euston, I struggle to spot the site of Blisworth Station. And no one else on the train looks up from their Sudoku or their BlackBerry.

As Coleman put it: 'There is hardly a branch line in Britain whose earthworks would not be marvelled at if they were those of a new road or an ancient fort.' And we never notice.

And the Dust Gathered on the Tables

The new railway opened fully on 17 September 1838, connecting with the Grand Junction and providing a direct link between what were becoming the four major cities of England: London, Birmingham, Liverpool and Manchester. The country now had the beginnings of a railway network and it would grow like some rampant exotic plant, checked occasionally by outbreaks of financial turmoil, but never for long.

The first train from London, containing the company's directors, arrived in Birmingham in four and a half hours, compared to the fourteen hours of the old Union stagecoach. The first public train, which left at 8.10am, was a little more leisurely and arrived at 1.50pm according to the Birmingham station clocks, and 1.58pm by the watches of the passengers, suddenly drawing attention to a problem the world had never previously considered.

Each town, living its own life, used to have its own time, according to its own reckoning of sunrise and sunset, without having to worry what time it was anywhere else. It was a new world, although the most obvious means of dealing with it – synchronizing all railway clocks – did not become universal until 1851 when the entire network adopted Greenwich time or, as it was generally known, 'railway time'.

The advantages of the train also became clear on Day 1: the London newspapers were available in Birmingham by two o'clock. 'Shortly we expect to see them some hours sooner,' said *The Times* correspondent. And the effect was felt in the stagecoach offices.

Before the Liverpool & Manchester opened, even the directors expected its business to come primarily from the carriage of freight, as on earlier prototypes like the Stockton & Darlington. The canal companies fought like fury against these upstart rivals; the stagecoach companies observed the process with what must have been either equanimity or fatalism. In the 1820s the canals were clogged with piled-up merchandise, and their owners reviled as monopolistic overchargers. But the roads were better than ever before: 'the finest public-transport system the world had ever seen'. The new system of turnpike trusts ensured that the highways were maintained, and the new methods of constructing roads, pioneered by Telford and McAdam, enormously improved them. New coach designs also made the ride faster and more comfortable (or less uncomfortable). The new coaches shared their names with the growing number of daily newspapers. So far as most people were concerned in the early nineteenth century, these coaches had the same sense of urgency as the papers. They seemed like the future. There was some rationale behind the squeal of pain by the Northamptonshire landowners against the coming of the railway.

Even after 1830 there was no absolute certainty that the railways would supplant the road. One of Sir Goldsworthy Gurney's steam carriages carried 13,000 passengers between London and Brighton in 1836, and was said to touch speeds of 20mph. Gurney was not the only inventor working along these lines: Walter Hancock had versions called the *Infant*, 'a great snorting vehicle', and the *Autopsy*. Which was very apt. Burst boilers were a major problem on the early railway locomotives, but they were a far more alarming possibility on these carriages because the passengers were sitting directly above the boiler. The road vehicles were noisy and dirty. And the turnpike trusts imposed penal toll rates on them claiming they chewed up the roads. And so, nearly two centuries later, George Stephenson was commemorated on the five-pound note; and Goldsworthy Gurney wasn't.

Either way – Stephenson's or Gurney's – the horse-drawn coaches were now doomed. Some of the stalwarts of the coaching business, like Pickford's, managed to jump on the gravy train, as it were, before it left the station. And some of their employees shifted nimbly across. But the aristocrats of the trade, the coachmen, could not forsake their air of command to start afresh. There is said to be no known case of a coachman becoming an engine driver. 'Hang up my old whip over the fireplace', Harry Littler, who held the reins of the Southampton *Telegraph*, allegedly cried after the London & Southampton Railway was opened in 1838, 'I shan't want it never no more.' Then he fell ill, turned his face to the wall, and died.

Yet there was very little nostalgia on the part of the public. The government paid no compensation, as they had done to the slaveowners. There was almost no attempt to preserve any of the lovingly painted and lacquered coaches. 'Up and down the country,' wrote David Mountfield, 'the coaching yards fell silent, and dust gathered on the tables at the roadside inns.' Ten years after the first train from Euston pulled into Birmingham, the last long-distance stagecoach in England, the *Bedford Times*, was withdrawn. The slogan inscribed on its door panels had long been *Tempus Fugit*. And now time really had flown.

Those who feared the railways would spell the

end of the horse were entirely mistaken though. The need for horses actually increased, both because of the needs of railway construction and for the short-haul journeys for both goods and passengers to and from the stations. Hence the late nineteenth-century prediction that by 1950 the streets of London would be six feet deep in dung.

In *Vanity Fair*, Thackeray wrote a wonderful elegy for the coaching era:

Where is the road now, and its merry incidents of life? Is old Weller alive or dead? And the waiters, yea, and the inns at which they waited, and the cold rounds of beef inside, and the stunted ostler, with his blue nose and clinking pail, where is he, and where is his generation?... These men and things will be as much legend and history as Nineveh, or Coeur de Lion ... stage-coaches will have become romances.

Actually, except for a brief nostalgic revival in the late 1860s, stagecoaches were almost totally forgotten except in the corners of the kingdom so remote that the railways never penetrated. But the names of the main stagecoaches were preserved, almost in their entirety, in a manner that became so familiar that soon no one knew how they had originated.

These were the names of some of the leading stagecoaches leaving London in 1836:

The *Express* to Hertford
The *Despatch* to Aylesbury
The *Courier* to Birmingham

The *Telegraph* to Bishops Stortford
The *Economist* to Birmingham
The *Times* to Brighton
The *Star* to Cambridge
The *Independent* to Chichester
The *Herald* to Exeter
The *Morning Star* to Tunbridge Wells

The notion of the *Morning Star,* now Britain's Communist paper, heading daily to Tunbridge Wells in four and a half hours with a team of four bays, is a particularly delicious one. But in the 1820s newspapers and stagecoaches were both the height of modernity and speed. It has just taken rather longer for newspapers to be superseded, that's all.

I met Andy Newbery at Blisworth on a warm July evening. After I left him, I went back to Milton and drove up Barn Lane until the road peters out. Then I tramped past fields high with ripening barley to find the old farm crossing. Now there is a huge steel footbridge complete with graffiti that would not look out of place in The Bronx. The wires sway in the summer breeze and, with only momentary warnings, the Virgin Pendolinos sweep through.

They are faster than the *Royal Scot,* just as the first trains were faster than the stagecoaches. We mourn our lost steam engines, and our lost childhood. Except in the memories of writers like Thackeray and a few disgruntled coachmen, the coaching age vanished without trace. It's all very puzzling.

CHAPTER FOUR

MONKWEARMOUTH

Monkwearmouth is an area of Sunderland of – how can one put it? – limited appeal to the visitor. It has the city's improbably named new football ground, the Stadium of Light, and not a great deal else. St Peter's Church was founded in AD 674; unfortunately the Vikings destroyed most of the building.

But there is something quite exceptional and striking: here in the midst of this hard city is an extraordinary classical building in russet-coloured stone with a huge four-column Ionic portico that would not look out of place in Pall Mall. Indeed, Pevsner compares it to 'a provincial Athenaeum'. This was the railway station, built in 1848 by the local MP, George Hudson, who happened to control this particular railway and much of the rest of the infant network besides. He was anxious to keep his constituents sweet, his passengers happy, and his vanity massaged.

The building is now a museum and, inside the ticket hall, Hudson – as painted by the fashion-able portraitist Sir Francis Grant – looks down with both the air and the sideburns of Harry Secombe playing Mr Bumble. Hudson never did get the knighthood or, indeed, the dukedom to which he might once have aspired. In the popular reckoning, he was more than that: he was The Railway King.

Hudson is a largely forgotten figure now, yet he bestrode the narrow world of the 1840s. This brand new industry was transforming the country, and he was its dominant, and certainly most dynamic, figure. One almost fancies one can hear him speaking, since he was a familiar type: an up-by-his-bootstraps Yorkshireman – short, stocky, pugnacious, abrasive, arrogant, domineering, chippy, ostentatious, uncouth. He was crooked too. Or as Lord Macaulay put it: 'a bloated, vulgar, insolent, purse-proud, greedy, drunken, blackguard'.

Hudson was an exemplar of a theory of mine that for a charlatan to storm the British establishment, it helps (as with Robert Maxwell or Jeffrey Archer) to be an outrageously obvious one. His reign was brief: he rose to power in 1841 when he knocked heads together, persuading eight separate companies to forget their differences and build a crucial section of line from Darlington to Newcastle. He was deposed in 1849 when his financial chicanery was exposed. In the meantime he had been powerful enough to lead the successful opposition to William Gladstone who, as a young president of the Board of Trade, had contemplated nationalizing the railways. And he was able to substitute his own charisma and instincts for even a semblance of normal business practice. 'I will have no statistics on my railway!' he is said to have roared at one meeting.

The question that divides biographers is whether Hudson was a rogue, or just a scamp.

Were his machinations a mere detail compared to the energy and determination so crucial to linking the unconnected strands of Britain's early railways into something vaguely approaching a coherent whole?

The more important question is why it should ever have been left to the likes of Hudson to create the network. The railways were the most powerful invention the world had yet seen. They were already transforming the countryside, the economy and the lives of the people. The British government – alone in Europe, almost alone in the world – concluded that, in such circumstances, it was its solemn duty to stand and watch.

It happened that the initial growth of the railways coincided with the peak of the political and intellectual power of laissez-faire, the belief that everyone is better off if capitalists are left alone to get on with making money. As seen from Britain, excessive government had been a catastrophic failure in the late eighteenth century: British official idiocy had caused the American revolution, while the French revolution had produced tyranny and terror. That was one factor.

And by now the notion of economic individualism had been given intellectual coherence by David Ricardo and mutated into what is often called 'classical economics'. Ricardo's first political disciple was William Huskisson, but his ideas found their clearest political expression in the Anti-Corn Law League, the campaign against tariffs on imported corn led from Manchester by Richard Cobden and John Bright.

The Corn Laws were gradually abolished in the

late 1840s, but only after about one million people had starved to death in the Irish famine, unable to afford any other food when the potato crop failed. The restraint on free trade was seen to be the mass murderer, although the truly lethal combination was the tariff on one side and non-intervention on the other.

This is a confusing era for modern students, since Cobden and Bright were called 'radicals'. Yet their supporters – the increasingly powerful northern industrial bourgeoisie – were the least likely to support the kind of reforms that might stop children being sent up chimneys or railway navvies being continually blown to bits.

They also financed and pioneered the railways (even some of the southern companies relied on northern brass). And they were the last people to want the government meddling in their business. Yet building a railway was an inherently political activity. Until 1856, a parliamentary act was required to form any limited liability company. Some plans were approved; some weren't – the process was whimsical, depending more on shifting parliamentary alliances than intrinsic merit.

There were voices raised in favour of greater government control, but these also tended to be confusing and improbable ones, such as the Marquis of Londonderry, given the credit for first suggesting, in 1836, that railways should revert to the public after twenty years. Londonderry particularly opposed those railways that were 'most prejudicial to the landed interest'. And the Duke of Wellington argued that 'the public should be secured in deriving those advantages from these speculations which it had the right to expect', which sounds suspiciously socialistic coming from the leading reactionary of the day. But then Wellington loathed the railways: he had seen enough blood shed in his life before witnessing Huskisson's fatal accident.

The chief supporter in the Commons of greater control was James Morrison, a liberal but mega-rich industrialist who sat for Ipswich. In 1836 he tried to introduce a bill giving parliament the power to regulate the companies' fares and charges every twenty or thirty years, which hardly sounds draconian. Yet, complained the Leeds Whig Edward Baines: 'there never was a measure more obnoxious to the majority of the House.' The other voice in favour of railway nationalization was that of the splendidly eccentric Colonel Sibthorp, MP for Lincoln, who was in favour of taking over railways the better to annihilate them and bring back the stagecoach.

The King and the Crash

William Gladstone would also have nationalized the railways if he could. And at the Board of Trade he fathered the 1844 Regulation of Railways Act which brought in various measures to curtail the new industry's abuses. It included a near-exact copy of Londonderry's suggestion, allowing companies to pass into public owner-ship after twenty-one years.

But it was never invoked: even Sir Robert Peel, the prime minister, seemed to regard the idea as

96

rather unsporting. And the thundering profits made in the early years (the Stockton & Darlington actually paid fifteen per cent dividends) soon declined, which reduced the pressure. In any case, the law only applied to *future* lines and by then many of England's main lines had already been built and were therefore exempt.

The 1844 act emerged in the same haphazard way as everything else, even the most fundamental decision underlying railway construction: the gauge. Brunel, mastermind of the Great Western Railway, rejected George Stephenson's gauge of 4ft 8½in, arguing that his preferred width-measure of 7ft permitted faster, more stable and more comfortable trains, which was probably true. It also helped lock in freight customers to using his system, and no one else's. But from a national perspective, the significant point about the gauge – and this is hardly an abstruse technicality – is that it does not matter that much which one you choose as long as the whole network has the same one. This fact seems to have struck surprisingly few people, until the inevitable day, in 1844, when the two systems met at Gloucester and everyone and everything had to change trains. With the memories of stage-coach travel still fresh, passengers were stoical about the inconvenience. But merchants were less stoical about the extra costs caused by the need for trans-shipment. And the live animals, now being transported in large numbers, were often very unstoical indeed when forced out of one wagon into another in some strange siding.

Gladstone's Act failed to impose a decision,

leading to half a century of mess until the broad gauge was finally scrapped. But the act was not a complete waste of time. It placed the first silken bonds of government regulation round the necks of the companies, and these would be tightened with exquisite slowness over the decades to come. The railways were forced to stop running open-top wagons for third-class passengers (the pampered darlings), to which some responded by briefly introducing fourth class. They were also forced to run at least one comparatively cheap, daily third-class service that became known, throughout the Victorian era, as the 'parliamentary train', a phrase that hadn't entirely disappeared in the 1930s.

This was a highly significant act in establishing that the government had some kind of say in how the railways were run, even if the how, why and where they were built was to be left largely to the likes of Hudson. But, as part of the general give-and-take of the legislative process, the act also abolished a rule forcing railway promoters to deposit part of the capital before they could introduce an enabling bill into parliament. This had been a serious curb on their idlest fancies, and its abolition must be regarded as an immediate cause of what happened next. What happened next was that railway capitalism was not merely rampant, but rampaging.

Mass hysteria can be dated back at least to Exodus chapter 32 when Aaron persuaded the children of Israel to hand over their earrings to be melted down into a worshipable golden calf. Actual speculative frenzy is generally held to have started with the Dutch tulip mania of the 1630s when whole estates were allegedly mortgaged to buy the paper ownership of a rare bulb. And in 1720, 'the year of the Bubbles', the French went berserk over the Mississippi Company and the British over the South Sea Company, which was going to revolutionize trade between Britain and the Americas and might have done, had the company actually possessed a boat.

The railway mania of the mid-1840s was different from these, in that it was founded on fact: a new, successful and transformational technology. The best analogy is with the dot-com bubble of the late 1990s, to which the same applies. After the millennium, people lost huge sums having invested in schemes to sell on-line dog food and the like. In the 1840s investors were duped into railway schemes that were quite simply dogs.

The railways were real and potentially lucrative, for which there was a pent-up demand. This did not mean that every half-baked scheme cooked up by con-men, chancers and shysters had a future. But the history of humanity shows that, when this mood takes hold, there is no stopping it. Did any of the children of Israel have the wit to hide their jewellery?

Britain wanted a railway network, and wanted it fast. The government had opted out of the process. Someone had to step into the breach. That someone, for a few short months in 1845, was just about everyone.

By late 1845 those someones included: Pilbrow's Atmospheric Railway and Canal Propulsion Company; the Great Kent Atmospheric Railway; the Wakefield, Ossett and Dewsbury Direct and Atmospheric; the Gloucester, Aberystwyth and Central Wales ('the Committee regret that in view of the unprecedented number of applications they have been obliged to reject many of respectable character'); the Alton, Farnham and South Western Junction; the Hull and Holyhead Direct; the Pontop and South Shields Railway; the Direct Western Railway; the Lynn and Dereham; the Wellhouse Bay Somersetshire Midland; the Clonmel and Kilkenny; the Direct Manchester Railway; the Thames Embankment and Atmospheric Railway ... not to mention the Jamaica, Kingston and North Midland; the Great Central Sardinian Railway; the Callao and Lima and Pacific Coast Railway; and the Great Western Railway of Bengal.

There was also the company which placed a long and expensive announcement on the front page of *The Times:*

THE GREAT EUROPEAN RAILWAYS COMPANY

The text consisted entirely of blather ('Most truly has it been observed that the philosophy of railroads is only now beginning to be comprehended by the universal world...') unadorned by fact, such as where these railways might actually be built. The implication was that they would fill the entire continent.

The Times was not actually fooled by this advertisement, but decided that (a) the advert was probably some kind of laboured satire – *Punch* had just been founded and was very fashionable – and that (b) it didn't matter what it was as long as the cash was paid up front. The notice did not even contain the by now customary and enticing list of distinguished supporters, some of whom would know their names were included and some of whom might not.

By the end of May there was so much railway business in the Commons that committees had to meet elsewhere. On 1 July the word 'mania' appeared in *The Times*. In August the mood was such that in Leeds the police had to be called to keep the pavement clear outside the stock exchange, and the exchange's chairman, Mr Ridsdale, was cautioning his colleagues to 'repress rather than foster the speculative spirit of the times'.

And then it changed. The technical term for this stage of a mania is 'revulsion'. It did not happen in an instant: as late as September 27 the *Railway Times*, one of scores of publications that had sprung up to meet the hysterical demand, carried eighty pages of advertisements for new companies. But in October the word 'ruin' was also mentioned. However, the promoters were in too deep. Those of them who wanted their enabling law enacted in the next parliamentary session had to lodge their documents by the end of November and were in a panic to make at least a pretence of surveying their routes: 'Young gentlemen with theodolites and chains marched about the fields; long white sticks with bits of paper attached were carried ruthlessly through fields, gardens, and sometimes even through houses.' Lists of new proposals appeared daily now, though some seemed like pairs of towns, grouped together at random, for euphony rather than sensible communication: the Didcot and Andover Railway; York and Lancaster; Bristol and Dover; Tring and Reigate.

The deadline was 30 November, a Sunday. The plans had to be deposited before midnight in the clerk of the peace's office in each county through which the proposed railway would pass. Parties of lawyers raced round the country, hiring special trains where the railways already existed, and where the companies would actually accommodate a potential rival. One group was refused tickets and had to disguise itself as a funeral party instead. A solicitor with the plan for the 'Great West of England Railway' arrived at the Golden Ball turnpike gate at Sherborne in a post-chaise and four in an attempt to reach the Dorset office just before the clock struck twelve. The gatekeeper was asleep, and stayed that way. The solicitor took the plans and ran – but was five minutes late.

The Great West of England Railway got as far as informing one gentleman, without a by-your-leave or may-we, that the line would pass through his garden twenty yards from his windows, on an embankment twenty-two feet high. Other than that, no more was heard of the Great West of England, except when it appeared on a list of 879 schemes that had failed to deposit their plans and were presumed defunct – a list of glorious poetic melancholy, stretching from the Abergavenny and Monmouth, and the Alrewas and Ashby-de-la-Zouch, to the Youghall, Cork and Port Valentin. Including Pilbrow's Atmospheric.

The crash was dramatic, according to John Francis, a Victorian railway writer with a flair for melodrama. 'It reached every hearth, it saddened every heart in the metropolis. Entire families were ruined. There was scarcely an important town in England but what beheld some wretched suicide. Daughters delicately nurtured went out to seek their bread. Sons were recalled from academies. Households were separated; homes were desecrated by the emissaries of the law...'

There is some dispute among academics as to what extent this really happened. And the crash might just have been a passing embarrassment, other than for those stupid and greedy enough to have courted financial ruin, except for one thing. Like the public, the existing railways (or those that were close to existing or had some chance of existing) did not know precisely which of these schemes were completely phoney and which might have been a genuine competitive threat to their business. Quite often, the safest response seemed to be to take them over, with a guaranteed dividend. Thus the railway companies, who had already paid the lawyers to get their bills through parliament and the landowners to get their rails across the ground, landed themselves with another financial impediment instead of getting the licence to print money that might have been expected.

While all this was going on, real people were building real railways. The year 1845 also saw the end of the brutal struggle to build the Woodhead Tunnel through the Pennines. Thirty-two men were reported killed in the process and 140 maimed. Though these figures are almost certainly underestimates, the social reformer Edwin Chadwick said that they made Woodhead, proportionate to the numbers involved, a bloodier battle than Talavera, Salamanca, Vittoria or Waterloo. A year later, the assistant engineer Wellington Purdon faced a Commons select committee and was asked if patent fuses were used in the blasting. Here is Terry Coleman's account:

'No,' he said. The committee persisted. Wasn't this sort of fuse safer? Purdon made his celebrated reply. 'Perhaps it is; but it is attended with such a loss of time, and the difference is so very small, I would not recommend the loss of time for the sake of all the extra lives it would save.'

Hard bastards like Purdon made railways happen. And through the late 1840s the tentacles spread and spread. In 1848 alone, more than 1,000 miles of track were opened, taking the network to over 5,000. And enough genuine companies emerged from the mania to ensure that by 1854, within nine years of it ending – nine years! – just about every town or city of substance in Britain had a railway connection. And amidst all the dross thrown up by the mania, one line stood out: the London & York Railway. This was the basis of what became the Great Northern and is now the East Coast Main Line from King's Cross.

In financial terms, Leeds was the city that supposedly lost most from the mania. Francis claimed that, while the police were clearing the hordes from the streets, shares selling in London for £21 sold in Leeds for more than £25. So much for the canny Tykes. But one Tyke came through the first phase unbroken. George Hudson correctly foresaw what was to prove an inexorable trend in British railway history for the next hundred years: a continual process of amalgamation into larger and larger units, a process that Victorian governments could never quite decide if they were for or against. However, Hudson incorrectly imagined this would be happening under his aegis and control.

In August 1845, when madness was endemic, he was involved in an epic by-election in Sunderland, where he fought off a high-profile free trade candidate and then sent a special train to London so the news of his victory could spread as fast as possible. As a politician, Hudson was as big a windbag as any other Victorian, with an extra coating of humbug: 'They tell you, gentlemen, that I want to rob and injure the poor. God forbid I should do any such thing!'

As a railway magnate, he was soon staring at trouble, not from the excesses of the mania, but from his own relentless ambition. He seemed to have it all now: several estates in Yorkshire, one of the best town houses in London, and a portfolio of companies that mutated into the Midland Railway. But he didn't have a route into London, and the inexorable progress of the Great Northern, which was beyond his grasp, threatened to block his way. Then he had what appeared to be a lucky break.

The inchoate line into East Anglia, the Eastern

Counties Railway, had been a basket case since it opened and lacked the money to expand. Hudson saw this as his way from York to London, taking an easterly path through Lincoln and Cambridge. He took over as chairman of the Eastern Counties, where he followed his instincts and started ruthlessly cutting costs. But in 1846 a fatal crash at Stratford caused by an inexperienced driver led to Hudson's methods being exposed. And his other habits were also starting to attract attention.

The previous year a letter-writer to *The Times*, using the modest pseudonym A London Trader, had denounced Hudson's 'villainous juggling' with figures, using formidable statistical evidence to back him up. Whatever sort of trader this was, he probably wasn't a Seven Dials barrow boy. Then, in 1848, a pamphleteer called Arthur Smith accused Hudson of paying dividends out of capital rather than revenue, dubious then, illegal now. The allegations mounted, and it became clear that his kingdom was built on manipulation and embezzlement. With railway shares now languishing, Hudson had no chance of even beginning to buy his way out of trouble. He lost control of his companies and retired to one of his estates, saved only from arrest for debt by his parliamentary immunity; understandably, he took to drink, a fact that was obvious on the rare occasions he appeared in the Commons.

But Hudson had promised Sunderland a dock, and that he delivered, which was enough to keep him an MP until 1859. After that, he had to go into exile, a shabby figure hanging pathetically round the docks at Boulogne, hoping to meet old friends. 'Surely I know that man,' said Charles Dickens to a companion as he returned from a trip to Paris. 'I should think you did,' whispered the other. '*Hudson!*'

The passage of time made the establishment not merely forgetful but forgiving. In 1865 Hudson dared to come back and was duly arrested. But his creditors relented (he couldn't pay them, anyway), his admirers raised a small annuity, he rented a modest house in London with his wife and was readmitted to the Carlton Club, eventually becoming chairman of the smoking room. The bell tolled at York Minster when his coffin passed by.

Railway historians mostly err on the side of kindness towards the old rascal, because they like the railways and he built them. But the most pertinent comment came in a leader in *The Times* on Hudson's death in 1871:

Looking back to the 1840s and Sir Robert Peel's then distant premiership, it noted:

He [Peel] decided on free trade in railway enterprise ... unlimited competition ... fierce parliamentary battles, useless branches, suicidal rivalry in traffic, and all that chiefly marks the railway system up to the present time.

Undoubtedly the non-interference allowed the activity of speculators full play, and England obtained a complete series of railways at an earlier period than would otherwise have been the case... But at what a cost all this was done! Consider the sums wasted in British railways, and judge whether it can be said that

107

the system adds to our reputation as a prudent and business-like people. George Hudson was the creature of such a system.

Even the French Pay Homage

In 1834 Peel had been summoned back from holiday in Rome to form a new Conservative government. His administration (120 days) lasted longer than his journey (34 days), but not by much. Europe by then was just trying to work out its response to the British invention that would make it possible to get from Rome to London in a couple of days, and start to give future politicians the first inkling of the modern delusion that they are indispensable.

Britain's achievement was the talk of Europe. And governments were trying to work out how to adapt this remarkable British innovation to their countries. You can see the effect of Britain's initial lead more clearly than ever these days. When Eurostar trains cross the Channel, they do not have to switch sides like cars; in a discreet act of homage, both the French and the Belgians made an early decision that their trains, unlike their road vehicles, would follow the British example and take the left-hand track. (One exception is the train depicted on the dust-jacket of this volume. This can be attributed to either artistic licence or engineering works). And virtually every country in Europe chose its gauge to match Stephenson's.

Belgium was the quickest to respond. The

country had only formally come into existence in 1831, after a rebellion against Dutch rule and – then as now – it had no real unity or obvious purpose. Its first king, Leopold I, saw railways as the means of making sense of his quirky little country, which was also desperately in need of a reliable means of exporting its coal. In 1834 its parliament voted unanimously to draw up a national plan of where the railways should go. Ten years later it was more or less achieved. And the consequences of this are still in place. The country seethes with suppressed hatred, and the residents of prosperous Flemish-speaking Antwerp have almost nothing to say to the French-speaking citizens of rundown Charleroi. But you can still get from one to the other by fast, direct trains every half-hour.

France also had a national railway programme, though in the early years the network of relationships involved – between central government, local authorities and private companies – was more complex than the actual system itself. Not surprisingly, development was slow. It was the 1850s before a proper spider's web of lines took shape, with Paris at the centre. Douai in northern France acquired a station in 1846 but it was so quiet for the first few years that it was used for ball games. Again, the consequences are there today. France has great trains from Paris, but the service between, for instance, Bordeaux and Lyons is non-existent.

Germany was not even a country as such at the time. But it built its system quickly and cheaply, with a mixture of state and private capital, at about a quarter of the cost of Britain's. Prussia took the lead, and trains played a crucial role in economic development: there were few roads in the countryside in 1840. Prussian obsessions pervaded the railways, for good and ill. Both the postal and railway service were run like a peacetime army: 'three-quarters of a million men who stood stiff at attention when their superior spoke to them'. Company directors were often generals. Of course, the trains were efficient and punctual and, underlying the construction of the lines, there was the thought of potential military use. And the effects of the nineteenth century have not disappeared there either. German railway employees slouch around like anyone else these days, and no longer take their orders from the Imperial General Staff. But their trains are still magnificent.

Nineteenth-century British travellers found that funny foreign railways had their peculiarities. At the start of the journey, the French forced passengers to hand over their luggage, which then had to be carefully examined before it would be given back. 'The examination of luggage is necessarily tedious and annoying,' advised *The Railway Traveller's Handy Book of Hints, Suggestions and Advice* in 1862, 'and a person wishing to escape it should leave the matter in the hands of his servant'.

Second-class on German railways, it went on, was so comfortable that there was no point in travelling first-class except to avoid the universal habit of smoking. Luggage regulations there, not surprisingly, were rigidly enforced. Accommodation in Austria was 'indifferent', Dutch trains were 'liberally conducted' (which presumably did not mean the use of marijuana was permitted), while Belgian first-class was 'luxurious'. However, the author did not recommend Belgian second-class to ladies because of a shortage of doors: 'The seats ... have to be clambered over in the most awkward and indelicate fashion'.

Having adopted the gauge and in some cases the left-hand rule of the road, none of these countries sought to emulate Britain's let-a-hundred-flowers-bloom approach to building the system. Sweden briefly got itself entangled with John Sadleir, a fraudster-MP like Hudson who, as chairman of the Royal Swedish Railway Company, issued himself with 20,000 extra shares. On discovery in 1856, he poisoned himself on Hampstead Heath. And the Swedish government then decided to build and operate its main lines on its own, thank you very much.

The only other country that proceeded in anything like the British manner was the United States, where federalism, size and the national culture made government control improbable. Often American railroads really were cheap and cheerful: rickety lines thrown across the prairies where there were no snotty aristocrats to try to out-greed the railroad barons (which would have been some feat), merely the Indians and buffalo whose role was to be shot at and stay dead.

The cheerfulness was a necessity because the distances were so vast and the trains so slow that the cold comforts of early European trains would have been beyond human endurance. No

American was going to travel hundreds of miles without access to food and a toilet. American luxury – epitomized by the Pullman car – eventually spread across the world. But the infrastructure rotted, producing a railway that became the reverse of the British one: vital for shifting bulk freight across the continent, but almost wholly useless for passengers.

The Americans are credited with beating even the Germans to the first use of a train for transporting troops. In 1831 Brigadier-General Steuart and a hundred volunteers left Baltimore to quell a riot by railroad workers. Meanwhile, in Germany and indeed France, the generals busily involved themselves with railway planning. In Britain, the government did not bother to give itself the right to commandeer trains for troops until 1844.

The military possibilities offered by railways were obvious. Less obvious, perhaps, was the potential for total fiasco. In 1850 the Austrians moved 75,000 troops, 1,000 carriages and 8,000 horses to the Silesian frontier. 'Due to shortage of rolling-stock and staff, bad weather and lack of previous arrangement, the 150-mile journey took twenty-six days,' according to Ernest F. Carter, author of *Railways in Wartime*. Not merely could they have marched the distance quicker, the men could have had a fortnight's leave as well. Britain's approach may have been crazy, but no one should imagine every other country was getting things *exactly* right.

Casson's Alternative Universe

So what if? What if Gladstone had triumphed over Hudson in 1844? What if Britain had constructed a logical and efficient railway system, to the specifications of a professor of economics, say, and not one that depended on, for example, whether the keeper of the turnpike-gate at Sherborne was awake or not?

There was one last chance for something like this to happen. Lord Dalhousie, first as Gladstone's deputy at the Board of Trade and then as his successor as board president, tried to establish a system of that sort, based on detailed regional investigations of the competing mania schemes. MPs, more spirited then than now, saw him off, preferring to do battle for their own local interests.

It would be more than 160 years before anyone dared make the attempt again. In his capacity as professor of economics at Reading University and a business historian, Mark Casson has recently considered conventional academic wisdom about the issue. This holds that the problems of Britain's railways can be traced back to the initial lack of planning and the inefficiencies that resulted, especially in the duplication of main lines. He concluded that 'the inefficiencies were not only large, but larger than anyone has ever suggested before'.

In his capacity as a railway enthusiast, Casson proceeded to move to the next phase, which was to construct his own railway system, something beyond even the most elaborate train set: an entire counterfactual network as he believes it could and should have developed after 1830. By

Casson's reckoning – and it involved far more complex study than ever went into building the real thing – a 12,000-mile network, properly thought out, would have had the same social benefit as the 20,000 route-miles that Britain did have at the peak just before the First World War.

Some of the follies of the British system that developed are obvious. It is not a mark of the city's grandeur that London has a dozen different main railway entrances instead of a single *Hauptbahn-hof*, *Termini* or Union Station, which even the Americans usually managed; it's a mark of national stupidity that has cost trillions of pounds in wasted time for travellers over the generations. Because the rival companies were fighting for dominance and each had its own station, the major provincial cities also failed to become major hubs. To this day changing trains to go north or south remains an infernal nuisance in Manchester and Glasgow. Swansea, for many years, had six different stations, enabling it – in this respect, if no other – to rival Paris. Even in a town as small as Dunstable, Casson points out, changing trains was difficult because the lines never linked up.

For Casson, the mania ('a redistribution of income from naive investors to street-wise lawyers') and its collapse meant that the eventual British railway network was a salvage job. 'The failure of Parliament to establish an integrated national system was the permanent and most serious aspect of the legacy,' he says. The early railway engineers were primarily concerned with getting from one end of the route to the other, rather than maximizing revenue by stopping at

114

the major centres in between. That is another reason why Robert Stephenson was unperturbed about missing Northampton, and why the Great Western avoided historically important Trowbridge, and opted for the tiddly village of Swindon instead. In the 1840s the pressures on the entrepreneurs changed: landowners desperately wanted a railway instead of trying to keep it away. The result was a shambles, based on local politics, engineers' whims, the state of the capital market and pure blind chance.

To put it right, Casson retreated into his dream world. This is a very academic dream world in that it is founded on eight main heuristics ('the Steiner principle, the triangle principle, the cut-off principle...') which are hard to criticize if you cannot quite understand what a heuristic is. The result was a very carefully ordered dream too, with just one trunk line to the north out of London, heading through Northampton to Rugby, where it branches off in different directions. This is, of course, the basis of Britain's motorway system. And his hubs and junctions are not necessarily the existing hubs and junctions: Wetherby, Melrose, Kirkby Lonsdale, Trowbridge and indeed Northampton become vital railway centres; Crewe is left alone as an obscure and peaceful Cheshire village.

Casson's analysis puts into perspective what was the first major catastrophe that shaped Britain's failing twenty-first century transportation system. His system is an awesome piece of work and far better than the real thing. In heaven, perhaps, I will be able to take a ride on such Cassonian confections as the Trowbridge cut-off and the Axminster loop. But though Casson appears to have taken everything into account, it is, I think, possible to identify some weaknesses, even without a clear understanding of heuristics.

Starting with the most trivial point: if Robert Stephenson did not have the technology in the 1830s to get trains by a direct route into Northampton, then no one else would have done, including Casson.

Secondly, I believe that Casson – as economists sometimes do – has underestimated the inevitability of politics. In 2008 Gordon Brown's government announced plans to distance consideration of major infrastructure projects from the democratic process, imagining that this way it would thus be possible to dump a nuclear power plant on some unsuspecting village without objectors being able to stop it. I suspect the British people will prove more resilient and resourceful than the would-be dictators expect. And even in the first half of the nineteenth century, when power was more concentrated, it was not possible to ignore local feelings – whether people were fighting to get a railway, or keep it out. Britain is not Belgium. Casson also ignores what was sensed instinctively then and we know for certain now: that British government involvement with the railways will always tend towards the calamitous. In an alternative universe, Britain would probably have matched France in the 1840s and talked about railways rather than building them.

Also, his single trunk line does sound awfully vulnerable. Even if it were designed as a ten- or twelve-lane highway, which is what would now be needed, it would be at the mercy – as the M1 is – of all manner of problems: crashes, weather, sabotage, incompetence. Cars can find an alternative route when the motorway is closed and trains need one too: a network has to be robust as well as intricate.

The final point is that all these supposedly wasteful alternative routes turned out, during the most crucial years of the twentieth century to have their uses, as we shall see. The construction of Britain's railways was a traditional British cock-up, but it was not an unmitigated cock-up.

Fear and Loving

From the day the Liverpool & Manchester opened, the overblown, generalized fears about what the railways might do to passengers, livestock and the countryside all rapidly disappeared. But the Huskisson business created a very specific fear, of the trains themselves.

There was a certain adventurousness in the early days. People accustomed to riding on top of stagecoaches happily rode on train roofs for a while, as they still do in parts of Africa and Asia. (What is really terrifying is when they ride on top of trains with electric overhead cables.) But they soon got the message not to wander off.

Small boys had raced the horse-drawn Stockton & Darlington, jumping on and off the wagons. Meanwhile, adults walked the line, which seemed natural at a time when the distinction between railways and highways was still fuzzy. This did not become a national habit. After Huskisson's death British railways were almost invariably fenced in. This was partly because landowners did not want passengers contaminating their estates with their mucky presence. But the idea rapidly took hold that trains were dangerous unless you were on one.

P.G. Wodehouse has a wonderful line about Aunt Agatha 'whose demeanour was now rather like one who, picking daisies on the railway, has just caught the down express in the small of the back'. But Wodehouse wrote that in 1923, by which time he was largely based in America where, if anyone did pick daisies, they would be quite likely to do so on the railway, or at any rate the railroad. In the US, trains marched through city streets (most famously in Syracuse, New York), and hobos leapt in and out of boxcars that often had more passengers than a subway in rush hour. In the cinema the oncoming train has been a constant motif from *The Perils of Pauline* to a modern rite-of-passage movie like Rob Reiner's *Stand by Me:* the casual walk across the trestle bridge in the sunshine, the distant toot of the freight train, the Huskissonian look of horror at the realization that there is nowhere to run or hide, the terrifying approach ... and the *deus ex machina* that enables the hero to escape.

In the Third World, the shantytowns of Nairobi and Dhaka nuzzle against the tracks, and the street vendors of Bangkok lay out their wares so close to the rails that their limes, mangoes and fingers all look certain to be crushed by the wheels. Unthinkable in Britain.

In the 1950s the British *chanteuse* Alma Cogan sang *The Railroad Runs through the Middle of the House;* it was one of the songs of my childhood, but the very word 'railroad' gives it away as American, as does the concept. The middle of the house? Totally against British planning regulations! Trains are segregated as if they are carriers of disease. The arrangement applies even in stations. From Euston to the remotest country halt, the platform, as the name implies, has always had to be raised high above the tracks. The expense has been massive. The French have much faster trains than we do yet, even at major stations, passengers potter quite happily along on platforms barely raised above ground level. American conductors just keep a set of portable steps.

Not merely did British railways require fences, but the company was responsible for maintaining them. This became more urgent after the Southern Railway introduced third-rail electrification in 1925. And the law was reinforced in 1972 (Herrington's case) when the House of Lords ruled that the British Railways Board owed a duty of care to trespassers. Get run over by a train and you can claim. The widow Huskisson should have sued too.

In Arnside, Cumbria, there is traditionally an annual mass trespass on the Kent Viaduct across Morecambe Bay. This is said to be the exercise of the parishioners' ancient right of way. However, it takes place on Christmas Day, when there are no trains. And its very rarity makes it worthy of note. Fear, I am convinced, is part of the British fascination with trains. But the conscious fear of actually *travelling* on trains faded very rapidly. Though the early financial support for railways came almost wholly from the northern bourgeoisie, the Lancashire capitalists and the north-eastern Quakers, it rapidly spread across the classes. The Liverpool & Manchester's initial assumption, remember, was that the main potential revenue would come from goods, particularly from raw cotton, whose volume had outgrown the canals' capacity to carry it.

Then the company discovered that the manufacturers themselves would also be travelling: the story of the Manchester gentleman who went to Liverpool *twice in one day* to buy cotton tickled the press's fancy. Then, slowly, the railway latched onto the potential of the workers as passengers. The weavers started to use the line to carry their finished work to their customers, with one weaver carrying the produce of two others. The managers responded by imposing a one-person, one-pack rule. So the weavers staged a boycott and got the rule rescinded: the first recorded instance, according to Nicholas Faith, of a popular revolt against 'the almighty, monopolistic railway'.

But it took a while for the working-classes to get much benefit. Third-class did not exist in the early days (although the Liverpool & Manchester experimented with a 'superior description of carriage' above first-class). This was partly because the companies were at first taxed per passenger mile, so there was a disincentive to selling cheap tickets. The Stockton & Darlington introduced a third-class in 1835, partly to draw in the walkers, who up there had not yet succumbed to the trespass taboo.

The notion of carrying the working-class developed from there, but even third-class fares were high, and third-class passengers were confined to the slowest and most inconvenient trains. Some thought they were actually worse off than before because the old wagons and carts that used to carry them were being driven out of business along with the stagecoaches. So there was no alternative to the new railways, where conditions for the poor might range from the bad to the unspeakable. We might talk these days about cattle-class on Ryanair or First Great Western; this was the real thing.

Third-class generally comprised open trucks and while, on the face of it, they were similar to a carter's wagon, even a slow steam locomotive travelled about two or three times the speed of a horse, and so its passengers got a great deal colder. And if there was any danger going, they got the brunt of it. The Great Western, which opened its first stretch in 1838, did not bother with such riff-raff at all until it reached Reading in 1840, when it was announced – and you can imagine the official hand holding the official nose – that 'goods train passengers would be conveyed in uncovered trucks by the goods train only'. Since the Great Western's *second-class* was un-covered, the next rung down had to be disgust-ing. According to Charles E. Lee's splendid monograph on *Passenger Class Distinctions:* 'The seats for the goods train passengers were eighteen inches high, and were fitted in trucks with sides and ends only two feet above the floor; standing was thus very dangerous, especially as there were no spring buffers. The London-Bristol journey involved ten to twelve hours of exposure and discomfort.' And worse.

On Christmas Eve 1841 two of these trucks were put on a goods train to Bristol to carry home workers who were building the new Houses of Parliament. They were placed behind the locomotive and tender but in front of the freight wagons. The weather was bitter. The sides were so low that passengers might have been thrown out in the event of a sudden jolt. It was more than a jolt. Near Sonning the train ploughed into a landslide: eight dead, seventeen injured.

Remarkably, considering the hair-raising safety methods of the 1830s – no telegraph, no signals – this was the first high-profile accident since Day One. And it did lead to stricter regulations in the 1844 Act. But a Commons enquiry soon revealed that none of the companies had fully complied with the Act and, though third-class was normally now covered, that in many ways made things worse. The closed wagons had appalling ventilation, making them a haven for germs; and they had little light by day and, normally, none at night which converted the carriage, as one press report put it, into 'a den of infamy'. The Lee monograph is one of those splendid works that, by its concentration on the arcane, illuminates far greater historical truths. It includes a drawing of a post-1841 Great Western third-class wagon. It is hard to decide what it most resembles: a Black Maria or a poultry lorry.

Even in 1850, alfresco travel had evidently not disappeared entirely. In his short story *The Fiddler's Reel,* Thomas Hardy describes the arrival of an excursion train from Wessex at Waterloo for the 1851 Great Exhibition at Crystal Palace:

The unfortunate occupants of these vehicles were ... in a pitiable condition from their long journey; blue-faced, stiff-necked, sneezing, rain-beaten, chilled to the marrow, many of the men being hatless; in fact, they resembled people who had been out all night in an open boat on a rough sea, rather than inland excursionists for pleasure. The women had in some degree protected themselves by turning up the skirts of their gowns over their heads, but as by this arrangement they were additionally exposed about the hips, they were all more or less in a sorry plight.

The stoicism of our ancestors beggars belief, and they embraced the excursion train from the first opportunity. The precise first instance is unknown, but we know that in the 1830s the horse-drawn Whitby-Pickering line in Yorkshire issued cheap tickets to a church bazaar. Thomas Cook's first enterprise was undertaken in his capacity as secretary of his local branch of the South Midland Temperance Association. In 1841 he took 570 people from Leicester to Lough-borough for an anti-alcohol rally. We assume the company did not have to worry about passengers overdosing on cheap lager and wrecking the carriages.

When the Great Exhibition opened ten years

123

later, Cook was hired by the Midland Railway to use his skills in drumming up business for their trips from Yorkshire to London. A fares war broke out between the Midland and its rival, the Great Northern, and the cost was slashed from fifteen shillings(75p) to five; one estimate is that Cook alone organized travel for 165,000 passengers.

By then the masses were accustomed to using their rare days off to get on a cheap train, however congested and uncomfortable it might be, and wherever it might be going. There were even trips to factories as well as to zoos and seaside resorts. Indeed, there were treats available that are denied to modern day-trippers. In 1849 John Gleeson Wilson murdered all the other occupants of the house where he lodged in Liverpool: a pregnant woman, her two children and her maid. A crowd estimated at 100,000 turned up to watch him hang: 'The railway turned the occasion to a business purpose,' said *The Times*, 'by running cheap trains, all of which were densely packed.' Later in the century public executions were abolished, and professional football became popular instead.

In those first few extraordinary years, every kind of business was affected by the railways. The London 'magsman' – or street trickster – experienced a splendid boom when the provincial innocents made their first visit to the big city. However, according to the historian of the underworld Kellow Chesney, this was a temporary phenomenon: 'The magsmen reaped the harvest, but in the long run the transport revolution worked against them by helping to form a more sophisticated town-centred society... On the whole the social and technological changes of the nineteenth century tended to favour the higher grades of fraud.'

Quite so. Crooked railway entrepreneurs often did extremely well.

So Excessively Improper

From the reign of Elizabeth I until 1844 Eton College held a ceremony on Salt Hill in the middle of what is now Slough. It was known as 'Montem', and was replete with traditions of an obscure and complicated nature, even by Etonian standards. It had started as an initiation rite for new boys but, by the end, had become a major public occasion: in May 1844 Her Majesty graciously lent the college the immense tent of Tippoo Sahib, captured at the storming of Seringapatam, for the Eton boys to dine in.

Victoria's consort, Prince Albert, attended that year, travelling by rail from Paddington to Slough in the Great Western's state carriage. The whole day, reported *The Times*, 'came off with all those accompaniments, of crowds, equipages, processions, gay dresses, juvenile joy, beauty, drums and dust, which usually attend this triennial Saturnalia'. However, Etonians, their relatives and Royalty were not the only ones present. As the late Victorian historian of Eton, H.C. Maxwell Lyte, put it: 'The opening of the Great Western railway had the effect of bringing down a promiscuous horde of sightseers.' And the

125

headmaster, Edward Craven Hawtrey, returned to his quarters with a steely resolve.

He bided his time. But in November 1846, six months before the next Montem was scheduled, the news seeped out. The whole business was being abolished forthwith. 'One could hardly help regretting the abolition of so very picturesque a ceremony,' *The Times* said now, in a much lower key, 'but still the alteration of circumstances may render such a step expedient. The great facilities afforded by railways for conveying vast multitudes of people to Eton and Salt Hill render it hazardous to encourage the assemblage of such a mixed crowd as is now certain to be collected at the Montem.'

Ex officio, headmasters do not care for any kind of Saturnalia, and headmasters of Eton tend not to be enthusiasts for a 'mixed crowd'. Under Hawtrey's predecessor, the enthusiastic flogger John Keate, Eton had objected to the proposal for the Great Western, even though the line was a full mile and a half away. Keate was worried not only about the arrival of a mixed crowd, but about the possibility of his own boys taking the train for the purpose of 'degrading dissipation'.

At Rugby, the higher-minded Dr Thomas Arnold welcomed the first train through the town on the London & Birmingham with the words: 'I rejoice to see it and think that feudality is gone forever'. But the school had certainly not rejoiced when the planned route was first published, showing the tracks right by the school. The governing body acted quickly to get them shifted across town.

The coming of the railways confused the upper classes. The initial response was one of horror but then, as the reality hit home, the more pragmatic landed proprietors realized there was money to be made from discreet blackmail if a company wanted to cross your land and from improved commerce if it arrived nearby. And the fact was, that once people used the railway, they were won over. Even first-class was less than luxurious in those early days. When the young Gladstone went home to North Wales to get married in 1839 he wrote in his diary: '200 miles to Hawarden. Dust from engine annoying to the eyes and filthy in the carriage. I had dreaded the motion backward.' But it was infinitely better than the stagecoach.

Prince Albert ('Not quite so fast next time, Mr Conductor, if you please,') made his railway debut that same year, and that embodiment of sturdy Victorian virtues encouraged the Queen to have a go three years later between Slough and Paddington. She wrote to her Uncle Leopold that she was quite charmed.

Victoria, though now presumed to have been born at the age of eighty, was in her twenties at the time. Her generation was to be the railway generation. Their parents and, particularly, grandparents remained wary, fearful of the speed (Albert was always a little elderly) and of the change the railway was bringing. The Devon squire Cecil Torr, looking back in 1918, recalled his father's relish as the journey from London to their house near Lustleigh became less arduous. It took twenty-one hours in the *Defiance* coach in 1841. By 1845 the express from Paddington got him to Exeter in four and a half hours, with another three hours to get home. But Grandfather Torr was never quite reconciled. 'However glad I should be to receive my call,' he said, as he looked forward to death, 'I would prefer home to a railway carriage.'

His contemporaries felt the same. Lord Melbourne, prime minister from 1835 to 1841 and Queen Victoria's mentor, told her years later that he had never liked railways because 'they brought such a shocking set of people who commit every horror'. (His view may have been coloured because at the moment he took office, he had just made a very rash investment in the Nottingham Railway.) The Duke of Wellington understandably left it thirteen years after the unfortunate Huskisson business before using a train again. He complained that railways would only 'encourage the lower classes to travel about'.

The fears of the 1820s had been apocalyptic; in the 1830s they were more specific and real, but still verging on the hysterical. 'Your scheme is preposterous in the extreme!' the royal surgeon Sir Astley Cooper told Robert Stephenson and his colleagues as he explained just what he was planning to plonk by his estate at Berkhamsted. 'Do you think for one moment of the destruction of property involved in it? Why, gentlemen, if this sort of thing be permitted to go on, you will in a very few years destroy the noblesse!' By the 1840s as the upper-classes began to see the advantages and seize them when they presented themselves, opposition evaporated into, at worst, a grudging acceptance.

There were a handful of hold-outs. The most splendidly vindictive must have been John Younghusband of Cumberland who left his property to a relative 'on condition that he should never travel on the Carlisle & Silloth Bay Railway or receive into his house any of the promoters of that undertaking'. Apparently, it had used its compulsory powers to acquire some of his land.

There was also old Lady Suffield who continued to ride up to London in her own carriage to avoid other people. But most of the nobility tried to get the best of both worlds: they didn't want the railway in their back yards necessarily, but out of sight and sound just a short distance away was very handy. Even Wellington, who had been given a special deal that no station would be placed within five miles of his home, Stratfield Saye in Hampshire, gave way to his neighbours and permitted one at Mortimer, three miles away.

They tried to get the best of both worlds while travelling too. The ever-snotty Great Western Railway was particularly anxious to help in this regard, maintaining, at Bath, separate pens on the platform for first- and second-class. The third-class passengers are presumed to have been in the goods shed.

The aristocracy maintained their own superior version of first-class by travelling in their own private carriages, lashed to a flatbed truck, as though they were still on the road. This had one huge advantage – it offered the speed of the railway rather than the road, while maintaining privacy. But there were a number of disadvantages: for a start, it must have been fearfully bumpy. Also the horses had to travel separately, and frequently ended up somewhere totally different, especially if the journey involved the change of gauge at Gloucester.

The biggest problem of all became clear to the Countess of Zetland when a spark from the engine ignited an umbrella, and then her whole carriage, near Rugby in 1847. She and her maid took refuge outside on the truck but, with the train still travelling at 40mph, the maid hurled herself off and was badly injured. 'How long,' asked *The Times* wearily, 'will railway companies delay establishing a means of communication between passengers and the guard?' A surprisingly long time, actually.

Through want of imagination, mixed with inertia and snobbery, British trains had been modelled on the stagecoach from the start. The long survival of this system, according to Philip Bagwell, was explained by 'the Englishman's fixed determination to remain as isolated as possible from those who have the effrontery to travel on the same train as himself'. Visiting Americans, used to the conviviality and convenience of their trains, looked on aghast. The practice of conveying private road carriages disappeared in the 1850s and, gradually, the upper classes made their own accommodation with the new reality though, for some, it took longer than others. The writer Augustus Hare told how his mother would refuse to take the train all the way into London, but would get horses to meet her at a convenient station so she would not actually be seen in town alighting from a train. Sitting opposite strangers, she said, was 'so excessively improper'.

Even first-class strangers.

Every Fool in Buxton

Eventually, new forms of etiquette emerged to cope with the disagreeable situation of sharing carriages with people to whom one has not been introduced. Britain's love-hate relationship with the railways was starting to take shape. But one highly influential group did its best to remain aloof, and moulded that relationship into the tortured shape that it would assume forever.

The British intellectual response to the advent of the railways is usually summed up in two much-quoted literary references. Just two. One was Dickens' representation – in 1848 – of an engine as the inexorable agent of doom in *Dombey and Son*, first in the tormented mind of Dombey, mourning his son ('Away, with a shriek, and a roar, and a rattle ... the remorseless monster, Death!'), and then as the instrument of retribution against the villainous Carker.

The other reference was Ruskin's withering denunciation of what became the Midland main line from St Pancras to Manchester.

There was a rocky valley between Buxton and Bakewell, once upon a time, divine as the Vale of Tempe; you might have seen the Gods there morning and evening – Apollo and all the sweet Muses of the light – walking in fair procession on the lawns of it, to and fro among the pinnacles of its crags... You Enterprised a Railroad through the valley – you blasted its rocks away, heaped thousands of tons of shale upon its lovely stream. The valley is gone, and the Gods with it; and now every fool in Buxton can be in Bakewell in half an hour and every fool in Bakewell at Buxton.

Neither of these passages is characteristic of what you might call a consistent intellectual position. Nostalgia was always strong in Dickens. Like Thackeray – and unlike most of their readers – he harked back to coaching days. There is a far more effective piece of Dickensian writing, it seems to me, in *The Uncommercial Traveller*, the now little-read collection of sketches he wrote in the last decade of his life, the 1860s. Here he returns to his boyhood home in Kent.

As I left Dullborough [presumably Chatham] in the days when there were no railroads in the land, I left it in a stage-coach... With this tender remembrance upon me, I was cavalierly shunted back into Dullborough the other day, by train ... and the first discovery I made, was, that the Station had swallowed up the playing-field. It was gone. The two beautiful hawthorn-trees, the hedge, the turf, and all those buttercups and daisies, had given place to the stoniest of jolting roads. The coach that had carried me away, was melodiously called Timpson's Blue-Eyed Maid, *and belonged to Timpson, at the coach-office up-street; the locomotive that had brought me back was called severely No. 97 and belonged to S.E.R., and was spitting ashes and hot water over the blighted ground.*

In reality, no traveller was more commercial than Dickens, and he travelled frequently by train, as did Ruskin, usually cited as the ultimate railway-hater. Ruskin's works, being even more voluminous than Dickens', contain, like the Bible, pretty much any quotation that might suit one's purpose. At various times he expressed support for nationalization, a bizarre hatred of ornamentation on railway stations and a tender affection for the steam engine: 'I cannot express the amazed awe, the crushed humility, with which I sometimes watch a locomotive take its breath.'

Matthew Arnold, obliged to make a living as a schools inspector and spend his life enduring missed connections, cold platforms and draughty waiting rooms, saw the railways as part of the embodiment of middle-class philistinism, a word he popularized. There was also Wordsworth who, in 1833, extended a grudging welcome to this strange new creature called the locomotive:

In spite of all that beauty may disown
In your harsh features, Nature doth embrace
Her lawful offspring in Man's art.

That lasted until someone tried to stick a line through to Windermere:

Is there no nook of English ground secure
From rash assault?

Yet in Britain, in what became the home of railway enthusiasm, it was difficult, in those early days, to find writers willing to admit that they welcomed the trains. The intellectual classes always have a problem with change. They reacted with almost unanimous distaste to the crudities of Thatcherism, without rejecting the financial benefits it brought most of them. They even shuddered at the first sight of a word processor, and said that they could not possibly give up their typewriter, until they realized the machine's liberating power.

What the *literati* say and do is not always the same. Ruskin's attacks on capitalism were funded by his inheritance and his investments. The mania's improbable victims included the Brontë sisters who, at Emily's urging, invested their aunt's legacy in Hudson's Yorkshire & North Midland. Darwin, more prudently, sat out the mania and then built up a portfolio of railway investments that gave him the financial security to write *On the Origin of Species*.

When the railway age began, the few writers to enthuse about it were at the solid-good-sense end of the spectrum like that fount of wit, wisdom and humanity, the Rev. Sydney Smith:

Railroad travelling is a delightful improvement of human life. Man is become a bird; he can fly longer and quicker than the Solan goose. The mamma rushes sixty miles in two hours to the aching finger of her conjugating and declining grammar boy. The early Scotchman scratches himself in the morning mists of the North, and has his porridge in Piccadilly before the setting sun...

That was his softening-up exercise for a furious

campaign against the Great Western Railway for locking their passengers inside the trains leaving them open to possible incineration, as had happened at Versailles in 1842. As he wrote to the publisher, John Murray:

Every fresh accident on the railroads is an advantage, and leads to an improvement. What we want is an overturn which would kill a bishop, or at least a dean. The mood of conveyance would then become perfect.

Smith never did get his bishop. But otherwise that is a pretty accurate prediction of how safety would progress on the railways, which any health and safety inspector could endorse. Among British novelists of the era, the only out-and-out enthusiast for the railways seems to have been the foxhunting bard R.S. Surtees, as in *Mr Facey Romford's Hounds* (1864):

People can now pick and choose wives all the world over, instead of having to pursue the old Pelion on Ossa or Pig upon Bacon system of always marrying a neighbour's child. So we now have an amalgamation of countries and counties, and a consequent improvement in society – improvement in wit, improvement in wine, improvement in 'wittles', improvement in everything.

The high priests of Victorian culture and conscience looked on with disdain. Yet this pattern was peculiarly British. France, with far less reason to look back to an idealized past, was divided between Saint-Simonians and Parnassians, modernizers and sceptics. In railway terms, there were loathers (like Flaubert) and lovers (like Balzac). Flaubert would compile lists of his pet hates, which varied from time to time. 'Railways, factories, chemists and mathematicians' was one version. 'Railways, poisons, enema pumps, cream tarts, royalty and the guillotine' was a more resonant one. But the railways remained a constant.

Later, Zola, in *La Bête Humaine*, used trains not merely as a setting but as characters in a fearful story of love and vengeance. Jacques the engine driver no longer had his much-loved locomotive, *Lison*. This new one was grimly called No. 608. Just like the change from *Timpson's Blue-eyed Maid* to No. 97 – except that the railway itself is not seen as the source of unwanted change. We are catching our first glimpse of railway nostalgia.

In British literary fiction, a locomotive's main purpose was as a device to bump off unwanted characters (like Carker, or Lopez in Trollope's *The Prime Minister)* more effectively than any stagecoach. You wouldn't catch a Victorian British novelist becoming lyrical about one, any more than you would be likely to see Martin Amis or Will Self standing on a platform writing down engine numbers. But one great nineteenth-century European artist did exactly that: the composer Antonin Dvořák, even in his distinguished old age when he was probably the most famous man in Prague. Dvořák habitually made a daily journey to the station to find out which engine was pulling his favourite train; unable to get there one day, he sent his favourite student, Josef Suk, instead. 'Himself no railway enthusiast, Suk dutifully noted the number: but took it from the tender, not the locomotive,' according to Ian Carter. 'This solecism almost cost him the chance to marry Dvořák's daughter.'

In the US technological progress has always been received with far more gratitude than in Britain. 'Railroad iron is a magician's rod, in its power to evoke the sleeping energies of land and water,' said Ralph Waldo Emerson in 1844. 'The bountiful continent is ours, state on state, and territory on territory, to the waves of the Pacific sea.' And there even the Arcadians were comparatively relaxed. In the midst of his masterpiece *Walden*, Henry David Thoreau burst into song:

What's the railroad to me?
I never go to see
Where it ends.
It fills a few hollows,
And makes banks for the swallows,
It sets the sand a-blowing,
And the blackberries a-growing,

but I cross it like a cart-path in the woods. I will not have my eyes put out and my ears spoiled by its smoke and steam and hissing.

This was fair enough. But the moment passed quickly.

Now that the cars are gone by and all the restless world with them, and the fishes in the pond no longer

137

feel their rumbling, I am more alone than ever. For the rest of the long afternoon, perhaps, my meditations are interrupted only by the faint rattle of a carriage or team along the distant highway.

A British Thoreau would have been apoplectic. I did wonder if I was reading too much into the literary responses, and over-elaborating British attitudes compared to everyone else's simply because I was writing a book and needed a theory. Then I went to Liverpool.

The exhibition 'The Railway: Art in the Age of Steam' was shown at the Walker Art Gallery in Liverpool and the Nelson-Atkins Museum of Art in Kansas City in 2008 and early 2009, bringing together more than one hundred works from across the world. And it was possible to see the same national distinctions at work on canvas as on the page.

Here was American triumphalism in full cry. *Westward the Star of Empire Takes its Way* proclaimed Andrew Melrose as the title of an 1867 painting of an engine at dawn scattering the deer in Iowa. Here was the French fascination with the interplay of the machine and the landscape. Indeed, perhaps the most charming of all paintings of British railways came from both Camille Pissarro, and his son Lucien, in the improbable settings of Dulwich, Bedford Park and Acton. And here – most delightfully – was the magnificent twentieth-century Belgian surrealist Paul Delvaux, who was obsessed with painting naked women and railway stations and sometimes *(The Iron Age*, 1951) both together. (What more could

138

a boy ask for?)

Contrast British railway art. *The Night Train* by David Cox (1849) is terrifying the horses. Frank Holl's 1867 depiction of the aftermath of an emigrant's farewell is entitled simply *Gone*. And a pair by Abraham Solomon (1855) had the titles *First Class: The Meeting* and *Second Class: The Parting*. Just in case anyone missed the point, they also had heavy-handed subtitles: 'and at First Meeting loved' and 'Thus part we rich in sorrow, Parting poor.' Fortunately, perhaps, he never got round to third-class. His original version of the first-class picture showed a young man flirting outrageously with a girl while the father dozed but, after it was attacked in the *Art-Journal* as 'vulgar', Solomon bowdlerized it so he was talking instead to a very wide-awake father while the girl looked on demurely.

There are exceptions, of course. But it is important to draw a distinction between art that might have appealed to the *Art-Journal* and representational art, aimed squarely at popular taste – as purveyed by the Victorian art-as-narrative merchant W.P. Frith or the twentieth-century droolers-over-steam Terence Cuneo and David Shepherd.

American artists, even in their post-triumphalist phase, have always been fascinated with the tracks themselves, particularly as they stretched ever further west: linear elements in a regular landscape. Note the work of Edward Hopper or the drawings of Bob Dylan. But even in pictures not shown in Liverpool, the overriding theme in British railway art is the train as threat: an agent

139

of unwelcome change, misery and social division. That reached its apotheosis in John Martin's huge apocalyptic vision, *The Last Judgement* showing a train crashing into the abyss of hellfire. And Martin was at least as popular as Frith in his day. (The picture is now in Tate Britain, but it is dark, confused and hung well above eye level, so it is impossible to see the train. However, a curator assured me it was there).

Even the best-loved of all British railway pictures, Turner's *Rain, Steam and Speed* – a Great Western train as ethereal as a will-o'-the-wisp battling its way across Maidenhead Bridge – had to overcome the artist's belief that trains were ugly. That's what Ruskin said, anyway, if we trust him. Certainly, there is something very strange here, a paradox that seems to lie deep in the British subconscious.

A Note on Sex

When I began researching this book, I asked an analyst friend whether there was any published work on the psycho-sexual implications of railway travel. She said that they were too obvious to be worth discussing.

But then she is a Jungian. Sigmund Freud had no problem discussing them.

It is a puzzling fact that boys take such an extraordinarily intense interest in things connected with railways, and, at the age at which the production of phantasies is most active (shortly before puberty) use

140

those things as a nucleus of a symbolism that is peculiarly sexual. A compulsive link of this kind between railway-travel and sexuality is clearly derived from the pleasurable character of the sensations of movement.

Freud noted that 'every boy' had at some time wanted to be an engine driver or a coachman. Had he been writing later than the very start of the twentieth century, he would doubtless have added motor cars or even planes. But there are two features that are particularly germane to trains. One is the jolting that was characteristic of the early days. Another is the thrusting produced by the faster and more obviously phallic modern locomotive. Even in the nineteenth century, the train was regularly described as a projectile.

The sexual arousal produced by trains, Freud said, also had its counterpart:

In the event of repression, which turns so many childish preferences into their opposite, these same individuals, when they are adolescents or adults, will react to rocking or swinging with a feeling of nausea, will be terribly exhausted by a railway journey, or will be subject to attacks of anxiety on the journey...

Freud's disciple Karl Abraham did a great deal of research into the behaviour of neurotics.

Many neurotics experience a pronounced bodily pleasure in travelling. As a particularly characteristic example I may mention one patient of mine who used to make long railway journeys and to keep awake all

141

through even the longest of them in order not to lose his pleasure in travelling; and who used to travel chiefly for the sake of that pleasure. It may be mentioned that in many persons a long railway journey always brings on a pollution during the following night.

'A pollution' is what we would less pejoratively call an emission. The Freudian psychohistorian Peter Gay found sexual overtones throughout Victorian railway writing: 'the railroad became, for the nineteenth-century bourgeois imagination, a favourite actor in the theatre of libido'. Gay finds it even in *Dombey and Son,* which seems to be a stretch, but elsewhere it is not a stretch at all. Consider Walt Whitman. *To a Locomotive in Winter:*

Thee in the driving storm, even as now – the snow –
  the winter-day declining;
Thee in thy panoply, thy measured dual throbbing,
  and thy beat convulsive;
Thy black cylindric body, golden brass, and silvery
  steel;
Thy ponderous side-bars, parallel and connecting
  rods, gyrating, shuttling at thy sides;
Thy metrical, now swelling pant and roar – now
  tapering in the distance;

Steady on, old chap, one might say. But then Whitman was an American, and assumed to be homosexual. For anything similar in the British context it is necessary to turn, quite startlingly, to Elizabeth Barrett Browning. In the deep unread recesses of her verse-novel *Aurora Leigh* is this astonishing passage:

So we passed
The liberal open country and the close,
And shot through tunnels, like a lightning-wedge
By great Thor-hammers driven through the rock,
Which, quivering through the intestine blackness,
  splits,
And lets it in at once: the train swept in
Athrob with effort, trembling with resolve,
The fierce denouncing whistle wailing on
And dying off smothered in the shuddering dark,
While we, self-awed, drew troubled breath, oppressed
As other Titans, underneath the pile...

Contrast that with the repressed writing of all the male British Victorians. Indeed, contrast that with the contents of any of the 13,000-plus works listed in Ottley's *Bibliography of British Railway History*, nearly all of them written by men.

We might perhaps disregard as irrelevant the exchange in the Commons in July 2008 between the MP for Lichfield, Michael Fabricant, angry because fast trains pass through his constituency without stopping, and the transport secretary, Ruth Kelly:

Fabricant: Does the right honourable Lady understand that it is not much fun standing on a platform and a high-speed train sucks you off...
Kelly: The honourable Gentleman is of course right; it would not be much fun.

But then these trains are run by a company

143

called Virgin. Deep within the artistic and literary contempt, and the unanimous unwillingness to confront the erotic significance of railways, there must be something that leads on to the catastrophic failure of British transport policy, which would be a more fitting subject for parliamentary question time.

Let's go back to Alma Cogan. The original (American) title of *The Railroad Runs through the Middle of the House,* I now discover, was *The Railroad COMES through the Middle of the House.* As Cary Grant said in *North by Northwest,* when he momentarily removed his mouth from that of Eva Marie Saint; 'Beats flying, doesn't it?' Perhaps we should move on swiftly.

CHAPTER FIVE

THE BRIDGES

The *Pasty'n'Haggis* train from Cornwall to Dundee or Aberdeen crosses what might be called the three major structures of the British railway network: Brunel's Royal Albert Bridge over the Tamar, the Forth Bridge from Edinburgh into Fife and the Tay Bridge between Fife and Dundee.

You could also add a fourth: the comparatively unpretentious Royal Border Bridge at Berwick, for its (growing) political significance. But the Forth Bridge, the last to be built, is pre-eminent, both as a symbol of Victorian endeavour and ingenuity, and as part of the language, even to people who would struggle to place it on the map.

'It's like painting the Forth Bridge,' we say of any task that has to be repeated endlessly. The idea that it is necessary to start repainting the bridge the moment the job is finished is said to be a myth. But 200 workers are still required to provide constant maintenance of various kinds, at least until 2012 when engineers are due to complete the application of a special coating supposed to last twenty or thirty years.

It won't affect the language. And it won't change the bridge's appeal, unless someone tries to alter the trademark red. It is the colour, however often it is applied, that (as with the Golden Gate) makes it stand out from the grey crowd. Its stature is that, uniquely in Britain, the upstart road bridge has to be known as "the Forth *Road* Bridge" to distinguish it from the real thing.

Railway writers have long been reduced to gibbering wrecks by the sight of the bridge. It is as 'full of moods as a mountain', drooled C. Hamilton Ellis. 'It should be seen at sunrise; it should be seen in the evening; it should be seen in a storm; it should be seen when a white sea mist drifts up the firth, hiding all but the tops of the towers; it should be seen at night, when the fireman of a crossing engine opens his firedoor and floods the girders momentarily with an orange glare up to the topmost booms.'

Actually, you don't see much of it from the train. And when once, while driving, I found a vantage point to stare at it on a clear Scottish afternoon, I was struck by the lack of symmetry

145

between the hulking great superstructure and the pathetic little three-car diesels that now constitute the bulk of its traffic. No more do firemen flood the girders with an orange glare.

Its status is also partly by way of contrast. Work began on the Forth Bridge in January 1883, barely three years after its counterpart across the Tay was destroyed in a gale of such ferocity that it has blown down the years to make it Britain's most infamous railway disaster: the *Titanic* of the tracks. In the long and melancholy history of train crashes, this was something of a one-off. Unlike so many other accidents, it did not reveal some terrible defect in the railway system that could have produced a similar tragedy anytime, anywhere. But like the 'unsinkable' *Titanic*, this disaster spoke of the ever-popular conjunction of hubris and nemesis.

The Tay Bridge – the longest in the world – was opened in 1878; it had eighty-five spans, combining cast and wrought iron, with thirteen high girders to allow extra clearance for shipping. The following summer Queen Victoria went across, and graciously conferred on the designer Thomas Bouch the order of knighthood. On 26 December 1879 *The Times* published a gushing account of Bouch's plans to complete the rail network north of Edinburgh by bridging the Forth:

Vast as the undertaking seems, there is every reason to have confidence in its practicability. The engineer is Sir Thomas Bouch, whose greatest achievement hitherto – the Tay Bridge – has turned out a splendid success.

That was Friday's paper. Monday's paper told a different story.

Seventy-five passengers were thought to have been on the mail train making the return journey from Burntisland to Dundee through a fierce westerly gale in the early evening of 28 December. Modern accounts of the catastrophe retain an extraordinary poetic power.

When the train passed the signal box at Wormit, south of the bridge, Signalman Barclay entered the time in the train book – 7.14 – and let it pass. He and his colleague Watt saw it reach the high girders... 'A sudden violent gust of wind shook the cabin,' wrote L.T.C. Rolt.

At the same moment both men saw a sudden brilliant flash of light followed by total darkness; tail-lights, sparks and flash all instantly vanishing. Barclay tested his block instruments and found that they were dead. He and Watt then attempted to go out along the bridge but were driven back by the force of the wind. They next went down to the shore of the Firth. As they stood there the moon momentarily broke through the flying cloud wrack and by its fitful light they saw to their horror that all the high girders had gone.

And the train too. The official report was less graphic but totally damning: inadequate bracing of the ironwork of the tall piers, probably combined with defects in casting the columns. You could say there was a seventy-sixth victim of the disaster: Bouch, broken, was dead within the year. Yet the name now most closely associated with the Tay Bridge disaster is not Bouch but the

Dundee cod-poet William McGonagall, whose opening verse, somewhat less poetic than Rolt's description, is as infamous as the event itself:

Beautiful Railway Bridge of the Silv'ry Tay!
Alas! I am very sorry to say
That ninety lives have been taken away
On the last Sabbath day of 1879,
Which will be remember'd for a very long time.

Less well-known is the fact that it gets worse:

As soon as the catastrophe came to be known
The alarm from mouth to mouth was blown,
And the cry rang out all oe'r the town,
Good Heavens ! The Tay Bridge is blown down...

And almost forgotten, but equally execrable, is the account by A.J. Cronin, creator of *Dr Finlay's Casebook*, who originally became famous as a result of his 1931 novel *Hatter's Castle*. The heroine's lover Denis is on a train:

The wheels clanked with the ceaseless insistence of a passing-bell, still protesting endlessly: 'God help us! God help us! God help us!' Then, abruptly, when the whole train lay enwrapped within the iron lamellae of the middle link of the bridge, the wind elevated itself with a culminating, exultant roar to the orgasm of its power and passion. The bridge broke...

Meanwhile, the heroine, having been kicked by her father and then nearly drowned, is giving birth in a barn to a premature and sickly baby,

148

not that we're talking sudsy and overblown melodrama or anything...

Then the train with incredible speed, curving like a rocket, arched the darkness in a glittering parabola of light, and plunged soundlessly into the black hell of water below, where, like a rocket, it was instantly extinguished – for ever obliterated! For the infinity of a second, as he hurtled through the air, Denis knew what had happened. He knew everything, then instantly he ceased to know.

There really is no accounting for public taste.

As you cross the Tay even now, it is possible to see, alongside the innocuous new bridge, the foundations of the old one still sitting in the water. A *memento mori* in perpetuity. It is impossible to look at them without a shudder.

It's Safer with Jesse James

And yet train crashes of all kinds do exert an extraordinary hold on public attention. The complaint that every death on the railways attracts disproportionate media attention is not new. '"Dreadful loss of life on railways" was a stereotyped line,' complained John Francis in 1851, 'the casualties were always exaggerated, and for a long time it was the custom to treat railway travelling as very dangerous compared with that by coaches ... railway accidents were treated as special judgments on the sins of the people.' Two days after the crash outside Paddington in 1999 the *Daily*

Mail reported that the death toll could reach 170. The correct figure was thirty-one.

There is an obvious partial explanation for the exaggeration. It is easier to verify who might have been on a crashed car or plane than on a train or, more relevantly, a particular part of a train. And the media are not in the business of underplaying possible casualties.

In terms of news value, plane crashes, even small ones, also get more attention than car accidents. There is a logic here, I think. People are used either to driving themselves or being driven by someone they know. Even on a bus, the driver and the road ahead are both visible presences. On a train or plane the passengers entrust themselves to an unseen pilot facing perils we also can't see. It is amazing that we ever travel on either.

The Freudians have their own version of events. Freud found that the underlying sexual pleasure of riding trains had its counterpart whenever it was repressed, which he termed 'fear of trains', while his apostle Karl Abraham interpreted 'the fear experienced by neurotics in the face of accelerating or uncontrollable motion as the fear of their own sexuality going out of control'. It could, of course, just be their fear of being killed.

After the gung-ho early days, train travel was not outrageously dangerous, but it was nowhere near as safe as it could and should have been. Through the 1850s, 1860s and 1870s the lapses in safety were frequent but never quite egregious enough to shock the Victorians' rather blunted sensibilities sufficiently to make the government do anything.

The three most significant possibilities for improvement were points and signals that inter-locked to prevent any conflicting movement of trains; block-working to ensure that each train had its own inviolable space on a stretch of line; and continuous brakes to provide instant control over every wheel of every carriage.

These all came in, but more or less at random. According to Rolt: 'successive Railway Inspecting Officers urged the adoption of these safety precautions upon the railway companies (not all very willing to listen) with such tireless and un-daunted persistence that "lock, block and brake" became a kind of theme song of the Board of Trade.'

Victorian train crashes had a certain theatrical quality, and perhaps that is in the nature of rail-ways. (Staging crashes was one of the main delights of playing with my train set, and I don't care what Karl Abraham would make of that.) There was, for instance, the incident at Aynho in 1852 on the opening day of the Great Western's broad-gauge route to Birmingham. The special train, pulled by the *Lord of the Isles*, and driven by Daniel Gooch, Brunel's right-hand man, ran into a mixed goods and passenger train of the Oxford & Rugby Railway, whose driver was evidently unaware that the pace of life in the vicinity had just been stepped up: 'The guard of the mixed was unloading cheeses,' recorded Rolt, 'when upon this pleasant and leisurely rural scene there burst in swift and awful majesty the *Lord of the Isles* running at over fifty miles per hour.' No one

151

was even seriously hurt on this occasion, which was held by some to demonstrate the stability of the broad gauge.

In 1865 there was nearly a far more famous victim than Huskisson. Trackwork was being carried out near Staplehurst in Kent, and the foreman misunderstood the timing of the boat train from Folkestone. The rails were not replaced in time, and part of the train fell into the river below. Among those technically unhurt was Charles Dickens who had the almost-complete manuscript of *Our Mutual Friend* with him.

Dickens received a commemorative plate from the railway company for his work in succouring the wounded with brandy and water. He was also granted his wish not to give evidence at the inquest; he was particularly insistent on this point, which was not surprising since he was travelling with his mistress, Ellen Ternan, and very anxious to avoid mentioning this. But, according to his son Henry, Dickens himself did not recover: he was a very anxious train traveller ever after, thrown into panic by the slightest jolt. 'Was it as if some terror from his own imagination had now come alive?' asked his biographer, Peter Ackroyd. *Our Mutual Friend* was his last completed novel and he died five years to the day after the crash.

But Dickens, who inspired reform of so many nineteenth-century evils, could have no impact on railway safety. The crashes kept happening; the companies and government remained indifferent.

In 1873, on the first Friday in August, the 'Tourist Special' carrying twenty-two carriages from Euston to Scotland derailed at Wigan, one

of many stations on the network where investment had not kept up with the volume of traffic.
Expresses had to navigate an obstacle course of
different kinds of points and crossings, of slow
trains and shunting wagons. This express was
going too fast, and it started a mysterious spate
of crashes, so much so that by September *The
Times* had a column headed 'Friday's Railway
Accidents', along the lines of 'Court and Social'
or 'Today's Racecards'.

'It is a national scandal,' the paper fulminated,
'after a collision or other accident that has numbered its victims by the score, to have to proclaim
that the whole was due to the want of a continuous brake, or of a locked connecting rod, or of
some other mechanical contrivance as well known
and as effectual as the lock on a street door.' It
added that the railway interest in parliament
should be countered by a 'passenger interest'.

Even the Americans began mocking the British
indifference to railway safety. 'If the choice lay
between going safely and at a moderate speed, or
going fast with a good chance of being killed,
most Englishmen would unhesitatingly pro-
nounce for the latter,' said the London correspondent of the *New York Times*. And this in the
year when American trains were at the mercy of
Jesse James and his gang.

There is something very curious here, since the
Americans always appeared to take these issues
very lightly. Thirty years later, the crash at Dan-
ville, Virginia (nine dead), was turned into a
rollicking ballad, *The Wreck of the Ole '97*, still
sung today, and the subject of a remarkably jolly

painting by Thomas Hart Benton. In the 1890s, simulated collisions between locomotives became a regular American fairground attraction. In a twelve-month period spanning 1911–12, 5,284 people were reportedly run down by unfenced American trains. And even now the phrase 'train-wreck' is part of the American language to describe a minor cock-up or a dysfunctional celebrity. (British newspapers have now, in their intellectually sloppy way, begun adopting the phrase.) It was hard to imagine that Wigan really was more dangerous than the Wild West in 1873 but, in many aspects of rail safety, Britain was definitely behind the US where the Westinghouse brake system was already in use.

The train derailed at Wigan contained a substantial cross-section of the upper classes, copying Queen Victoria by taking their summer holidays in the Highlands. Many of them hardly knew what had happened: the train was so long that most of it continued its journey after a remarkably brief delay. Thirteen died, including Sir John Anson Bt and three children of the Wark family of Highgate. Lady Florence Leveson-Gower, daughter of the train-loving Duke of Sutherland, had a particularly remarkable escape since her carriage was the first to leave the track. But there were hundreds aboard the train. Unlike plane crashes, it was and is very rare to have a passenger train crash in which everyone or even most passengers are killed (Tay Bridge being an obvious exception). So most of the *prominenti* just dined out on their near miss when they got to Scotland. And very little was done for the next sixteen years.

The catalyst for change, when it finally came, did not involve the privileged classes at all, or even what is now regarded as the British railway system. On an Ulster summer's morning in 1889 an excursion special carrying a huge number of people on a Sunday school outing from Armagh to the seaside resort of Warrenpoint became decoupled on a steep incline close to Armagh station. Ten carriages fell back down the hill to meet the full force of an ordinary passenger train behind them. About eighty-eight people were killed, most of them children. Despite Sydney Smith's campaign nearly fifty years earlier, they were locked in and could not escape. The inspectors reported that continuous brakes would probably have prevented the disaster. The railway interest fell silent and within three months lock, block and brake were all enshrined in statute.

It was a turning-point: you could argue that laissez-faire also died that day. The number of fatalities started to fall: in both 1901 and 1908 there were more than a billion passenger journeys on the British railway system, and yet not a single paying customer was killed through the railways' fault.

'I'm Afraid I've Wrecked the Scotch Express'

It never has been and never will be possible to eliminate human error. The worst disaster of all in Britain came at Quintinshill on the Scottish border in 1915, when two feckless signalmen, Meakin and Tinsley, caused a pile-up of five separate trains, one of them carrying the Seventh Battalion of the Royal Scots in obsolete, death-trap, gas-lit wooden coaches, brought out of retirement because of the war.

Burning coals ignited the gas, which destroyed all fifteen coaches of the troop train. Out of 500 soldiers, only 60 were at roll call the following morning. The exact death toll was never known because the military records were destroyed, but 227 is a commonly quoted figure – more than double the 112 killed at Harrow and Wealdstone, its nearest rival for fatalities, in a triple pile-up in 1952. Quintinshill was also exceptional because the signalmen, who were jailed under Scottish law for culpable homicide, were almost wholly to blame. Most accidents revealed a story of conscientious but overworked railwaymen doing their best to adhere to the company's rule book.

Right from the start, the railways offered an attractive form of employment: much better-paid than farm work, more interesting than a factory, and secure above all. The companies knew this well, and enforced their will through rigid hierarchy and iron discipline. 'The countrymen of England worked within squirearchies which had altered little since feudal times,' noted the labour historian Frank McKenna. 'Slipping from one type of feudal power to another caused little difficulty.' And, in contrast to the traditional rural class system, this one offered promotion prospects.

The drawback was that the company owned their staff, body and soul. 'The railwaymen were from the beginning ruled by instructions as detailed as those of the Koran,' said McKenna. 'They were the first "organization men", stitched firmly into the fabric of their company, noted for punctuality, cleanliness and the smart execution of orders.' And the slightest breach of those obligations – real or fancied – could lead to instant dismissal.

Employees had no right of redress against unscrupulous owners. The North British Railway recruited staff by offering sixpence more per day than its rival, the Edinburgh and Glasgow. When they had signed up, the company withdrew the sixpence. A driver and fireman who quit without notice on this line in 1850 were jailed for three months. There was a similar case on the London & South Western. Always notably high-handed, the Great Western transferred a man it considered a troublemaker to a punishment-job working twelve hours a day on a guillotine papercutter for £1 a week. And that was in the 1930s.

These were extremes. But many railway managers had a military background, and the principles of military discipline ran through the industry, mostly to its benefit. Rigid adherence to regulations must have prevented thousands of other Quintinshills. However, saving human life is not the main function of an army and the Victorian companies' casual disregard for their passengers' lives was magnified at least tenfold when it came to their own employees. In the mid-1870s an average of 750 railway workers were being killed every year. Over the last quarter of the nineteenth century, the figure still averaged

157

500. Who cared? That same *Times* leader of 1873 which so eloquently condemned the 'national scandal' of passenger safety also referred contemptuously to 'the injuries to which railway servants so recklessly expose themselves'.

Many railway jobs were inherently nasty and dangerous. Before corridor trains, guards had to get from carriage to carriage by clambering along the outside. The companies rejected the idea of running boards because passengers might use them to get to better-class compartments. There were the men in the engine shed amid the hissing boilers and, above all, those in the ashpit, clearing out the allegedly cold clinker, which was not always cold. There were the shunters, constantly at the mercy of the combination of rogue couplings and a train of goods wagons.

And then there were the number takers, an obscure group – barely 500 strong – who had to stand at junctions across the country noting the movements of every wagon and carriage, reporting back to the Railway Clearing House in London so that the clerks could balance the companies' competing claims. Paid trainspotters, if you like.

But they were not paid much, they were out in all weathers and their thirteen-hour night shift persisted until 1919. They were run down or crushed, quite regularly, especially in the dark. 'When number taker Casey was squeezed between the buffers and severely injured in March 1865,' wrote Philip Bagwell, the historian of the Clearing House, 'the superintending committee decided to make up his pay, less the 7s 6d obtained from the Passenger Assurance Company, for a period of

158

one month.' Such a job would have seemed entirely quaint to modern readers, until the 1990s when similar staff had to be employed, now sitting behind computers, to cope with the effects of re-Balkanization after the abolition of British Rail.

Men whose sleepiness could endanger passengers also worked long hours. One story concerns a guard who had worked for eighteen hours and was then told to go out again. When he protested, he was told: 'You've got twenty-four hours in the day like every other man and they are all ours if we want them.' Twelve-hour shifts were normal, but a foreman could insist on double or treble that if he felt like it. Drivers were always on call, and twenty-six-hour turns were not unheard of.

The growth of trade unionism did not change the essentials until after the First World War. The driver responsible for the Salisbury train crash in 1906 (twenty-eight dead) had been on duty for nearly ten hours with another two to go before Waterloo. The same applied to other workers. Signalman Sutton was a weary man alone in the remote box at Hawes Junction in Yorkshire on a wild winter's night when he momentarily forgot the presence of two light engines on the Midland main line. He let the midnight express from St Pancras into the section. The normally celebratory writer Philip Unwin put it this way: 'When Signalman Sutton saw the low-hanging clouds to his north turn to an angry red in the distance, he realised his terrible mistake.' When his relief arrived at 6am Sutton uttered perhaps the most desolate sentence in the history of Britain's railways: 'Will you go to Stationmaster Bunce and say I am afraid I have wrecked the Scotch express.' He had. Twelve people were dead, some burnt beyond all recognition.

Unwin added that the Midland Railway, Sutton's employer, did not use the lever collar, a red object slipped over the signal lever to remind the signalman not to pull it if the line was occupied. The Midland said it could 'foster carelessness in the signalmen'.

What if Somebody Speaks?

The Victorian traveller had a far greater fear than the outside possibility of crashing: the terror of other people. The traditional British railway carriage contained a succession of private compartments, usually with six or eight seats facing each other. Given a reasonably empty train, good fortune and a sufficiently repulsive expression to use on potential interlopers, it might therefore be possible to avert the presence of strangers entirely.

This reproduced the pattern not so much of the often disagreeably communal stagecoach but of the smaller and more intimate post-chaise. It also faithfully replicated the familiar patterns of British life: the stratified taverns, walled off into different saloons and snugs; the locked London squares; the gardens guarded by dense privet; the private family pews.

On trains – if not in daily life – the British way became the continental way in this respect too. The Prussians even trumped the three-class system, and opted for five, including a special military class. And the Europeans also compartmentalized their carriages, so that they too escaped the community life of an American train, on which, even in the 1870s, you were in danger of meeting a travelling salesman from Minneapolis and hearing his entire life story.

The British instinctively preferred silence. But many early train travellers found it difficult just to look at the landscape: the speed caused what Wolfgang Schivelbusch called 'the dissolution of reality and its resurrection as panorama', which travellers found disorientating. They thus took refuge in reading. The railways provided an enormous stimulus to the sale of books, by no means all of them mindless – the third and fourth volumes of Macaulay's *History of England* were 'cried up and down the platform at York' – or even readable: in 1854 Matthew Arnold said he had seen a copy of his dramatic poem *Empedocles on Etna* on sale at Derby station, though it is hard to imagine any train journey being quite long and boring enough for *that*.

The unwritten rules of British train travel were well understood. 'Fellow passengers could converse lightly,' said one student of Victorian manners, 'so long as they did not interrupt or force their attentions on one another.' That much has not changed. 'It was permissible to smoke,' said another authority, 'after obtaining the consent of everyone present – but never if ladies were among the occupants.' The first part of that applied even in non-smoking carriages until at least the 1960s, when the balance of power between smokers and non-smokers started to change.

The greatest bone of contention – the mobile phone question of its day – concerned the windows, which could waft in not merely fresh air but all the smoke and smuts from the engine. It was understood that the person facing forward and next to the window had the right to control it. This did not diminish the subject's ability to give rise to the most ferocious disputes. The following letter appeared in the *Daily Mail* in 1906:

Sir, – I think it would be a popular move on the part of our railway companies if they would label some of the carriages 'Fresh Air Compartments'. Some passengers seem to love an atmosphere composed of used-up, mixed-up human breath; they take corner seats facing the engine and then claim a right to keep the windows closed. The selfishness of travellers upon this point is beyond belief and growing worse every year ... FRESH AIR

The riposte appeared just twenty-four hours later.

Sir, – Had your correspondent 'Fresh Air' added the word 'Fanatic' to his nom de plume, it would probably have more accurately described him and his truculent class. Every one is agreed that fresh air is desirable – if taken rationally; but to be compelled to sit in a railway carriage for an hour with an icy blast concentrated on one's head through a small aperture in the side of a train travelling at 50 miles an hour is desirable only from a faddist's point of view... We are better off without 'Fresh Air's' miniature tornado and

This dispute lasted about 150 years and was ended only by the introduction of air conditioning, and the near-total abolition of windows that opened.

Third-class carriages were more public and noisier. And, on the Continent, there was a certain shabby chic among writers in professing to admire the happy camaraderie of the cheap seats. 'How often I have ... envied the travellers of the third and fourth class,' wrote P.D. Fischer, a German traveller, in 1895, 'from whose heavily populated carriages merry conversation and laughter rang all the way into the boredom of my isolation cell.'

Unlike Fischer, the novelist Alphonse Daudet – 'the French Dickens' – actually plucked up the courage one day to travel with the merry throng. 'I'll never forget my trip to Paris in a third-class carriage,' he wrote, 'in the midst of drunken sailors singing, big fat peasants sleeping with their mouths open like those of dead fish, little old ladies with their baskets, children, fleas, wet-nurses, the whole paraphernalia of the carriage of the poor with its odour of pipe smoke, brandy, garlic sausage and wet straw. I think I'm still there.'

That presumably means he did not make a habit of travelling that way. Still, I have not found a report of a nineteenth-century English writer doing anything similar. It might have smacked of enthusiasm.

Early in *The Hound of the Baskervilles*, Sherlock Homes sends Dr Watson down to Devon to keep an eye on the strange goings-on. At Holmes's instruction, Watson meets his companions for the journey, Sir Henry Baskerville and Dr Mortimer, at Paddington in time for the 10.30 train and he later reports brightly: 'The journey was a swift and pleasant one, and I spent it in making the more intimate acquaintance of my two companions, and in playing with Dr Mortimer's spaniel.' (The spaniel was not the hound essential to the plot.)

The novel was first published, in serial form, in 1901–02, but is presumed to have been set in the early 1870s, and learned Sherlockians have since spent a great deal of time worrying about the precise details of this trip. The 2006 annotated edition of the Holmes novels contains the following note:

In The Railways of Dartmoor in the Days of Sherlock Holmes, *B.J.D. Walsh concludes that Watson and company would have taken the 10.30 or the 10.35 to Exeter, arriving at 2.28 pm, where they would have had to change for Coombe Tracey which Walsh identifies with Bovey Tracey on the Moretonhampstead Branch. Although there was a slower train at 11.45, only by taking the 10.30 or 10.35 could they have had the chance of obtaining lunch at Exeter. Neither the 10.30 nor the 10.35 train had yet acquired a restaurant car, and they did not do so until July 1899 and October 1899 respectively. From*

Exeter, Walsh concludes, Watson and his friends would have caught the *4.12 pm* train and, after changing at Newton Abbot, would have reached Bovey Tracey at *5.40.*

This may perhaps represent more detail than the average reader wishes to hear, and Holmes himself once described the brain as an attic, which ought to be kept clear of unnecessary clutter. Conan Doyle certainly abided by that rule: he was a notoriously slapdash writer, and Mr Walsh seems to me rather lucky that the author sent Watson to the right station and failed to give the Exeter train an intermediate stop at, say, Stoke-on-Trent. The fact that there really was a 10.30 train must have been a remarkable coincidence (and the 10.35 a red herring). *The Hound of the Baskervilles* is not *Bradshaw's Monthly Railway Guide;* it is a work of fiction, and Conan Doyle is entitled to send Watson to Devon however and whenever he wants.

But Walsh's researches are not useless. For the travels of Holmes and Watson are, more than anything else, the embodiment of our image of Victorian train travel, filtered not just by Conan Doyle but by the various TV and film versions which sometimes take even more liberties with his writing than he took with the facts. The hansom to the station, the cheery porter, a first-class compartment ... what could be more agreeable? Actually, almost anything could have been more agreeable, barring a return to the stagecoach. Until the closing years of the century, train travel was not merely unnecessarily dangerous – thanks to the obstinacy of the companies and the indifference of the politicians – it was also very unpleasant.

For the Englishman's privacy came at a price. The side corridor, allowing both individual compartments and free movement between them (an invention credited to the German engineer Edmund Heusinger von Waldegg) had not yet appeared. Nor had the gangway connection between carriages. The choice was between Fischer's 'isolation cell' and the open American carriage. The second option was specifically rejected at a meeting of company general managers in 1853: 'It is obvious that it is so opposed to the social habits of the English, and would interfere so much with the privacy and comfort they now enjoy that these considerations would forbid its adoption in this country.' Gangways did not appear until 1882, and the first through-corridor train in 1892.

This ruled out any question of food on the train, hence Walsh's obsession with lunch at Exeter. While American passengers were already dining luxuriously on board and French stations were offering some of the best food in town, British stations were building the reputation for culinary vileness that they have never lost. In his story *Mugby Junction* Dickens sends 'Our Missis' from the refreshment room (said to have been inspired by Wolverton) with its 'sawdust sandwiches' to France, and she is horrified by what she sees: 'roast fowls, hot and cold ... smoking roast veal surrounded with browned potatoes ... hot soup ... FRESH pastry, and that of a light construction ... a luscious show of fruit ... bottles and decanters of sound small wine...'

'The baseness of the French,' says Our Missis, 'as displayed in the fawning nature of their Refreshmenting, equals, if not surpasses, anythink as was ever heard of the baseness of the celebrated Bonaparte.'

In Britain, certain stations, such as York, specialized in victualling passengers in a mad scramble; the emphasis was on speed. Swindon (aka Swindleum), had a particularly bad reputation but the buffet still cashed in: until 1895 nearly all Great Western trains to Bristol were obliged to stop for ten minutes owing to a contractual deal signed by Brunel when he was strapped for cash. It was 1879 before the first restaurant car appeared on a British train and, since there were no corridors, it was only open to the first-class passengers who were already in that carriage.

There was another more delicate consequence of long-distance, non-corridor trains, that difficult Victorian question – 'Where do you go?' The answer was down your trousers. According to Philip Unwin: 'There were to be found at the approaches to many terminal stations certain shops which sold curious rubber appliances known as "secret travelling lavatories" which gentlemen could strap to the leg.' Ladies, as usual, were expected to have more fortitude.

Much later, some first-class compartments had their own private lavatories, though even these could be daunting, for in normal circumstances it was considered indelicate simply to be seen making the journey to the 'excuse-me'. And for the unprepared there was still a horror to come. 'The simple apparatus just "gave" straight on to the track,' Unwin recalled, 'and when the seat lid was raised you heard an exciting plonkety-plonkety sound from the rail joints below.' The problem could not be solved for other travellers until corridors became general.

But there were also fears in a non-corridor train that, even for the English, were greater than lavatorial ones. There was a sensational murder in France in 1860 when the body of one of the judges of the imperial court, Monsieur Poinsot, was found in a pool of blood in a train from Troyes when it arrived in Paris, which is the sort of news the British expected to hear from abroad. Then, in July 1863, an Irish schoolteacher on the London & North Western's Liverpool to London express suddenly stabbed two fellow-passengers for no apparent reason (there is no record that they had insisted on opening the window).

If it was madness, it was well-calculated madness, because the attacker waited until after the train had just left Bletchley, knowing there was no further stop until Camden Town, forty-five miles away. And the victims and the only other occupant of the carriage (an elderly lady who had in any case fainted) had no means of making the train stop, or raising the alarm. The managers, meeting in conclave, had already considered the idea of a primitive communication cord – a continuous rope attached to a bell in the driver's cabin – but shied away because they were less concerned about its use than its misuse. And the legislature, as usual, had declined to legislate.

The following year there was worse. Thomas Briggs, chief clerk of the Lombard Street bankers Robarts, Lubbock & Co, was found with his skull bashed in by the side of the line between Bow and Hackney Wick. He died without regaining consciousness, having evidently been robbed and thrown out of the train window. An eminently suitable foreign suspect, Franz Müller, was identified, traced to a ship bound for New York, arrested on arrival, extradited, tried and hanged – all on rather dubious evidence, rounded off by an even more dubious reported confession beside the gallows. (Inspector Lestrade would have had the sense to call in Mr Holmes.)

A huge crowd gathered at Newgate for the execution, four months after the murder, chanting 'Müller, Müller, he's the man!' and 'Oh, my! Think I've got to die!' These scenes helped bring about the end of public executions four years later. More to the point, the murder finally forced the government to do something about railway safety, and an 1868 Act obliged companies to install bells on all trains that went more than twenty miles without stopping. Unfortunately, the bells failed to work, and the government gave up trying to enforce the law.

Even for those passengers who prepared their own sandwiches, went to the toilet beforehand and did not find themselves sitting opposite a murderous maniac (or someone who looked foreign and so might be a murderous maniac), Victorian train journeys were rarely comfortable.

Until the 1870s carriages only had four or six wheels and a rigid under-frame. Philip Unwin recalled that it was quite normal to find oneself on a four-wheeler, even on expresses from King's Cross and Liverpool Street, into the twentieth century: 'Its rhythm on the short 30-foot lengths of rail was a reverberating "boom-boom, boom-boom" and the short body was apt to work up an uncomfortable waggle at any speed.' The newer six-wheelers with bogeys ('boom-boom-boom, boom-boom-boom') were not as bumpy but still oscillated enough to make passengers feel sick – which was another reason to need the toilet.

Lighting on trains – from oil to gas to electricity – improved only sluggishly, especially in the downmarket carriages, and a suggestion in 1859 that there should be a light in every carriage at night was rejected. The heating situation was far worse: all through those frigid Victorian winters, British trains were almost entirely unheated. Instead, passengers were expected to make do with coats, travelling rugs and an extraordinary contraption called a footwarmer. This was a metal container filled with hot water (or, later, a chemical solution) on the platform, and rented out for a small charge, though it was late in the century before third-class passengers were allowed to use them. Even in 1905, by which time there were several well-tested heating systems available, the Midland Railway owned 27,000 footwarmers. In Devon the struggling Lynton & Barnstaple Railway only got rid of them in 1933, two years before it closed down.

Punch, that repository of often laboured railway humour, summed up public feelings on this subject.

To a Railway Foot-warmer

At first I loved thee – thou wast warm –
The porter called thee 'ot', nay, bilin'.'
I tipped him as thy welcome form
He carried, with a grateful smile in.

Alas! Thou art a faithless friend,
Thy warmth was but dissimulation;
Thy tepid glow is at an end,
And I am nowhere near my station!

I shiver, cold in feet and hands,
It is a legal form of slaughter,
They don't warm (!) trains in other lands
With half a pint of tepid water.

I spurn thy coldness with a kick,
And pile on rugs as my protectors,
I'd send – to warm them – to Old Nick,
Thy parsimonious directors!

Queen Victoria had been granted an oil-burning boiler in the Royal Train as early as 1843, and in 1872 she delightedly wrote in her journal about her traditional summer pilgrimage from the Isle of Wight to Edinburgh:

We had our own usual large travelling railway carriages, which are indeed charming. It was a splendid night ... I had a good deal of rest.

For everyone else, sleeping cars did not come in

171

until the following year. However, even Her Majesty was not wholly immune from the sort of nonsense her subjects endured more regularly. In 1867 the journey had been rather more vexing:

I had been much annoyed to hear just before dinner that our saloon carriage could not go under some tunnel or arch beyond Carlisle and that I must get out and change carriages there. The railway carriage swung a good deal, and it was very hot, so that I did not get much sleep. At half-past seven I was woke up to dress and hurry out at Carlisle, ... we had some breakfast and waited an hour till our carriage was taken off and another put on (which they have since found out was quite unnecessary!).

Welcome to *our* world, ma'am.

The Arrogance of Power

The trains were not even getting that much faster. In 1852 the Great Western was running trains to Bristol in just over two and a half hours. A year later they were taking three and a quarter hours. Financial cutbacks were presumed to be the cause. 'Having demonstrated their effortless superiority,' Professor Jack Simmons wrote of the company's directors, 'they sat back and dozed off.' Dr Watson's train to Exeter would not have done the journey much quicker than in the earliest days of the railways.

Yet these were the great years for the railway companies. In the third quarter of the nineteenth

172

century they formed the most powerful industry in the world's most powerful country, a situation that began to change as Britain's economic position became more difficult. For most of that time the Conservative Party was split because of the repeal of the Corn Laws, and governmental control over parliament was weaker than it would ever be again. That made it hard for government to thwart the railways' wishes even if ministers were inclined to do so.

There was a brief wobble after the financial crisis of 1866 when the contractor Samuel Peto was ruined, and share prices collapsed so much that the railway titans went to Downing Street and begged to be nationalized. The shares soon recovered their value, and the directors their nerve. Governments could never form a consistent policy as to whether they considered amalgamations a boon or a menace, but by now the big companies were very big indeed. Early in the 1860s the number of route-miles in Great Britain passed 10,000, almost the same as in 2008, but it was not yet halfway to its peak figure. The railways were still expanding rapidly.

By 1870 only the furthest reaches of the country and the most inconsequential of towns did not have a railway, but the pace hardly slackened. The Forth and Tay still had to be spanned, and so did the equally daunting barrier of the Severn Estuary – finally conquered when the Great Western opened the Severn Tunnel in 1886.

In 1868 the Midland Railway, determined to compete with its rivals to the east and west, pushed through a new line south from Bedford into its awesome new cathedral at St Pancras. Then it marched north to conquer Scotland by building the Settle and Carlisle line through some of the bleakest landscape in the kingdom at a terrifying cost of men and treasure.

No more did the railways plead and wheedle for the right to cross private property. They cheerfully bulldozed the homes of the poor, especially in north and east London, and called it slum clearance. At least 120,000 people were displaced in London alone after 1850, according to Professor Simmons; some received inadequate compensation, some didn't even get that, and they all had to trudge off and find somewhere else to live. To build St Pancras, the Midland removed an estimated 20,000 living bodies from the rookeries of Agar Town and a good many dead ones from Old St Pancras churchyard, which was also in the way.

The railway pioneers – the Stephensons, Brunel, Hudson – were all gone by 1860, either to churchyards or disgrace. They were replaced by hard-driving managers like Mark Huish of the London & North Western, an instinctive monopolist, and Brunel's former assistant Sir Daniel Gooch, as rigid a cost-cutter as his old boss had been expansive. The leading contractors now were globetrotters like Peto (before his fall) and the ubiquitous Thomas Brassey, who is said to have built one-sixth of the British network, and worked together with Peto on such exotica as the Grand Trunk Railway of Canada and the Grand Crimean Central.

The benefits of the railway system began to

flow into the homes of ordinary Britons, at least those who still had homes to live in. London's winter comfort had been at the mercy of the Tyne coalowners, who offered high prices and an uncertain supply whenever the winds blew unfavourably for their coasters. Now the coalfields of Britain competed for Londoners' custom. The urban working-class had the chance to enjoy a much greater supply of fresh meat, fresh fish, fresh fruit and fresh milk from the countryside, the dairy farmers of Derbyshire and Berkshire eventually driving out of business the sad and stunted old moos who were kept in city-dwellers' backyards and cellars. And people could travel.

The companies ran genuinely cheap excursions to the countryside and seaside from London and the great cities of the north, often charging only a farthing or ha'penny a mile instead of the normal penny-a-mile third-class fare. But travel on Sunday, the one complete day of leisure available to most working men, was sometimes impeded by the opposition of sabbatarians (this was before the railways lost interest in running Sunday trains at all), and the more fastidious were regularly discouraged by the contemptuous attitude of the companies towards their customers. And though conditions had improved since Hardy's description of travel to the Great Exhibition, they were still grim. 'Excursion trains meant all that was horrible,' wrote John Pimlott in his history of English holidays, 'long and unearthly hours, packed carriages, queer company, continual shunting aside and waiting for regular trains to go by, and worst of all the contempt of decent travellers'. Thus it would be in the football specials of a century later, at least for the rare passenger who happened to be sober.

This was not wholly different from the experience of travellers on ordinary third-class trains, even though third-class receipts had begun to outweigh those from the other two classes combined. The railway companies had not yet discovered that self-interest could be enlightened self-interest. Nor had they yet begun to contemplate the limits of their own seemingly boundless strength.

CHAPTER SIX

NORBITON AND SURBITON

There are few suburbs anywhere in the world that inspire quite the same instant comic recognition as Surbiton. (Neasden, maybe, New Rochelle, Moonee Ponds, but it's a short list.) Here is the epitome of south London commuterdom, the refuge of the introverted middle class, the epitome of dull respectability.

It was the obvious place to set *The Good Life*, the 1970s BBC comedy in which Richard Briers and Felicity Kendal opt out of rat-racing and attempt self-sufficiency, with pigs and a goat instead. They could more sensibly have done this by moving to Herefordshire or Devon and doing

B&B as well, but the comic potential for upsetting the snooty neighbours would have been far more limited.

In the same era, on the same channel, Reggie Perrin was staging his own more surreal rebellion against corporate conformity and middle-aged angst by faking his own suicide. *The Fall and Rise of Reginald Perrin* is remembered for David Nobbs' nifty scripts, splendid character acting (led by Leonard Rossiter as Reggie) and catchphrases such as 'I didn't get where I am today by...'

There was also the running gag in which Reggie would march into his office, unsuccessfully throw his umbrella at the hatstand and announce to his secretary, 'Eleven minutes late, Joan', followed by a familiar railway excuse: 'staff difficulties, Hampton Wick'; or 'defective junction box, New Malden'; or 'defective axle at Wandsworth'; or (finally) 'Twenty-two minutes late, escaped puma, Chessington North'.

Reggie was said to live in 'Climthorpe', but on TV he was regularly seen leaving his detached suburban villa, and marching past Frederick W. Paine's funeral parlour to the station at Norbiton (just up the road from Surbiton) to catch a train due in at Waterloo at 0858, or more usually 0909 due to staff difficulties, defective junction box etc.

Perhaps the Goods and the Perrins knew each other socially. But unlike Surbiton, Norbiton is so obscure that most viewers alert enough to notice the name probably thought it was made up. It does exist, though, and has become popular among clued-up locals because it is in Transport for London's Zone 5 compared to

Surbiton's Zone 6, making fares to Waterloo cheaper.

It's hard for those of us who remember the original series to realize that if Reggie were real, he would have been long retired by now. In his day Norbiton would not have had self-storage warehouses, nightclubs, Japanese delis and Oriental fusion restaurants, as it does now. The commuters would not have carried BlackBerries, iPods, Nokias, Macchiatos or semi-compulsory bottled water. Frederick W. Paine is still in place though, rebranded as 'funeral directors and memorial consultants' with a new sign in fetching maroon.

If this doesn't sound too much like a piece of Sherlock Holmes scholarship, Reggie's train must have been what is now the 0828, due at Waterloo 0857. He sat with the crossword in a compartment of six. Now the train is a Class 455, with no toilets or first-class, essentially a glorified bus. The day I travelled, about fifty people were in my carriage from Norbiton and we ran out of seats at Raynes Park. Reggie would not have recognized his fellow-passengers. Only one was wearing a tie. But in his day, outward conformity sometimes disguised inner rebelliousness; this lot seemed the reverse, casually dressed, slavish in their attitude – and they lined up at the exact place to get into the open doors like well-trained dogs.

Only two were reading paid-for newspapers, though about fifteen were reading the give-away. Nearly half were women; at a guess, about a third were foreign. The train was efficient and on time;

178

the passengers all looked tired, joyless and put-upon. Reggie would have recognized that all right.

Norbiton does not have much of a reputation but Surbiton's image is accurate enough. It was probably the first suburb in the world to be created by the railway. The royal borough of Kingston upon Thames was a centre for the coaching trade, and uninterested in the blandishments of the new-fangled London & Southampton Railway. So the line was built through Surbiton, which was just a nearby hamlet, with a station originally called Kingston-upon-Railway, opened in 1838. And of course it grew.

Surbiton was dominated by commuters before the word assumed its present meaning (a person who holds a cheap or commutation ticket). And its function has not changed in 170 years. The last bowler hat may have retired and ties have almost followed, but there still cannot be much point in living here unless you take one of the ten trains an hour into Waterloo. The self-conscious 1930s modern station is much admired, though to me it seems far too reminiscent of a toy garage; the pub next door (The Surbiton Flyer) is characterless, like the rest of the high street. There are far better places to keep goats.

For Philip Unwin, however, it was a wonderful place to grow up. He was a publisher (his greatest business coup was unearthing the explorer Thor Heyerdahl's account of the KonTiki expedition) and part-time railway nostalgist and none of his memories is more evocative than his account of a well-off Edwardian family's holiday from the old

179

Surbiton station.

For most of the day after the rush hour the middle platform was shut to the public while fast trains roared through but it was opened up for the fast Portsmouth train and for the 'West of England Express' (as the staff rather grandly termed the semi-fast corridor train for Exeter and Plymouth)... Even the stationmaster himself would usually be upon the platform to see these important trains away and to make sure a large party like ours found its EN-GAGED carriage safely...

The first premonition of the delights to come was the titter-titter of the signal wires below the platform edge... Next came the loud ring of the big electric bell on the outside-wall of the waiting room ... in another minute or so, the great moment was at hand and the front of the engine appeared round the gentle curve of the deep cutting by which Joseph Locke, builder of the line, had sliced through Surbiton Hill seventy years before.

Variety was one of the great charms of railways then, and the locomotive might be one of three or four different types from an old 4–4–0 or a newer 4–4–0 to one of the latest 4–6–0s designed by that fierce old Scot, Dugald Drummond. To be able to identify it correctly at some distance was an essential of boyish pride. As it approached, free-wheeling easily with steam shut off and the vacuum brake being applied, a bluish haze hung over the train.

Engine and its separate tender swayed independently for a second or two as they swept over the points, due probably to the three or four thousand gallons of water sloshing about in the tender, then in came the train. As usual it seemed to miss the platform edge by only an inch or two, wheels rattled heavily and rhythmically over the rail joints and over all was that delectable, unforgettable whiff of coal smoke, steam and warm oil.

There are no frock coats or 4–6–0s or whiffs of coal smoke at Surbiton now. And even South West Trains' faster trains (whatever happened to that lovely word 'express'?) are pretty sluggish and oppressively cramped. There was an incident, reported in the *Sunday Times*, on a train to Waterloo in 2008 when a particularly officious conductor ordered passengers to sit down. 'Will all passengers sit down for their own safety,' she barked. 'Now! I've told you once already.'

There followed one of those rare and wonderful moments in modern British life: a Perrinesque show of spirit from members of the public against overbearing authority. Inured to standing, repeatedly told by officials to get used to standing and in any case uninterested in the small, squashed middle seats that had miraculously become available, the standing passengers stayed where they were.

'It's the rules, so sit down!' screeched the conductor. 'You've made your point,' replied one commuter. 'Now do shut up.'

The incident brought forth a suggestion from economist Dr Tim Leunig of the London School of Economics, who suggested ripping out all the seats in some commuter carriages and reinstituting third-class, with much cheaper fares, for those passengers content to stand. Now that would have brought a smile to the face of Philip Unwin, and any other railway historian of his era. Because...

Faster, Cheaper, Plusher

James Allport was general manager of the Midland Railway for all but three of the years between 1853 and 1880. He was one of the driving forces in the expansion of the company's network north to Scotland and south into St Pancras. Then in the early 1870s, with the company mired in the heroic, hubristic battle to complete the Settle & Carlisle route, he suddenly broke free of the mental shackles that had imprisoned British railway thinking, and did so in two contrasting directions.

Aware that the Midland's tortuous new line would never compete with its rivals on speed, he decided to trump them on comfort. In 1872 he went over to the US and met George Pullman, the pioneer of luxury train travel, and arranged for the Pullman company to operate sleeping cars on the Midland. The new trains appeared in 1874 with great bronze lamps instead of what C. Hamilton Ellis called 'smoky stink-pots', an oil-fired heater and crimson plush ... the British had never seen anything like it.

Allport brought in corridor trains and more comfortable six-wheel carriages, with twelve-wheelers for the Scottish run, all of which was within the rules of fair competition as understood by his rival managers. And before dining cars became general, he stopped his trains at Normanton, widely believed to have the least worst railway food in the country. Most crucially, he also announced that henceforth there would be third-class compartments on all Midland trains instead of confining the proles to the slowest services. In 1875 the Midland reduced its first-class fares, abolished second-class, and immediately upgraded its third-class carriages with upholstered seats and more acceptable legroom. This was not playing fair at all, and the other companies were very cross indeed. But they had to respond and, as a result, slatted seats were abolished throughout Britain, except on the 'paddy trains' reserved for the grimiest of pitmen and labourers travelling to and from their shift. Italians were still riding in such carriages a century later.

In retirement, Sir James, as he now was, looked back on these decisions in a manner that can only be read with justice to the sound of plaintive violins.

I have felt saddened to see third-class passengers shunted on to a siding in cold and bitter weather – a train containing amongst others many lightly-clad women and children – for the convenience of allowing the more comfortable and warmly-clad passengers to pass them. I have even known third-class trains to be shunted into a siding to allow express goods to pass. When the rich man travels, or if he lies in bed, his capital remains undiminished, and perhaps his income flows in all the same. But when the poor man travels, he has not only to pay his fare, but to sink his capital, for his time is his capital; and if he now consumes only five hours instead of ten in making a journey, he has saved five hours of time for useful labour – useful to himself, his family and to society. And I think with even more pleasure of the comfort in travelling we have been able to confer on women and children. But it took 25 years to get it done.

He would presumably never have convinced his board if this was intended as pure philanthropy. 'Our only objects are to increase the profits of the Midland Company,' the chairman E.S. Ellis assured worried shareholders, alarmed at the health of their seven per cent dividends. It was good business because passenger numbers were now increasing exponentially, and the growth was in third-class, not first.

Surbiton had not started an immediate trend, and there were very few new suburbs specifically created by the railway before 1870. But now they proliferated, especially to the north and east of London in places like Tottenham, Walthamstow and Edmonton. These old villages now had to house the very people bulldozed out of the inner city by the railway companies, who thus skilfully managed to convert them into regular customers. The main beneficiary was the Great Eastern Railway, which offered cheap fares and brought the working-class into London in huge numbers: Walthamstow had more than a hundred trains a day to London by 1914, including a half-hourly all-night service designed for Fleet Street print workers. Unlike Allport, the Great Eastern did not derive much pleasure from conferring comfort.

However, change was coming fast by the 1890s. Parliament became increasingly interventionist, and it became harder for railways to avoid all kinds of obligations, including cheap fares, and compensation to those who lost their homes. Politicians' attempts to regulate the railways' freight monopoly were more cack-handed and for a time led to higher prices rather than lower. Then they just imposed a price freeze, which caused terrible trouble later. But for passengers of all classes, the experience of travel at the turn of the century was far better than it had been. The broad gauge was finally abolished in 1892, and the country at last had a unified railway system. Five thousand men performed the conversion work over a single weekend, and 'through the liberality of Mr Wills, of Bristol, one of the Great Western directors' they were each served with 2oz of tobacco. Above all, trains were less uncomfortable, as we have seen, and they were faster.

During the mad, magnificent month of August 1895, the east coast and west coast lines started racing each other from London to Aberdeen, a journey that before the Forth and Tay Bridges had taken more than fourteen hours but was now just eight and a half. (It takes about seven hours in 2009.) It thrilled the public, who flocked to the stations to cheer the combatants, and an excited *Times* correspondent who announced: 'I can boast to have flown from the Thames to the Tay in the short darkness of a summer's night.' It appears to have been less of a thrill for some of the passengers trapped aboard these careering monsters, especially if they then got dumped on

Dundee station at four in the morning. The battle cooled, although the renewed emphasis on speed persisted, not merely in the north but also in the west, where the Great Western had long considered itself above such childish tricks. Racing in slightly less obvious form continued until a serious crash at Preston a year later put a damper on the fun.

There was even a new competitor, a fourth line to the north, the Great Central – forced through in the 1890s by the splendidly combative Sir Edward Watkin, chairman of the Manchester, Sheffield & Lincolnshire Railway, the Metropolitan Railway and the South Eastern Railway, whose dream was to put this ragbag portfolio together, slip a tunnel under the Channel and create a route from Manchester to Paris. He did achieve the first part of his aim, the Great Central, built through virgin country from Annesley Junction north of Nottingham to a new London station at Marylebone.

Just about everyone tried to stop the Great Central. The only substantial places it served were Nottingham, Leicester and Rugby, all of which, as the other companies argued, had plenty of trains already. And he had a far more influential opponent than his bleating rivals: the Marylebone Cricket Club, since he was planning to blithely run his trains across the Nursery Ground at Lord's. But Watkin knew how to make a deal, eventually got the right to tunnel underneath Lord's (in exchange for giving MCC the site of the nearby Clergy Female Orphanage School), and one way and another got the route open in 1899.

No one else seemed to know quite what it was for. There was talk about the northern coalfields and the Grimsby fish docks but the Great Central never paid a dividend, and most of it was despatched in Dr Beeching's cuts, against only token opposition, less than seventy years later.

Its remnant, the Chiltern Line, still rumbles under Lord's on its way to the gin-and-tonic belt of Buckinghamshire. And Marylebone now has the charming new service from Wrexham and Gobowen to cheer things up. But it has always been a very subdued terminus.

Watkin was right enough about the need for a Channel Tunnel, though it is characteristic of British railway history that the visionaries see the right things at the wrong time. The Great Central was built to a higher specification than most earlier lines, with more space. If it existed now, it would never be closed: it would be a vital freight route to Europe, unclogging the other routes. Watkin was a hundred years ahead of his time. He had some idea about the twenty-first century but, like his competitors, had not got the foggiest what was about to whack him over the head in the twentieth. In 1899 there were only thirty-three petrol stockists for all the automobiles in Britain.

The Absurdity! The Impertinence!

In 1900 an article appeared in the *Railway Magazine* with the cheering title 'Decline and Fall of Britain'. This might have referred to just about anything: in this case it was the relative speeds of express trains. Ten years earlier, said the author, Charles Rous-Marten, a study had shown that British trains were the fastest in the world: 'it was a case of England first, and the rest nowhere!'

But, he went on, 'the hard, unpalatable fact is that we are as completely beaten *now* as all other countries *then*. It is childish and unworthy to blink at the truth'. Despite the higher speeds of the 1890s, Britain had been overtaken: it had five express runs, that is between individual stations, scheduled at more than 55mph, compared to twenty-six in the US and twenty-seven in France. The US had four runs over 66mph. The figures for complete journeys were even more damning. A 'home-made humiliation', Rous-Marten called it, 'if smartness and progress be any credit or advantage to a nation'.

If he found those figures humiliating, it was lucky Rous-Marten was not around in 2008 when only one train in Britain, the Eurostar, could go even half the speed of the Shanghai maglev. But, all in all, Britain's railway companies were not in triumphalist mood at the start of the new century.

On 1 January 1901 there was news in the financial columns of a boom in American railroad shares: 'the reports of the Vanderbilt Western lines for the calendar year have served to add to the feeling of confidence and strength so widely prevailing'. Meanwhile, their British equivalents were deflated, with dividend cuts expected later in the year. And the reality was grim too, with terrible New Year weather causing floods, landslides and a near-disaster on a weakened bridge in Leicestershire.

Two years later the £100 stock of the largest British company, London & North Western, had fallen further from £179 to £169, and at the annual meeting, Lord Stalbridge, the chairman, was stung by criticism from dissident share-holders who were advocating the introduction of American business and accounting methods that would offer a clearer breakdown of the firm's various activities.

'Is it just or reasonable,' Stalbridge enquired, 'that the management of your railway, conducted as it is by highly experienced officials, who have had a life-training in the service, and who have been selected because of their special qualifi-cations for the positions they occupy, should be condemned wholesale by gentlemen who have no practical acquaintance with these difficult and technical questions?'

'The absurdity, not to say the *impertinence* of this attitude!' responded one of his critics, Percy Williams, in a tract called *Our Decrepit Railway System*. The London & North Western had long had a reputation, as the *Manchester Guardian* put it, for both autocracy and complacency: 'Its brains and influence appear sometimes to be more earnestly engaged in discovering and creating obstacles to progress than in removing them.' And, as the leader of the industry, it must be seen to a large extent as its embodiment.

Queen Victoria died in the first month of 1901, and the years between then and the outbreak of war in 1914 are often seen as the most golden of golden ages: an endless summer's afternoon when life in Britain reached a pitch of perfection, after the drains and before the trenches. Of course they were seen that way in retrospect, given the horrors that would be unleashed. This was not how they were generally seen at the time. The failure to subdue the Afrikaaner farmers in the Boer War was a national humiliation somewhat greater than the comparative speeds of American locomotives. This was followed by a succession of German invasion scares, political crises, economic crises, the loss of the *Titanic* and near-insurrection in Ireland. An obscure *Frenchman*, of all things, was even first to fly across the Channel, not a heroic British aviator.

For some people at some moments, the perfection felt real enough. The lovely summer of 1911 left 'a consistent impression of commingled happiness' for the poet Siegfried Sassoon. 'Sitting under the Irish yew,' he wrote, 'we seemed to have forgotten that there was such a thing as the future.' In her account of that summer, Juliet Nicholson conjured up life for the young Sassoon:

Walking at dawn in a garden filled with tea roses, tree peonies and lavender he would hear the distant sound of the early morning milk train leaving Paddock Wood station where the stationmaster wore a top hat and a baggy black frock coat to greet the arriving London trains. He would hear the sound of pigeons cooing monotonously in their dovecot, awake too early with the rising sun and already bored. He would watch the old white pony pull the mowing machine up and down the lawn, as he always had.

But the station master of Paddock Wood in 1911 would have seen things rather differently because, for two days in August, the unthinkable happened – there was a national rail strike.

The companies were well used to coping with grumbles from shareholders, passengers and traders who had to endure their monopoly of goods traffic. Their methods of dealing with their own staff had always been brisker. Thirty years earlier, they had known how to cope with meetings of the Amalgamated Society of Railway Servants, whose very name spoke of cringe – they would have a spy outside the door taking names. But a new generation had grown up, and the folk-memory of rural serfdom was growing dimmer.

In 1901 the House of Lords had ruled, in the Taff Vale case, that trade unions could be sued for going on strike. At the time, this was seen as a huge blow to the labour movement. In practice, it caused a galvanizing surge of anger. The 1906 Liberal government reversed the decision, and now there was an avowed socialist, John Burns, in the government and twenty-nine Labour MPs in the Commons.

Servitude was no longer on the agenda. In 1907 the ASRS was bought off with the promise of 'conciliation boards'. Four years later, the railwaymen – convinced that more aggressively unionized workers were doing better than they were – finally walked out to demand recognition. The absurdity! The impertinence! A strike!

Presumably Sassoon did not attempt to go up

to London on the third weekend in August. Had he done so, he would have found the Grenadier Guards, with bayonets fixed, at Charing Cross. In Llanelly, South Wales, there was far worse: troops shot dead two young men, one of whom had just come into his garden to see what the fuss was about. But within two days it was over: David Lloyd George, as Chancellor of the Exchequer, cajoled the employers into negotiating, and the balance of power in the industry changed for ever.

The Knights were Still Bold

Yet seen from other perspectives, there was no hint of alarm about the future of Britain's trains. On a good day, even Charles Rous-Marten could get enthusiastic: 'Mr G. Whale's new express engines on the London and North Western Railway not only are very handsome and attractive-looking machines, but what is much better, are doing excellent work.'

In 1904, Rous-Marten travelled from Crewe to London behind No. 1419 *Tamerlane* – 'two hours, fifty minutes, forty-three seconds for the 158 miles, with a load of 360 tons… Bravo, Mr Whale.'

That same year the Great Western introduced the *Cornish Riviera Limited*, non-stop from Paddington to Plymouth, the longest non-stop journey in the world, at an average 55mph. That joined their other crack expresses: the *Cornishman*, the *Flying Dutchman*, the *Afghan* (to Chester rather than Kabul), the *Jubilee*, the *Zulu* (to Plymouth not Pietermaritzburg), the *Flying Welshman* and the *North Star*.

And, oh, the colours! The engines on the Brighton line were 'gamboge' – tropical yellow – with brass fittings, until they were toned down to chocolate. The London and South Western had olive green engines and salmon-coloured coaches. Everything about the Midland was crimson. The Great Western's chocolate-and-cream coaches were pulled by bright green engines. The Caledonian Railway was Prussian blue. The London and North Western engines were a boring black, but they *gleamed*.

No longer forced to stop to feed its passengers, the LNWR in 1906 offered lunch of 'Soup, Poached Salmon, Roast Sirloin, Roast Chicken and Salad, Asparagus, Diplomat Pudding, Cheese and Dessert'. There was no mention of either/or in that menu. (The price was three shillings and sixpence (17½p), about £14 in 2008 prices. Coffee was fourpence (1½p) extra. The restaurant seems to have been open to all classes).

And still the railways were expanding. The GWR introduced various cut-offs that helped counter its alternative nickname of the Great Way Round. It also joined forces with the Great Central to open a new line through the undiscovered countryside of Beaconsfield and Gerrards Cross. This line still functions today, complete with the pagoda-style, corrugated-iron waiting rooms (now listed) at Denham Golf Club station. By 1914 the largest town in Britain more than three miles from a station was Painswick in Gloucestershire, which had fewer than 3,000 people. However, the vast majority of these late additions were both charming and – on the face of it – useless, the daydreams of over-optimistic local landowners made flesh, offering trains that went nowhere. Slowly.

There was the Invergarry and Fort Augustus Railway, pushed north for twenty-four miles from Spean Bridge to the southern edge of Loch Ness, which, *The Times* reported, 'will be a great boon to the West Highlands'. It was not. C. Hamilton Ellis called this route 'A child of sorrow'.

Many of the new lines were operated under the Light Railways Act of 1896 which, forty years too late, reduced the inappropriately onerous standards – high platforms, complex signalling, gated crossings, elaborate fencing – as long as they stuck to a 25mph speed limit. Further south in Scotland there was the Campbeltown & Machrihanish Light Railway, running across the six miles of plain that constitute the southern tip of Kintyre. It was so remote from the rest of the system that the nearest connecting station was in Ireland. The *Campbeltown Courier*'s resident poet 'C.M.' greeted its arrival, in 1909, with a flush of pride:

A railway a'oor ain, nae less,
A railway a'oor ain;
Gin ye've yer doots, jist come an' see't;
This railway o' oor ain.

There was no poem to mark its demise. In fact, even the *Courier* failed to report this event (*c.*

194

1931), and the line's historian, A. D. Farr, was unable to date it exactly.

In Sussex there was the gloriously named Hundred of Manhood & Selsey Tramway, from Chichester to Selsey Beach, built by Colonel H. F. Stephens, a businessman for whom the word 'eccentric' is wholly inadequate. Before the end, in 1935, it was operating what appeared to be Model T Fords mounted on railway axles.

Stephens also reopened what may well be, despite much competition, the most economically hopeless of all Britain's railways, 'the Potts line', which ran trains from an inconvenient station in Shrewsbury – having been denied access to Shrewsbury General – across the Welsh border to the well-known megalopolis of Llanymynech or, alternatively, to the skyscrapers and shopping malls of Criggion. Originally opened in August 1866, it closed in December 1866.

The Potts line opened and went bust twice more (on one occasion the bailiff very conspicuously boarded the train, so he was shunted into a siding and left there) before Stephens rode to the rescue in 1911. He brought in locomotives called *Pyramus*, *Thisbe*, *Daphne* and *Dido* (Stephens was a great classicist) and one officially known as *Gazelle*, but more usually as the *Coffee-Pot*, said to be the smallest engine ever used on a British standard-gauge railway. He acquired an old London horse tram as a carriage, ripped out the top deck and used the seats on station platforms. With few costs but even fewer passengers, the line (finally closed to the public 1933) just about outlasted Stephens (who died 1931). Hilarious? I think so. Mad? Yes, but... The notion that Britain had built too many railways, which was already current in Edwardian times, turned out not to be the whole truth, as we will discover later.

Everyone still wanted 'a railway a'oor ain' because the railway was not merely the predominant means of transport but, for many purposes, the only practical one. Only in the suburbs, where electric trams were spreading, was there any serious competitive nuisance. To take one small but staggering example, on one October Sunday in 1911, the London & North Western alone transported 112 theatrical companies from one town to another: 30 special trains (some companies took scheduled services), 2,374 passengers, 182 scenery trucks and 8 horseboxes.

Just one of those specials, from Manchester to Carlisle, carried the following cast which – like the railways themselves – covered everything from historical drama to farce:

The *Florodora* Company
– Eccles to Preston
Miss Glossop Harris' Company
– Birkenhead to Carlisle
The Master of the Mill Company
– Leeds to Lancaster
When Knights Were Bold Company
– Bradford to Glasgow
A Royal Divorce Company
– Hyde to Glasgow
For Wife and Kingdom Company
– Barrow to Leith

And train travel did not even end with death. Brookwood in Surrey, the largest cemetery in Britain, had not one station but two: one for Church of England funerals, one for everyone else. The Necropolis Company also kept its own private station in a quiet corner of Waterloo and transported both mourners and the deceased to the graveyard. Naturally, class distinctions were maintained on the journey: there were first-class, second-class and third-class funerals and even three classes of coffin tickets. (Yes, yes, singles not returns.) All this lasted until the Necropolis station at Waterloo was bombed in 1941.

The railways still had no sense of their own mortality. In 1906 an officer of the Great Western, believed to be the revered chief mechanical engineer G.J. Churchward, threw out the *Lord of the Isles*, the most famous of the company's now obsolete broad-gauge locomotives, and had it broken up for scrap. He needed the space in the engine shed. From our perspective, that sounds crass but it does at least suggest an industry thrusting towards the future rather than one lost in its own historical drama. Or indeed, farce.

It's Cheaper via New York

The Edwardian era was also a time when collectivist ideas were gaining in intellectual credibility. Victorian certainties were under siege, and the railways were far from immune.

The companies were under consistent pressure

to cooperate more with their rivals. By September 1907 (with London & North Western stock now down to 137) Lord Brassey, the politician son of the engineer, was getting a thoughtful hearing from the Associated Chambers of Commerce for an extraordinary idea: 'Competition is carried to excess,' he said. 'An immense amount of capital is wasted on duplicate lines not called for by the public... In and out of parliament there is a growing demand that railways should be managed with a single eye to the service of the public, not for the benefit of the shareholders.'

This demand increased as the unions' victory in 1911 obliged the government to let the companies increase their fares and charges to pay for the extra wages. (This would become a very familiar story.) Furthermore, a Commons committee under Russell Rea MP concluded that prices were no higher in areas where different rail companies were cooperating with each other than when they were in full competition. This led to the setting-up of a Royal Commission under Lord Loreburn to consider the possibility of nationalization. It started to do this, without quite using the word (preferring 'state control' or 'administrative interference') before the war put a stop to the discussions.

As the commission deliberated, there emerged a brilliant tract, written by Emil Davies, a writer associated with the infant *New Statesman* and chairman of the Railway Nationalization Society. Davies might have made a more effective advocate had he shaved off his goatee and made himself look a little less like an anarchist bomb-thrower. But in print he made a devastating case against the massive pile of ramps, rip-offs, complexities and complications built up by the railway companies over the years.

He skewered the labyrinthine list of illogical charges and fares offered by the 217 different surviving companies. He quoted the assistant goods manager of the Great Western as saying that his company had thirty million different freight rates. He cited the 'celebrated case' of the hundred tons of potatoes sent from Dundee to New York, which were not landed because of high duties and were shipped back to Liverpool, all of which cost less than sending them from Dundee to Liverpool by rail.

In 1911, he said, a trader inquired about the rate for goods from Wokingham to Charlton goods siding and was quoted eleven shillings and eightpence (58p) per ton. He also asked for a price from the same place to Angerstein's Wharf, Charlton – same companies involved, but a quarter of a mile further on. The answer was five shillings (25p) per ton.

Davies explained, just as the sainted Barry Doe does nowadays in *Rail* magazine, how passengers could save themselves money by taking advantage of the anomalies, and buying tickets for longer journeys. He then offered a *tour d'horizon* of the Continent, a bountiful place of comfortable carriages, cheap and logical fares, magnificent food, happy well-paid workers and safe trains.

There were just two problems with this argument. First, since confiscation was not an option, the state would have had to buy out the companies at a fair price. At that point LNWR shares were down to 132, much cheaper than they had been but far more expensive than they would be in 1918, when they were down to 93, or about half their 1901 value, the assets having been completely clapped out by four years of wartime usage. In other words, nationalization in 1913 would have been a terrible deal for the taxpayer. In the context of British railway history, it is surprising that the government did not choose this least propitious moment to buy out the shareholders at a generous price.

The most terrible and whimsical of wars might not have been easily foreseeable. The evidence for the other problem was becoming clearer. After the 1911 strike, the Railway Servants mutated into the National Union of Railwaymen, and strikes increased. With each hint of disruption, businesses – if not yet passengers – began to explore other possibilities.

In September 1913 *The Times* reported that mail was once again travelling regularly by road, after three-quarters of a century on the rails. And it cited a large Edinburgh store that was using motor vans to deliver over a far wider area than was ever possible with horses. 'The present state of unrest in the railway and transport world is acting as a wonderful stimulus to the increasing use of the highway,' said the report.

Country roads had been almost forgotten for seventy years: they had been given a little life by the fashion for bicycling, but not much. Some of the old highways were sprouting grass from lack of use. The few railwayless towns, like Shaftesbury in Dorset, were now deathly quiet. 'The only sound that would disturb the nocturnal slumbers of a citizen,' Sir Charles Petrie later recalled, 'would be the faltering footsteps of a late reveller, or the hooves of a horse when his master rode in to fetch the doctor to some urgent case at an outlying farm or cottage.'

The world was about to turn upside down.

CHAPTER SEVEN

CARNFORTH

Carnforth station, in North Lancashire, was once the setting for a dramatic moment in political history. Gladstone, as prime minister, was staying with the Duke of Devonshire at Holker Hall, near Cartmel, in February 1885 when word came through of the massacre of Khartoum, and the death of General Gordon, Queen Victoria's favourite warrior.

Gladstone immediately left for London via Carnforth, where the stationmaster handed him a telegram from his monarch, so furious that she had abandoned her customary code, con-stitutional restraint and regard for grammar: 'These news from Khartoum are frightful and to think that all this might have been prevented and many precious lives saved by earlier action is too fearful.' This was potential political dynamite – the sovereign blaming her prime minister – and, according to one version, Gladstone's first reaction was to try to ascertain the stationmaster's politics and thus the chances of the telegram being leaked to the press.

And now Carnforth is perhaps the only station in Britain that is a genuine tourist attraction in its own right, a place which people come to see rather than just catch trains. It would be nice to report that the place was crawling with Gladstone buffs, anxious to see the stationmaster's office and a glass case containing his electric telegraph. But of course hardly anyone remembers this story.

People come here because Carnforth refreshment room is thought to be the place where Trevor Howard once removed a piece of grit from the doe-like eye of Celia Johnson, a routine kindness that was the starting point of *Brief Encounter*, perhaps the most enduring film in the entire history of the British cinema.

In fact, the refreshment room was built in the studio. But Carnforth station, thinly disguised as 'Milford Junction', and its clock were used for all the platform shots. The accents and attitudes of *Brief Encounter* make it clear that it was set in the Home Counties, though careful viewers may have noted the quick shot of destination boards showing such imaginary destinations as Barrow and Leeds rather than the far more vivid ones of Ketchworth and Churley. The film was made in the winter of 1945, with the war still on, but Carnforth was far enough north to be immune from V2 rockets and could be exempted from the blackout.

There are, I think, three reasons for the film's success. First, it was exquisitely acted, written (by Noel Coward) and directed (by David Lean), leaving aside the unfortunate lapse with the destination boards. Second, it is a love story in which the couple never get round to doing anything at all beyond the odd embrace, speaking directly to the British national difficulty with this area of life. (*Brève Rencontre* was apparently a complete flop in France, where audiences could not understand the point of a romance that was never consummated.)

And third, it is a love story *with trains*, and steam trains at that. It has the nostalgic appeal of the Second World War, which remains the fundamental reference point of British life, when the priorities were straightforward and obvious, without the messy compromises and doubts of peacetime. All wartime trains are a symbolic representation of that aspect of the English imagination. And there are expresses, rushing through, packed with sexual symbolism.

Nostalgia for the benighted trains of both world wars is rather absurd. Indeed the same might be said of the trains between the wars as well. However, this false-memory syndrome, probably helped by the images of *Brief Encounter*, did play an important role in much later political events.

Carnforth station did not thrive after the film crew left. Lancaster took over its role as a junction, and main-line trains no longer stopped there. The clock disappeared, and the place fell into sorry decay before a major rejuvenation effort in 2003. Now there is a visitor centre, a railway model shop and scope for hospitality way beyond that offered in the fictional buffet (you can 'Have your Brief Encounter at Carnforth station...We offer facilities for Business Meetings, Corporate Events and Private Functions'). The clock was rediscovered, repaired and re-hung and, though the main-line platforms are railed off, to make it clear this is not a *serious* station, the railings are attractive and painted a fetching green. There is a nasty concrete wall on the remaining northbound platform, behind which British Rail's last steam depot still awaits restoration. To balance that, there is still an amazing Furness Railway signal box (built *c.* 1870), looking vaguely like a miniature fairy-tale castle.

There is also the Brief Encounter Tearoom. Trudging in wearily at 4.15 one afternoon, I discovered Andrew, the owner, clearing up, having closed at four. I won't hear a word said against the Brief Encounter Tearoom: he recognized an emergency when he saw one, served me a pot of tea and lemon drizzle cake and did everything possible to make me feel comfortable short of removing grit from my eye.

And, sitting on the platform, I met a character called Jim Walker who told me of his own role in another piece of railway history: he was the fireman on the Stanier 8F engine that did the Blackburn-Carnforth run on the last actual working day of steam in 1968. He is not an admirer of the modern-day railway.

'We were watching *The Alamo* on TV,' he was saying, 'and I said to the wife "If that were the English, they wouldn't have fired a shot". They'll put up with owt. The whole transport system is a shambles. Get Deutsche Bahn to run this lot, they'd sort it out. What makes this nation go down is that we're apathetic people, I'm afraid it's the truth.'

Well, I nodded of course. You could say he has hit upon one theme of this book. But Carnforth is not the worst place to consider the matter of German railways, and the forgotten stories that helped Britain win both wars.

'Your Majesty, It Cannot Be Done'

The bald statement is associated mainly with the historian A.J.P. Taylor: The First World War 'came about mainly because of railway timetables'.

The basis for his argument lies in the Schlieffen Plan, which had long laid down, in intricate detail, the precise orchestration for *Der Tag* – the day when Germany could start the European war that large elements in its military structure desperately craved. Taylor explained:

The railway timetables which in other countries brought men to their mobilising centres, in the Schlieffen Plan continued and brought the troops not to their barracks, but into Belgium and Northern France. The German mobilisation plan actually laid down the first forty days of the German invasion of France and none of it could be altered because if it did all the timetables would go wrong. Thus the decision for mobilisation ... was a decision for a general European war.

Taylor was a somewhat individualistic historian, not a plodding defensive player but a purveyor of flashy strokes aimed at the boundary, sometimes off the edge. But on this subject his position is not so different from that of more consensual scholars. Yes, it was a war partly caused by railway timetables. But perhaps it would be more accurate to say not that they could not be altered, but that the high command *believed* they could not be altered.

The plan was based on the theory that it was necessary to see off France and Britain before concentrating on the eastern front. The story, as told by Barbara Tuchman, is that at the last moment – 1 August – the Kaiser got cold feet and belatedly tried to press upon the chief of the general staff, Helmuth von Moltke the younger, the less arrogant and more intuitive idea of merely defending the Western Front and fighting one war at a time. Moltke replied: 'Your Majesty, it cannot be done.'

The arrangements were indeed almost ineffable in their scale: one army corps alone – out of the total of forty in the German forces – required 6,010 railway carriages grouped in 140 trains for humans and the same number again for their supplies. The timetable was fixed: there were 11,000 trains, scheduled at ten-minute intervals. But if that could be achieved, it could also have been changed. Or so General von Staab, chief of von Moltke's railway division, insisted after the war when he learned of what he considered this slur on his department. And he wrote a book showing, in elaborate detail, how he could have moved four of Germany's seven armies to the Eastern Front in a fortnight, and left three to defend the west.

Germany had been using its railway system to prepare for war since the first tracks were laid. There was no unified national system – until 1871 there was no unified nation – but most of the trains were run by Prussia, and Prussian military values and requirements imbued the whole network. From the earliest days, discussions about the desirability of a new line always reflected its military potential. This policy proved extremely successful against the French in 1870, and it continued thereafter. There was a staff officer assigned to each line, and every year railway officials took part in war games. The best brains produced by the War College, it was said, went into the railway section and ended up in lunatic asylums. Before 1914 the Germans even sweetly helped Belgium construct a new light railway across the frontier; the Belgians probably thought it might bring in German tourists. And so it did, but they were wearing uniforms.

German railways always preferred punctuality to raw speed (they still do) but in 1903 two experimental electric coaches reached 130mph on a special military stretch. However, the high command rejected the idea of electrification as a strategy, partly on the grounds that having some lines electrified and not others would endanger the timetable of mobilization, and partly because it would render the whole railway more vulnerable to attack.

The difference between this elaborate planning and the genesis of the British system hardly needs repeating. In Britain the government as a whole had hardly had a say where railways were built, never mind the War Office. Totally uneconomic lines like the Stratford & Midland Junction, the Golden Valley Line in Herefordshire and the Potts line out of Shrewsbury had been built out of local pride and hope, not because they would ever save the country. But in 1914 and 1939, the nation was called upon to muddle through, as the railways had always done. And the combination proved curiously well-adapted to the task.

Aunt Sally's Triumph

On August Bank Holiday 1914, as war broke out, there were strange scenes at the London stations as the last boat trains made it back from the coast. When the Folkestone train arrived at Victoria, a sign said: 'Passengers: 603. Pieces of luggage: 223.' It might have been the Test score.

There was no indication when the missing bags might arrive, though it was assumed this would be a short war. At Charing Cross, the *Manchester Guardian* reported, passengers from Ostend arrived with breathless stories of catching the last boat. 'They said the other foreigners had left days before, but a great many of the English visitors refused to budge. They would stay, they had said, until they were pushed off, or until an English boat went to fetch them.'

This nation was not going to be panicked. In

208

April parliament had discussed the Northern Junction Railway, one of the few proposed lines which, though the idea had been around for about fifty years, had never been built. It was to run round London from Palmers Green to Brentford; the War Office said it was 'a national necessity' as a means of transporting its forces and avoiding the London termini. Parliament was not impressed. 'If you suggested a railway to the moon,' snorted the Earl of Ronaldshay, 'the War Office would say it was a splendid thing, and would afford them additional facilities for the movement of troops.' The existing railway companies objected and so did the residents of Hampstead Garden Suburb. The bill was thrown out.

But Britain was not entirely unprepared. Victoria's angry telegram to Gladstone at Carnforth had been the start of some dynamic action. When Kitchener set out to reconquer Sudan in 1896, the sappers built railways to use as supply lines, and the War Office had become, as the Earl of Ronaldshay hinted, rather keen on trains – although still nothing had been done to build the kind of strategic coastal route that armchair strategists had been advocating for decades.

And there *were* emergency plans. A railway executive committee was rapidly formed in 1914, comprising the general managers of the largest companies acting under the government's aegis. The first job was to get 118,000 members of the British Expeditionary Force to Southampton Docks. This was accomplished in a fortnight and, in the words of Christian Wolmar, 'with such remarkable efficiency that it transformed the status of the railways overnight. No longer were they Aunt Sallys but national heroes.' The operation would have been easier had the Northern Junction existed.

The railway unions declared a truce for the duration, and huge numbers went on active service, putting further strain on the system and forcing the recruitment of women for some jobs, although they were kept well away from the footplate. In July 1915 six women were being trained as ticket collectors at Manchester Victoria, an unthinkable idea a year earlier. 'The company seem to have no doubt that the women will prove able to perform their new duties,' the *Manchester Guardian* reported, adding churlishly, 'which to an outsider appear quite light'.

But as the war developed – or, more precisely, failed to develop – with the opposing armies fighting each other to a standstill, the haphazard British system found itself strangely suited to the job in hand. Routes like the Stratford and Midland Junction, for instance, played a vital role in shifting raw materials without clogging up the main lines.

Also crucial was the Far North line, which served two of the biggest naval bases, at Cromarty and Scapa Flow. To get sailors north, there was a Daily Naval Special from February 1917: fourteen coaches (no buffet) from Euston to Thurso, taking about twenty-two hours to do the 717 miles on a good day. There was a bad day in January 1918 when the train got stuck in snow ten miles short of Thurso, and 300 men, Wrens and nurses had to walk the rest of the way through a blizzard. Railway nostalgia was not an overwhelmingly obvious feature of the *zeitgeist* in the years after this war.

By the start of 1917, almost all the restaurant cars had gone and the old non-corridor carriages had re-appeared. Then the government imposed draconian cutbacks on non-essential travel to help divert resources towards the war: fares rose by fifty per cent; expresses were replaced by slow trains; and slow trains were replaced by no trains at all. Furthermore, it became a requirement that season tickets had to be shown, which apparently had not been the case. (No wonder the ticket collectors had little to do.) And dozens of stations were closed for the duration.

The immediate response was a brief rally in railway shares, in the hope that the companies would be allowed to keep the price rises when the war was over. But the more pertinent question was whether they would be allowed to keep anything at all.

Fur Coat, No Knickers

The soldiers who did make it back from the trenches, leaving so many fallen comrades, left behind any enthusiasm they might have had for fighting. They also left behind much of their traditional working-class deference. In September 1919, less than a year after the armistice, there was another full-scale and highly effective national railway strike.

In the immediate aftermath of war, the government was still effectively the employer while ministers worked out what to do with the railways. They had quickly conceded the principle of the eight-hour day. And the footplatemen, now organized into the Amalgamated Society of Locomotive Engineers and Firemen (ASLEF, initials that would henceforth strike intermittent terror into the hearts of commuters), got a deal protecting their wages and conditions. But with the economy under severe deflationary pressure, the other grades (seemingly less well-organized in the sprawling National Union of Railwaymen) were selected for pay cuts.

Morally and intellectually, the government's position was pretty weak: Lloyd George, the prime minister, can hardly have believed his own ears when he called the strike 'an anarchist conspiracy' and sent the railwaymen's old military comrades to patrol the stations. With ASLEF supporting its colleagues (which did not set a precedent), the NUR secured what appeared to be victory after a single week of national panic. 'The strike came because the Government were living in the atmosphere of the old industrial system,' the socialist J.L. Hammond proclaimed triumphantly, 'under which the employer gives orders and the worker takes them.' The only question, it seemed, was exactly how and when this new Eden would come into being.

There was a more mundane reality for the railway industry. With the help of management, blacklegs and volunteers, some kind of train service had been maintained during the strike. And the railways' customers found their own way round the situation. One party of holidaymakers stranded in Blackpool had walked home to Tipton near Wolverhampton: 113 miles in three days. But Victorian endurance was out of fashion; new technology and ingenuity were in. The new-fangled motor omnibuses kept running. For the wealthy, Daimler Hire Services started running daily private car services out of London. And in Paris, just ten years after Louis Blériot, crowds besieged the parcels office to have their goods air-freighted to London. The real victor of the strike was accurately proclaimed in a *Times* headline on 1 October, with the strike in full cry: THE TRIUMPH OF THE MOTOR LORRY.

Of all the ill-timed decisions to have bedevilled Britain's railways over the years, this strike was the killer. The workers, who played lickspittle for decades while their owners grew richer, had chosen the worst possible moment to get off their knees. It is hard to imagine events unfolding in any other way, given the greater historic context. But the new militancy was just one of the problems now besetting the industry.

Tens of thousands of railwaymen came back from the forces to their old jobs determined not to spend the rest of their lives offering un-questioning obedience to absurd instructions, as they had done during the war. However, a good many did not return to the railways: they took their gratuities and the mechanical skills they had acquired in the army, put together some bits and pieces, gave them a lick of paint, and – da-dum – they had something resembling a lorry.

Almost no regulations governed this infant

industry, no incomprehensible table with thirty million different rates, no legal requirement to take anything and everything, no hanging around in the sidings, no mucking about getting the goods from road to rail and back again. Might Mr Jones the draper like me to take the latest fashions ordered by Lady so-and-so twenty miles down the road, this moment, and at a very favourable price? Even when there was no railway strike, you bet Mr Jones would. 'That motor lorry services of some kind will be run as a permanent feature of our means of communication, particularly for light goods traffic, may be regarded as certain,' *The Times* concluded.

The old railway companies were no longer in a position to even think of responding because they had lost control of their own businesses. The political debate concerned how the railways would be transformed, not whether. The Labour Party was now the official opposition, and nationalization was a serious option. The government instead chose compromise, lumping the old companies together into four regional groupings. 'A bastard nationalization,' complained Sir Frederick Banbury, Tory MP and former chairman of the Great Northern.

But the minister of transport was Sir Eric Geddes, the Great Northern's former general manager, who knew whereof he spoke. And his speech introducing the new bill in 1921 was a forensic denunciation of his old industry's practices: the US got twenty-five tons of freight into the average wagon, and Britain five, for instance. Geddes was above all a cost-cutter, remembered for the 'Geddes Axe' on public expenditure (more of a bastard than a nationalizer, some thought). He had no intention of investing the kind of money that would have put the new companies on a firm footing: 'In the view of the Government there was no obligation on the state ... to put the railways back in any pre-war position,' he told the Commons.

The new companies started in 1923 and slowly they swallowed almost everything else that moved. The London, Midland & Scottish was a monster, with the Midland Railway stripped of its independence and dignity and added to the old London & North Western and the western Scottish routes; the London & North Eastern had the King's Cross and Liverpool Street empires and just about everything feeding off them, plus the Great Central out of Marylebone; and the Southern Railway controlled everything going south of the river. Alone, the Great Western survived intact, gaining the Welsh coal lines and other minor routes.

In their twenty-five years of existence these new initials, LMS, LNER and SR never did attract much loyalty from either staff or customers. A quarter-century was no time at all to get established. (To this day, the old railway bridge over the Ribble at Preston is known as the North Union Bridge, although the North Union Railway was taken over in 1846.)

The rates and fares set by the new companies were heavily regulated, with maximums that were now meaningless given falling prices, and an inherent inflexibility that made it almost impossible for them to compete. Strapped for cash for investment, facing obstreperous workers and a rapidly deteriorating competitive position, they were indeed born with all the disadvantages that attended bastard children in that era.

The coal and mineral traffic, the bedrock of railway freight, could not switch to road – but these industries were now stagnating. And soon passenger numbers began to be hit by the growth of buses and long-distance coaches and the first shiny new motors that began to appear, to the envy of the neighbours, on streets all over the country. The 'Big Four', their prices constrained by government controls, were like tethered giants, perpetually being taunted by the Lilliputian upstarts who had the freedom of the open road.

What a miserable life they led. The 1926 General Strike again chipped away at the notion of the railways' indispensability. And in 1931, at the LMS's annual meeting, the chairman, Sir Josiah Stamp, issued an even gloomier report than usual ('heavy decline in receipts') then took a sideswipe at the tormenters. 'In my opinion, road transport should be made liable for the whole of the costs it involves,' he said, 'and not be placed in a more favourable position than the railways.' It has been the cry of the beleaguered railway manager ever since.

Geddes had blithely predicted huge savings from the mergers, but the new companies were barely profitable. What no one in the government ever did, or ever had done, was to consider what the railways were for.

All the new companies were good at *something*.

Sir Josiah, despite his uncompromisingly Victorian name, was an enthusiast for modern American business practices and management accounting, precisely the kind of cost control the LMS's predecessor company, the London & North Western, had contemptuously rejected thirty years earlier. The LNER and the Southern avoided paying dividends, but the one invested heavily in faster trains on its main line to the north, and the other embarked on a huge campaign of third-rail electrification that was the salvation of the London commuter belt: by 1933 London to Brighton took only an hour.

The Great Western was the most adept of all at selling not just itself, but its region. In the twentieth century, the west country became seen as the most uniformly desirable part of Britain – soft airs, soft climate, soft countryside, soft accents. That had not been true in the early days of railways. In 1857, even *Bradshaw's Monthly Descriptive Guide* could not bring itself to sell the product:

Cornwall, from its soil, appearance and climate, is one of the least inviting of the English counties. A ridge of bare and rugged hills, intermixed with bleak moors, runs through the midst of its whole length, and exhibits the appearance of a dreary waste.

Fishermen's cottages in Padstow were pretty cheap in the 1850s. And it's still true that Cornwall looks dull from the main line, but that is not how it is perceived. 'The GWR set out to develop this image of the West Country as a desirable place, using luxurious images in its advertising,' explained Professor Colin Divall. 'In the 1920s and 30s, they realized that if they didn't do that they would go under against road competition.'

'The car had a cachet but the real competitor was the coach. Once you get pneumatic tyres and improved suspension you start to get some fairly serious long-distance road services. So the rail companies really did start marketing. All the companies used the word "customer" in the 1920s.'

The Big Four also showed some skill at putting their best face forward. Every self-respecting schoolboy used to know that Sir Nigel Gresley's streamlined LNER Class A4 4468 *Mallard* broke the world record for a steam locomotive by reaching 126mph south of Grantham in 1938. They were probably not aware that it travelled at that speed for just a single second, going downhill, that it was a deliberate record run milked by the publicity department, and that the engine never even made it back to King's Cross because the big end went long before Peterborough.

And that remains the world record, which is a pretty good indication of the limitations of steam in the modern world. Ten years after the war, even the expresses were slower than they had been before it. The frontline trains from Euston and King's Cross did eventually get faster, averaging just over half the speed of *Mallard* (which could have gone much faster, just as meaningfully, over a cliff).

The *Flying Scotsman* acquired the ability to run non-stop from King's Cross to Edinburgh thanks to the invention by Gresley, the LNER's chief mechanical engineer, of the corridor tender to allow a relief crew to nip through into the locomotive. By 1935 he was able to run the *Silver Jubilee* the 270 miles to Newcastle in four hours, and eventually the more lumbering LMS brought in the *Coronation Scot*. The chief mechanical engineers – Gresley, Stanier, Collett, Bulleid – became almost as well-known as the contractors had been in Victorian times. And the companies did offer both new luxury and new ideas.

There were trains with audio in the headrest, offering a selection of gramophone records; a cocktail bar ('thirty-two different cocktails') on the *Flying Scotsman;* and, on some King's Cross to Leeds services, a Pathé cinema van showing 'topical and other films'. The 1930s was also the era when all the companies followed the Great Western, and produced the Art Deco posters, much cherished today, advertising the charms of, for instance, a Southport lido full of improbably gorgeous bathing belles.

'It was a golden age for the railway,' said an auctioneer, trying to flog one of the posters in 2006. No, it was not. It was a golden age for the railway poster. And it was this classic misjudgment that still distorts the folk-memory of the railway before nationalization in 1948 and which led John Major towards his fateful decision to break up British Rail. The elite expresses sped past thousands of slow, dirty trains carrying disgruntled commuters dreaming of a new motor car. This was especially true outside London, where passengers got little benefit from the 'sparks effect' which bumped up business on the newly electrified lines. The *Manchester Guardian* letters column was full of complaints along these lines. To use an old Lancastrianism, what Britain had was a fur-coat-and-no-knickers railway, the opulence of the show disguising the threadbare reality underneath.

What the railways had was the worst of both worlds: bastard nationalization, as Banbury had said. The companies were too large and too regulated to be nimble, with the government preventing them making cutbacks (e.g. the closure of engine sheds) that might have improved profitability but increased unemployment. Yet there was no clear commitment to the maintenance of services or a coherent investment policy. In 1931 a government committee, under the industrialist Lord Weir, proposed that this programme of electrification should be extended nationally. It was received politely, and given the traditional response used by British governments when faced with the possibility of long-term investment projects. *The Times* said the idea was 'premature, to say the least'.

Well, quite so. As everyone in Whitehall knows, it is extremely important not to rush to judgment in these matters, as those excitable foreigners, the Swiss and the Swedes, had done by electrifying their lines. 'There is very good reason to suppose that for the purposes of ordinary main-line traffic the coal-burning locomotive is still the cheapest for Great Britain,' the Establishment's newspaper went on. It was the British way: when in doubt, do nothing.

Better Never than Late

And yet, in spite of everything, there were still railway optimists in the years between the wars. 'A NEW RAILWAY' said a headline in 1922.

The plan was to build a line from Halwill Junction north through the uncharted territory of west Devon to link up with the branch line from Barnstaple to Torrington. It would open up the area for tourism, and help both the farmers and the china clay industry. That was the theory; the government was so impressed that it chipped in half the cost.

The North Devon & Cornwall Junction Light Railway – a name full of Victorian exuberance rather than the knowing weariness of the 1920s – duly opened for business three years later and the small market town of Hatherleigh became the last in Britain to acquire its own railway station.

Better never than late, perhaps. Hatherleigh Station was a good mile out of town. In 1880, when the line was first discussed, the townspeople might have been content to put up with that familiar West Country inconvenience; in 1925 attitudes were somewhat different, especially as most townspeople wanted to get to Okehampton, which was seven miles away by road, and twenty by the new railway. 'It turned up too late, in the wrong place and going to the wrong places,' according to the local historian Brian Abell. 'Within a few years of it opening there were Austin Sevens flying round all over the place.'

There was a certain amount of china clay traffic winding along the north of the route; and a single passenger coach, with maybe a little luggage and some dead rabbits, stopped at Hatherleigh twice daily. But, according to the Devonian railway bard David St John Thomas, passengers caused astonishment:

'We had two people on Monday, Mr and Mrs X going to see their daughter in Bude,' I remember the guard telling me by way of justifying his existence. Finding various excuses to visit this living but empty museum over the years, I once caught the evening train from Halwill and arrived at Petrockstowe so early (partly because the timetable allowed for unwanted shunting at Hole and Hatherleigh) that the crew played cards for half an hour in the station and still reached Torrington ahead of schedule.

The most serious of many level-crossing accidents on the line, Thomas went on, was between a full excursion bus and an empty passenger train. He theorized that perhaps the authorities were embarrassed to close a railway they had so recently opened, or perhaps they had simply forgotten about it.

I favour the second explanation myself.

Railways did close in the inter-war years, especially after 1930: 1,240 route miles, six per cent of the total. It is a surprisingly tiny amount given that the whole rationale of the groupings was 'competition, bad; co-operation, good', and that many rural routes had clearly been losers even before road traffic came along.

Some of the lines – as at Campbeltown – hardly even got local obsequies. The Brill tram in

Buckinghamshire, the furthermost expression of the Metropolitan Railway's former national ambitions, was closed in 1935 by the newly formed London Passenger Transport Board, sitting in judgment more than fifty miles away. In his 1973 TV film *Metro-land*, John Betjeman sat at the preserved old junction at Quainton Road and reminisced as only he could:

I can remember sitting here on a warm autumn evening in 1929 and seeing the Brill tram from the platform on the other side with steam up, ready to take two or three passengers through oil-lit halts and over level crossings, a rather bumpy journey to a station not far from the remote hill-top village of Brill.

The news from Brill rated one paragraph in *The Times*. Other lines attracted more attention. There was the Devil's Dyke Railway, from Hove up the airy downs above the shimmering sea (on a good day), to The Dyke station. But it is a hard climb up there, and the railway stopped half a mile from the summit, while the omnibuses and charabancs could go right up to the Devil's Dyke Hotel. People gave up using the train except on the final day, New Year's Eve 1938, when five hundred clambered aboard, including pub landlord Bob Pitt, who had been on the first train fifty-one years earlier.

Mostly, the victims were taken out quietly, piecemeal. There was the Basingstoke and Alton Light Railway, built in 1901 and closed in the First World War so that the rails could be reused in France. Local pressure got the line reopened in

1924: 'There was so much excitement at Cliddesden station that the Union Jack was hoisted
upside down, and the ex-stationmaster, Mr
Bushnell, stood on the platform wildly waving a
stick,' said *The Times*. It was shut again eight years
later, this time for ever, although Cliddesden later
attained far greater celebrity when it was used as
Buggleskelly station in the filming of the 1937
Will Hay comedy *Oh, Mr Porter!*. Somehow that
has never quite given it the cachet of Carnforth.

Poetic station names started to disappear along
with the eccentric lines: Bala Lake Halt, Banavie
Pier, Botanic Gardens (Glasgow), Checker
House, Defiance Platform, Denver (Norfolk not
Colorado) ... and Parracombe, Snapper and
Woody Bay, along with the rest of the old Lumpy
& Bumpy, the Lynton & Barnstaple.

Lynton, the clifftop town on the edge of
Exmoor, had been one of the first places in the
country to get electric light, thanks to a hydro
plant, and in 1888 got a water-powered cliff lift
(still in operation) down to the sea at Lynmouth.
Ten years later, it belatedly had a railway: a
narrow-gauge line from Barnstaple built to the
splendidly precise gauge of 1ft 11⅝ in. The history
of the line contains the sentence which in different forms is contained in just about every one of
the hundreds and hundreds of books on rural
railways: 'Traffic did not develop to the extent
which the promoters had optimistically assumed.'

Yet the line bumbled along, never losing that
much money. Then in 1935, having just taken the
momentous decision to get rid of its footwarmers
and install heating, the Southern Railway

suddenly decided it would be more sensible to get rid of the trains. The local roads had been improved with predictable consequences and now there was a need for £2,000 worth of track repairs. Management at Waterloo let the decision be known in response to a request for an extra halt at Barbrook. There was a furious protest, enough to persuade the Southern Railway managers to come down and hold a conference on the issue at Barnstaple. The protestors from Lynton were so anxious to be there that they decided to travel by the most modern, efficient and convenient means available. *They went by car.*

The line closed after the summer season, on 29 September 1935. There was *Auld Lang Syne* at Lynton, and a wreath of bronze chrysanthemums at Barnstaple Town from a Captain Woolf, with the words 'Perchance it is not dead, but sleepeth'. Just as lavish celebratory dinners were the traditional accompaniment to railway openings, the wreaths and songs, along with the occasional brass band and the setting-off of detonators, would become the familiar trappings of closures. The following day the LNER's new *Silver Jubilee* to Newcastle began, and did the 268 miles southbound in just under four hours at an average speed of 67mph. This compared to the nineteen miles in ninety minutes, or just under 13mph, achieved by the Lynton & Barnstaple.

Its demise did produce what I think is perhaps the most affecting elegy ever to be written on such an occasion. Credited to A. Fletcher, it was published in the *North Devon Journal* in September 1935.

Oh, little train to Lynton,
No more we see you glide,
Among the glades and valleys
And by the steep hillside.

The fairest sights in Devon
Were from your windows seen
The moorland's purple heather,
Blue sea and woodland green.

And onward like a river
In motion winding slow
Through fairylands enchanted
Thy course was wont to go.

Where still the hills and valleys
In sunshine and in rain
Will seem to wait for ever
The coming of the train.

An anachronism? Only in the sense that the
Lynton & Barnstaple was ahead of its time rather
than behind it. There probably was no better
route in the country – with its quaint gauge, lovely
countryside, and tourist market – better suited for
the bonanza business of preserved steam trains
that was to come. Diesel railcars, a technique
tried by the Great Western on several of their
branches, might have kept the line staggering
along until the 1950s, and then there might have
been a chance of keeping it going. But the
Southern was interested in electricity rather than
diesel and, for the Lynton & Barnstaple, the

future was too far away.

(The Lynton & Barnstaple Railway Trust reopened a mile-long stretch near Woody Bay in 2004, with ambitions of extension, and dreams of complete restoration. The words 'Perchance it is not dead, but sleepeth' are used as something of a motto by the revived L&BR. A wreath of bronze chrysanthemums is carried by the first train at the company's autumn gala, and laid on the captain's grave at Martinhoe. Perchance he will be proved triumphantly right.)

What no one saw was that the real anachronism was the *Silver Jubilee:* a huge investment in fast steam engines, a technology going nowhere...

To Milford junction, via Blood and Tears

...Except that once again war overturned the logic of running a peacetime railway. In 1939 Britain still had coal but not oil. Every drop of petrol was needed for operational purposes, and it was certainly lucky that British trains did not depend on diesel. And, as the Germans sensed before 1914, electricity supplies would have been more vulnerable to aerial bombardment.

No one blamed this war on the timetable and, in principle, both sides were far less dependent on trains. In practice, the railways were crucial from the start for transporting troops and, even more significantly, supplies and, in the case of the concentration camps, the victims. Even before the war formally began, Britain's major stations – and some of the most benighted rural branch

227

lines – were filled with tagged, scrubbed and bewildered children being evacuated from the cities into the countryside to avoid the supposedly imminent German air raids. More than 1.3 million children and vulnerable adults were moved on 3,800 special trains inside a fortnight. Unnecessarily, as it turned out.

And before September 1939, the first month of war, was over, severe petrol rationing was imposed, forcing anyone who did insist on travelling ('Is your journey really necessary?' as the slogan went) back onto the trains, which were already more unpleasant than they had been a month earlier.

Cheap fares, excursions, reservations and restaurant cars were abolished, daily timetables reduced to Sunday levels (things were *that* bad) and speed limits imposed. And Victorian gloom descended on night-time trains, at least until blackout curtains could be installed to allow faint blue lights inside the carriages. In 1914 these kinds of changes had happened gradually. This time the government acted at once, expecting imminent all-out war, then relented a little, then clamped down again in times of severe pressure, particularly before D-Day. By 1942 long-distance coach services were abolished, with bus services being diverted to the railway stations. The aim was to get travellers on the trains while simultaneously doing everything possible to keep them from travelling in the first place.

In this war, railway work was made a reserved occupation which exempted essential staff from conscription. And when the bombing did start, the railway engineers became vital workers, mucking in alongside the sappers to clear bomb damage and repair tracks. There were some 9,000 instances of enemy damage during the war, 247 of them bad enough to affect traffic for at least a week. The greatest need was the transportation of coal and, with coastal shipping out of the question, that put extra pressure on the main routes. The LNER was worst affected, both because it was so essential for coal traffic and because it was close to the east coast airbases, making it a particular target for enemy attack.

And so clapped-out, obscure and even closed-down railways were pressed into service, to a far greater extent than in 1914–18. Even the dear old Potts line in Shropshire – *Coffee-Pot* and all – was given a vital job. A huge ammunition dump was established at Kinnerley Junction. According to railway historian Leslie Oppitz: 'More than two hundred huge storage sheds, camouflaged and decked out with turfed roofs, were built around the village.' Each had its own siding. In Hereford-shire, a similar facility was established near Pon-trilas on the almost as moribund Golden Valley Line and is still known locally as 'the dump'.

These were railways which every serious ana-lyst believed should never have been built. And yet the British railway system, constructed with hardly any regard to military considerations, helped defeat Germany whose railway had been planned by generals with precisely that purpose in mind. Here was the quintessential triumph of British muddling-through: cock-ups elevated into guiding principles.

As D-Day approached, the pressure intensified. In the three weeks before 6 June 1944, there were nearly 10,000 special trains, with their load carefully concealed to avoid attracting attention. Railway officials called this 'the tarpaulin armada'. In the month after the landings, with secrecy less obsessive, the number of special trains increased to more than 4,000 a week as troops and stores were moved to the south coast.

The man-in-the-street, and the man-in-the-railway-carriage most of all, was well beyond getting worked up about a little inconvenience and delay. But when *Brief Encounter* came out, a few months after the end of the war, it did not perhaps have quite the same impact on audiences that it does now. The British had had quite enough of stations like Milford Junction, slow trains, dim lighting, stale buns, imperious buffet manageresses, and perhaps also of lives in which their own impulses were always overridden by calls of duty.

The Times's critic was completely underwhelmed by the film: 'The composition is lacking in dramatic force and imaginative range'. He didn't even say he liked the trains.

CHAPTER EIGHT

MELTON CONSTABLE

The last stationmaster of Melton Constable sat back in his armchair. Nice people, Harold Drewry, and his wife Jill, both happy to talk about the old days.

Harold was third generation on the railways – his grandfather was an engine driver, and his father was a bricklayer. Two of his uncles worked there too. That was the pattern in Melton Constable: practically every family had three generations on the railway but not four.

He started in 1947, as a clerk in the goods office. Then they made him stationmaster, over at Gayton Road near King's Lynn, the youngest in British Railways' Eastern Region. Then they brought him home to be stationmaster at Melton. The last.

Most English villages have changed seamlessly, from generation to generation. There are three totally distinct eras in Melton's history. Before the railway, when it was just a hamlet close to Melton Constable Hall, ancestral home of the Lords Hastings. The railway era, lasting about sixty years. And afterwards.

For this was no ordinary country station. Melton Constable was at the heart of an extraordinary network of routes: the Midland and

Great Northern Joint Railway, stitched together in 1893 from a series of individual lines, and extending for 183 miles from its two separate junctions with the Great Northern north of Peterborough, across the wide open spaces of the Fens and rural Norfolk.

It was like a giant fantasy railway, with a map reminiscent of the Reverend W. Awdry's map of Sodor. The M&GN, the Muddle and Go No-where, barely seemed to intersect with the real world; little golden ochre engines pulled varnished wooden carriages to places an outsider might hardly believe existed: Twenty, Counter Drain, Whaplode, Clenchwarton, Hindolvestone, Corpusty & Saxford. As a joint operation, it effectively kept its independence even after the 1923 mergers and continued running its own sweet way to its own sweet stations.

And yet, up to 1959, there might be four trains simultaneously from Melton's two platforms, going east to Fakenham and King's Lynn, north to Sheringham and Cromer, east to Yarmouth, and south to Norwich. Unfortunately, this was not Norwich Thorpe, where you could catch a train to London, but the more glamorous-sounding if less useful Norwich City.

Who needed London? After the war, when Harold and Jill were young, Melton could seem like the centre of the universe. 'When the Midland trains came in at holiday times, they were packed,' said Jill. 'You couldn't prick a pin on them. We used to run down the line with newspapers and we learned how to let the coppers slide out of our hands so they'd tell us we could keep the change.'

And the railway was Melton's heart. 'The left-hand side of the village were the railway houses,' she said. 'The other side were "private houses". Posher, they thought they were. But we had flush toilets in the railway houses. You had to go across the yard, but they did flush. Pride, poverty and pianos, that was Melton Constable. Even if you couldn't play, you had to have a piano just to fool the neighbours.'

But then the 1950s came, and Midlanders started going on holiday in their own cars, and the trains grew emptier, and the whispers grew louder. Before Dr Beeching went near the railways, managers were looking for cutbacks, and the M&GN was an awfully tempting target.

'Did you know it would close?'

'We did know that traffic over the M&GN was being siphoned off, so there were little hints of what was going on,' said Harold. 'They were drawing so much into Norwich Thorpe we were just getting dribs and drabs. It was deliberately run down. Definitely.'

The news was announced in 1958, a payback from the British Transport Commission, which needed economies to fund a staff pay increase. Most of the line closed the following March, the biggest fell-swoop railway closure Britain had seen. The response was muted: just little wreaths or black flags at each station. The track was lifted within months, but Melton station lingered on, running diesel railcars up to Holt and Sheringham, before shutting for good in 1964. It was no more than a sad coda. 'The life went out of Melton when the main line closed,' said Harold.

'He was asked to be the under-stationmaster at Liverpool Street,' said Jill. 'We couldn't imagine him in a top hat. Didn't have a top hat at Melton. We've got one in the loft. That was Uncle Ernie's. But he was an undertaker, that's another story.'

So Harold spent most of his working life in insurance, and that was fine. And there are grandchildren, and that's great. But you can't escape the melancholy when they talk about the railway, and the way the village has changed since it vanished. 'They've got no idea,' said Jill. 'They're different people here now. They just dash in and dash out. They don't come here to settle.'

The bowling green is threatened; the school has merged; the Hastings Arms has closed down; and Melton Constable Hall, a seventeenth-century gem, is in a bad way. The Railway Institute – sold off cheaply to the locals – still thrives, under the improbable title of the Melton Constable Country Club. And the industrial estate, on the site of the old station, seems to be doing pretty well.

I told Harold I'd like to take a look and he said he would drive me, but he seemed uneasy: 'I haven't been up there in years. There's no reason at all for me to go.' And most of the industrial estate was as unfamiliar to him as to me: The Big Prawn, MC Dismantlers, SFX Signs, Flexsys and Portable Toilet Hire. Harold pointed out the loco shed, tucked away behind holly bushes and buddleias. The water tanks are still the most impressive sight in the village, and he proudly showed me where they were patched up from a German raid.

'So where was the station exactly?' I said. He

looked around at the anonymous modern buildings producing prawns and signs and portable toilets, and a look of alarm crossed his face. 'To be honest, I don't know... Oh dear me, I'm lost. I can't even tell you now where the East Box stood.'

He recovered his composure, showed me the Hastings estate with a local's aplomb and took me down to trace the cutting where the main line used to run. And then I left to catch the bus back to Sheringham, the nearest the modern British railway system gets to Melton Constable.

But I never got to Sheringham, not by bus. For as we passed the chi-chi little town of Holt, there – on a sunny afternoon in the spring of 2008 – was a J15 goods engine, the old workhorse of the LNER, in steam and waiting to pull half a dozen former British Rail carriages and a substantial number of tourists back to Sheringham. And just walking along the platform towards the cab was an elderly gent in fireman's overalls, wearing the biggest smile I've seen in years. Gosh, he was having fun.

This was the North Norfolk Railway – the Poppy Line – one of the most thriving heritage railways in a county that seems to have more preserved lines than actual ones. It is not normally the sort of train people race for, but I leapt off the bus and ran like hell.

Holt station, as it now exists, is a charming fake on the eastern edge of town. The Poppy people would like, in theory, to extend back to the old station in Holt and then to Melton Constable and then, heaven knows, to Peterborough if they thought it was do-able. But it isn't, and they are fairly content with what they have: ten miles of the old M&GN between Holt and Sheringham, where their station is the real thing, and very lovely it is too. It is separated by a sliver of road from the nasty, pinched little platform offering the National Express service to Cromer and Norwich which is marketed, not unsuccessfully, under the name of the Bittern Line.

The J15 pottered along at roughly the same pace as the Bittern Line, with far more elegance, conviction and charm, though of course none of the public service obligation. At Kelling Heath Park (where the train only stops when going downhill), we drew level with a massive very East Anglian ploughed field and there suddenly appeared a broad view across Weybourne Mill to the North Sea, a vista as sudden in its enchantment as anything on the remaining national network.

In defiance of all traditional railway instructions to passengers, I was leaning out of the window. And as we came into Weybourne, the breeze from the sea – just sweetly refreshing on a golden afternoon – slapped me gently in the face, as it must have hit Harold Drewry's grandfather when he drove this line a hundred years ago.

It's A Disgrace. Let's Buy It!

In 1948 Britain's railways were finally acquired by the people of Britain.

The nation woke up on the third New Year's

236

Day of peace to find itself the owner of about 19,000 route miles of track, 1,230,000 wagons, 45,000 passenger coaches, 20,000 locomotives, 50,000 houses, 25,000 horse vehicles, 7,000 horses, 1,640 miles of canals and waterways, 100 steamships, 70 hotels, plus 34,000 commercial lorries, acquired as a result of the partial takeover of the road haulage industry. It also acquired almost 700,000 new employees.

For reasons lost in the mists of railway history, the nation did not acquire the Talyllyn and Festiniog Railways in Wales, two omissions that would prove more significant than expected. It also failed to acquire the North Sunderland Line (rather a long way north of Sunderland, between Seahouses and Chathill) and also the two-mile railway between Grimsargh and the Lancashire County Mental Hospital at Whittingham. This hauled heavy goods to the hospital, and gave free rides to staff and villagers. These omissions proved less significant.

There were no celebrations, by order of the new British Transport Commission, which said there would be celebrations when there was something to celebrate. It also said it had no plans to repaint the trains and signs just for the sake of it.

However, a few months later, in September, there was a bit of a shindig at Liverpool Street station to mark the opening of the new electrified service to Shenfield, one of the few investment projects to survive all the government's post-war austerity cutbacks. The minister of transport, Alfred Barnes, was given the honour of driving the first train. As he was being shown how to start it, he asked, 'Do you mean like this?' sending the train on its way with its doors open and half the dignitaries still on the platform.

The analogy is of course irresistible. Clement Attlee's Labour government nationalized the railways because it had a huge majority and a manifesto commitment, and because nationalization was an idea whose time had come. The case for it was no stronger in 1948 than in 1836, 1844, 1867, 1907, 1913 or 1921 – possibly weaker. And the government certainly did not take possession because it hadn't the faintest idea how it would play with its new train set. It wasn't just that there was no new colour scheme for the trains to replace the old ones; there were no new ideas either.

The effect of the war was similar to that of 1914–18, only more so. The government was extremely anxious to emphasize the terrible state of the railways and talk down their value while it was in the process of buying them. 'A very poor bag of physical assets,' the Chancellor of the Exchequer, Hugh Dalton, told the Commons in 1946. 'Those dingy railway stations, those miserable, unprepossessing restaurants. The permanent way is badly worn. The rolling stock is in a state of great dilapidation. The railways are a disgrace to the country.'

This was not entirely the fault of the previous owners, who had been obliged to let the government wear down the permanent way and dilapidate the rolling stock to save the country from the Nazis. They also had to let the Treasury cream off a large dollop of the revenue that came in from extra wartime use. One might have assumed the chancellor might have some plans to invest in the system. Otherwise, why buy it?

The consensus view is that the government paid too much to the shareholders to buy this disgrace, a 'staggering' (to quote Christian Wolmar) £927 million – £27 billion at 2009 prices. That was not the view of the reluctant vendors: the future prime minister Harold Macmillan called it 'an act of robbery and confiscation', but then he was a director of the Great Western at the time. 'The terms,' said the chairman of the LNER, Sir Ronald Matthews, 'would bring a blush of shame to the leathery cheek of a Barbary pirate.'

Sir Ronald's other comments might have seemed worthier of further discussion as the years went by. 'Nationalization', he said, 'clogs the wheels of a developing industry. It places dictatorial powers and almost unlimited patronage in the hands of the Minister of Transport and creates another immense bureaucracy. It destroys every vestige of *esprit de corps* and competition.'

Certainly, the reality of British Railways quickly disillusioned the hopes of its most ardent admirers. On the day of the acquisition of the wagons (almost a million and a quarter of them!), the horses, the hotels and the 700,000 employees, one of the staff unions – the Railway Clerks' Association – urged the commission to announce that there will be 'a new staff relationship, on the concept that management and staff are partners in the task of serving the community'.

This charming new partnership was barely six months old before delegates at the National Union of Railwaymen's annual conference were

239

furiously complaining, apparently without dissent, that state capitalism was as bad as, or worse than, the old version. Nationalization had not provided a say for workers in 'the sort of round-table conference system that they had envisaged', said J. Martin, a relief signalman from Manningtree. J. Seaman of King's Lynn complained that the people who had mismanaged the industry in the past were still mismanaging it.

Nor was there any obvious change from the passengers' point of view. They didn't feel included in any new relationship. As John Betjeman wrote:

I'm paid by the buffet at Didcot
For insulting the passengers there.
The way they keeps rattlin' the doorknob
Disturbs me in doin' my hair.

That verse was not included in his Collected Poems: 'too hostile to the great British worker to be publishable in Attlee's Britain', said his biographer, A. N. Wilson.

Actually, it was not that clear who *was* mismanaging the industry. There was Barnes, the dangerous engine driver. Reporting to him was the British Transport Commission, under Sir Cyril Hurcomb, a former civil servant. The BTC also had responsibility for docks, inland waterways, London Transport, road haulage, buses and coaches. Reporting to Hurcomb was the Railway Executive, which was indeed controlled by former railway managers under Sir Eustace Missenden, from the old Southern Railway.

Below them were the regions which, after a difficult start, reasserted their old independence and did their utmost to ignore London's whims.

They all had knighthoods, in the British way, at the top of British Railways. And, in an equally British way, it is clear that they not only had no idea what they were doing but no idea what they were meant to be doing. Were the railways competing with road or co-operating with it? Was the BTC in charge of developing an over-arching transport strategy or making the trains run on time? According to British Railways official historian, Terry Gourvish, there was 'a series of morale-sapping conflicts at all levels of management'. On the one hand the Executive sent up reports about the collapse of a staircase at Alloway Station in Ayrshire and the question of advertisements on train lavatory mirrors. However, said Gourvish, its members were discussing genuinely important matters 'in an atmosphere of secrecy if not conspiracy'.

Whether the £927 million was fair or not, the cost was not absorbed by the government but remained as a charge on British Railways, so the new operation was minus £50 million every year before anyone had filled a shovel full of coal. The operation was legally obliged to pay its way, yet management had little freedom of action because it was expected to follow national directives and objectives. This was not just the Labour Party way. In April 1952 the government suspended a rise in rail fares because of growing fears among their own backbenchers about inflation, and here was a simple way of solving a political problem.

By then the Conservatives, under Sir Winston Churchill, were in power. The real mismanagers were the government, whoever they were.

The Billion Pound Hotchpotch

In 1954 Churchill called in an able and undemonstrative junior treasury minister called John Boyd-Carpenter, and asked him to become what was by then known as minister of transport and civil aviation.

It did not get him a seat in cabinet though he thought, as had happened to one previous incumbent, it might give him a nervous breakdown. His immediate predecessor and distant cousin, Alan Lennox-Boyd, had been ill several times in the job and was known to be desperate to escape: he was an expert in colonial affairs. The permanent secretary, Sir Gilmour Jenkins, was an expert in merchant shipping. 'He declined to interest himself in anything else,' recalled Boyd-Carpenter in his memoirs, 'although in fact shipping was the area in which fewer serious problems arose than any other.'

By then the Conservatives had abolished the Railway Executive and Hurcomb had gone from the BTC, to be replaced by General Sir Brian Robertson Bt, the former governor of the British zone of Germany, where he had been a sympathetic and effective presence as West Germany progressed from defeat to democracy. The railways though, that was a tough one. 'He was a splendid man, and a fine soldier,' wrote Boyd-Carpenter. 'It

242

was some months before I could get on human terms with him. He would come to my room, sit bolt upright in his chair – almost at attention – and very formally call me "Minister".'

Eventually Robertson loosened up, and the two men acquired an understanding. The hopeless railway lines would have to go, but Boyd-Carpenter would support modernization for the major routes. There had never been any mandate or appetite for denationalizing the railways, though Lennox-Boyd had successfully pushed through a bill sending almost all the road haulage business back to the private sector.

In any case, who would want the railways? Dalton's comments on their wretched condition were now even more applicable. As people became prosperous, the car was taking over: passenger numbers were stable, but only in the context of a huge general increase in travel; the freight sector was in meltdown; and BR as a whole was now losing money steadily. The trade unions had lost interest in being partners with management or having round-table conferences. They wanted higher wages, specifically to catch up on the increases given to other sectors in the early 1950s as post-war austerity began to lift. In particular, the two major unions – the NUR and ASLEF – wanted to ensure that their rises were higher than the other's.

It was a chastened, consensual, cautious Conservative Party that held power in the 1950s, very reluctant to take on the forces of the proletariat which had ejected it so brutally in 1945. Sir Walter Monckton, the minister of labour, was the pioneer of the beer-and-sandwiches approach to settling union disputes. Or, to be more precise, the large-neat-whisky-and-sandwiches approach, as Boyd-Carpenter discovered at one set of negotiations at the ministry, when he gulped down a glass intended for one of the union leaders, and choked.

This magic did not always work as quickly as intended: there was a seventeen-day ASLEF strike in 1955 and, continuing the process dating back to 1911, the nation was again obliged to make itself a little less dependent on the railways, and again found it was possible. It was settled, as usual, not by the employers but by the government.

The deal between Boyd-Carpenter and Robertson had borne fruit in January that year when the BTC's great modernization plan was announced. The underlying premise was now undeniable: Britain's trains were so dreadful, and already so far behind those elsewhere in Western Europe, that something had to be done. Since nothing had been done, certainly since 1939 and not much since 1914, the amount involved was staggering at the prices of the time: the newspapers did not even have an easy way of expressing amounts over £1,000 million – officially a billion still meant a million million. This was £1,300 million. Who ever used such numbers? Railwaymen were striking to get their wages up to ten quid a week.

Yet the plan sounded most enticing: an overhaul of track and signalling; replacement of steam by diesel and electrification; updating of rolling stock; a revamp of freight; and closure of branches. The public were bewildered to be told just how bad things had got. For instance, some goods trains had to be stopped at the bottom of hills and again at the top to alter the brakes manually, because they had no continuous braking. The immediate response was one of delight: the *Observer* summed up: 'heartening and exciting', although its columnist Paul Jennings had a slightly different take:

Once those gaunt strong engines, named after people and places one has never quite heard of – Sir Henry Thomkins, Stindon Hall – are replaced by secretive diesels; once continuous brakes in goods trains have silenced for ever the night-long mysterious bingbong-bang *from misty, moonlit yards that for generations has told millions, in our warm beds, of our ancient, endless commerce; once the fretwork stations are replaced by pin-bright foyers ... a certain openness, a certain ancestral earthy communion with fire and water and the lonely native hills, will have gone for ever. The British ... instead of thinking primeval, empirical thoughts in a sort of permanent pre-Creation mist, an aboriginal foggy steam or steamy fog, may become just another Scandinavian country, matter-of-fact under a pale, clear sun.*

There was no chance of that. A thousand million? A million million? Did this industry know the difference? The allegation that railway companies did not understand the economics of their own business had been flung at the London & North Western in 1904. Half a century on, it seemed truer than ever. Introducing the plan, the British Transport Commission had predicted the railways would break even in 1960. In fact, by

1960 the deficit was turning into an abyss, the modernization plan was regarded as complete madness, the Ministry of Transport was blaming the commission and the Treasury was blaming the ministry (which it had always considered hopeless, anyway). The economist Christopher Foster concluded that the commission had never had figures to tell what should be modernized and what should be closed, and was just guessing. Five years later officials had to admit to the Commons that they did not know whether the London–Manchester line was profitable or not.

Looking back in an interview more than half a century after the plan, Foster (by now Sir Christopher) also fingered the crucial non-financial error: 'It was full of mistakes but the absolutely key mistake was that they believed the future of the railways was freight, so enormous money was poured into it. They built a whole lot of marshalling yards that were virtual white elephants from the moment they were built.'

You could argue that, in other respects, the plan had been far too cautious. On electrification, it was a retreat from the proposals made in 1931. There was no suggestion that all the main lines out of London should be electrified, just those from Euston and King's Cross. But at least those schemes got a result, in remarkably quick time by modern British railway standards: less than twenty years for Euston to Glasgow; less that forty for King's Cross to Edinburgh.

The main effect of the fiasco, however, was to change attitudes in Whitehall. Previously, senior civil servants had thought for years that, sooner

246

or later (preferably later), something would have to be done to improve the railways. Now the mood was that something would have to be done *about* the railways. Quickly.

And yet, where did the blame really lie? Ministers wanted the railways to compete but would not allow them the freedom to set wages or prices or decide services that might have made that possible. In the words of the academic Charles Loft: 'Whatever the failings of management, the foundations of the BTC's eventual failure were all laid by the Government.'

A Drug-like Fascination

In August 1951 the *Manchester Guardian* sent one of its correspondents to investigate a newly discovered tribe, found wandering in a steamy jungle. *Guardian* expenses being what they were, this was in Crewe rather than New Guinea.

The tribe, about a hundred strong, apparently all male, and from as far afield as Shipley and Walsall, were on the 'sulphurous' footbridge north of Crewe station, all carrying their special notebooks. 'Some of them don't seem to have any homes to go to, they spend so much time here,' said a porter. 'There's no law against it once they have bought their platform tickets.'

The headline read:

THE ALLURE OF TRAIN-SPOTTING
SEARCH FOR AN EXPLANATION
AMONG THE ADDICTS AT CREWE

And so the word 'trainspotter' (the *Guardian* hyphen was an indication of its unfamiliarity) began its tortured journey through the public consciousness and the English language. It was puzzling that in the decade when one generation – politicians, civil servants and passengers alike – were losing their faith in the railways, their sons were flocking towards Crewe Station. Perhaps it constituted an obscure form of rebellion.

But it was also the perfect time. Travel was cheap and easy by bus and (for all its faults) train. It was a boom time for model railways too, but childhood then was not a period of imprisonment, unless you were sent to boarding school. Parents of that era did not go into paroxysms of fear if their pre-adolescent children could not be located by satellite tracking every second of the day. There was not a huge range of alternatives to trainspotting: in 1951 most households still did not have TV. And from the footbridge at Crewe there was an extraordinary panorama no little black and white telly could match: an astonishing variety of locomotives, representing a good half-century of railway history, still clanking and wheezing and occasionally whooshing their way up and down the old LMS system and beyond.

Railways as a hobby dated back to late Victorian times: there were two magazines and, in 1899, a London gentleman's club, the Railway Club, which still exists. But it only erupted among the young in the post-war years. One of the earliest references to it comes from 1946, when two teenage boys were sitting on a fence by the main line at Hatfield taking engine numbers, and saw the King's Cross to Aberdeen sleeper derailed. Eleven people were injured. The boys, Richard Shearman and Brian Clements, gave important evidence to the inquiry. Had their sons or grandsons been there for the more infamous Hatfield derailment fifty-four years later, they would probably have been locked up as terrorists.

By 1951 Ian Allan's Locospotters Club had 250,000 members, a number inflated by the fact that you had to pay only once, which left the secretary complaining that there were too many members to cope with. Yet still adults were left a bit baffled. John Grant, the *Guardian* representative at Crewe, did not get the explanation he sought. This worried him although most people, especially young ones, find it hard to explain why they enjoy something. (Why do you like strawberries or ale or sex then, Mister?)

And so Grant was left unimpressed. He talked of 'the drug-like fascination' the engines held for the boys, and decided: 'It is difficult for the uninitiated to see much positive value in standing on a grimy railway bridge to tick off the numbers of passing engines, unless it is that train-spotting inculcates a strict regard for truth.'

Soon, he wasn't the only one complaining. Before 1951 was out, Tamworth and Preston became the first stations to ban trainspotters as a nuisance. This policy spread. Three years later seven boys were summoned by Stockport magistrates for trespassing: a policeman had spotted one of the boys lying on his back on the Manchester to Euston main line. Asked what he was doing, he said: 'Listening out for trains.'

One of the fathers said books on trainspotting should be banned. But another pointed out that, since stations were barring the boys, trespass was their only recourse. That same summer an excursion train from Stockport to Blackpool was wrecked by 'drunken youths', probably not the first and certainly not the last. It was easier to pick on trainspotters than drunks. The whole saga does seem like an illustration of the managerial doltishness of British Railways in the 1950s. A decently run organization would have harnessed the enthusiasm to its own ends, and its infinite benefit. Instead petty officials used extreme cases to blacken the majority. The only other institutions that generally ban their most zealous customers are pubs.

By 1964 Crewe was also trying to mop up remaining pockets of resistance. Officials claimed that some boys had used railway communication systems to tell signalmen to get their trains moving. Oh, give over. By this time many teenagers were starting to find more direct ways of discovering 'drug-like fascination'. And these weren't ways that necessarily inculcated a strict regard for truth.

The End of Civilization

The young enthusiasts of the 1950s gathered for choice at the great junctions of the railway system, not on the little branches where the same old tank engine might reappear spasmodically with the same grubby old carriages. No one was much interested in that.

The adoration of Britain's branch lines is largely a retrospective romance. It was widely agreed, and assumed, that the new nationalized railway would act dynamically where the Big Four had been so dilatory, and embark on mass closures of hopeless railways. There was no real opposition to that in principle; there was nothing in the Transport Acts of 1947 and 1953 saying that British Railways had to keep lossmaking lines going because they were inherently a good thing. 'Is there any reason why a great many more branch lines and small stations should not be closed at once?' asked the *Manchester Guardian* in 1951. But which lines and stations? And how do you calculate loss in an industry that had difficulty calculating anything?

In any case the new organization quickly proved itself incapable of taking coherent decisions. The most ardent advocates of supporting branch lines wanted to replace steam with diesel railcars or railbuses. The world's shining example, somewhat improbably, was held to be County Donegal. There had also been some experiments on the Great Western in the 1930s, and they were said to decrease costs by up to two-thirds. They had to be worth a try. Instead, British Railways chose to build – as Owen Prosser of the Railway Development Association wailed despairingly – 'dozens and dozens and *dozens*' of tank engines, specifically for passenger use on rural branches.

The world's most famous tank engine had first appeared in book form in 1946, three years after the Revd W. Awdry began telling Thomas stories to his son Christopher. Thomas was popular enough in the 1950s, though without the world-wide adulation and marketing that followed later. But at that time the imaginary railways on the imaginary island of Sodor were no more improbable than a great many of those that still did exist – indeed rather less improbable than the Potts line or the East Kent Light Railway, perhaps Colonel Stephens' finest comic creation, where the laughter finally died in October 1948.

Elsewhere, however, the process kept proving rather troublesome. The 1947 Act had established a complicated – what else? – procedure before closure, involving a regional Transport Users' Consultative Committee and a central body. When the Railway Executive tried to halve the fifty miles of track left on the Isle of Wight, the county council hired Melford Stevenson QC, later a well-known and rather bad-tempered judge, who quickly elicited the fact that the Executive could not back up their own figures. That won a stay of execution, at least.

The Bluebell Line between East Grinstead and Lewes was closed in 1955 and then had to be resuscitated when a local resident, Miss Margery Bessemer, discovered a provision in an Act of 1878 specifying how many trains on the line had to stop where. British Railways was forced to reopen it and operate what was called the 'Sulky Service', fulfilling the minimum statutory requirement until they could get the law changed and the line shut again.

Almost every line had its stout defenders, most

of them totally unconvincing. A taxi-driver in Sedbergh called the twenty-seven-mile line through the Vale of Lune from Tebay to Clapham 'a mark of civilization and progress'. Everyone in the town was terribly upset about it closing, though a visiting journalist found it hard to find anyone who used it. In 1955 the Prison Commission objected 'very strongly' to the closure of the lonely, curvaceous Dartmoor line to Princetown. But it had to admit that the prisoners were transported by road. So was the jail's coal supply. *The Times* gave extensive coverage to protests against the loss of the branch from Oxford to Woodstock in 1954, even though there were said to be an average of five passengers per train.

And a succession of peers rose in the House of Lords to defend the Swansea to Mumbles railway, then running as a locally owned electric tram but first operated by a one-horsepower engine (to wit, a horse) in 1807. 'As a boy I often rode on this railway,' said Lord Silkin, 'and sometimes had to help it along because it got into difficulties on its journeys.' 'The thing that struck me most,' said the more lordly Lord Ogmore, 'was that, as we went along, there were little boys fumbling in the sands for pennies. I persuaded my mother to give me some money to throw out to them.'

But in every one of these cases it is possible, looking back fifty years, to think that they could have had a future, if anyone had loved them. The Isle of Wight is vilely overrun by cars; the Woodstock line, languid though it was then, could have been a major asset as Oxford jammed solid. And the Bluebell Line opened a third time in 1960, as the first fully fledged standard-gauge preserved passenger line, and as such thrives to this day.

The pioneer had been the Talyllyn Railway, a narrow-gauge slate line somewhere in the wastes of gawd-knows-where-in-mid-Wales, rescued from the edge of extinction in 1950 by a group of eccentrics/visionaries, led by the author L.T.C. (Tom) Rolt. Next came the Festiniog Railway, further north into Snowdon, which was brought back from extinction itself. They do well too. You could imagine that similar things might have happened in the Vale of Lune, the Isle of Wight and Dartmoor if anyone had had the wit, energy and bloody-mindedness to *make* it happen. The Ealing comedy *The Titfield Thunderbolt*, in which George Relph, John Gregson and Stanley Holloway make it happen, was filmed in 1953 after the writer T.E.B. (Tibby) Clarke paid a visit to the Talyllyn.

And in the case of Swansea, this story should break the local council's heart. The Swansea & Mumbles Railway, that lovely name curving along that lovely (on a good day) bay, could have been billed as the oldest passenger line in the world and knocked the Blackpool trams into a cocked hat.

But it was impossible in the 1950s to envisage the sentimentality for old railways that would develop later. It was even hard to imagine the extent to which the car would choke our cities. However, at least one of the closures of that era just beggars belief. Before the war, London Underground had been planning to take over the

GNER line from Finsbury Park to Alexandra Palace, and add it to the Northern Line, as with the High Barnet and Mill Hill East branches. Those works were completed before the war, but the Ally-Pally line was never converted. So it mouldered, and was closed in 1954, leaving the otherwise desirable suburbs of Crouch End, Stroud Green and Muswell Hill with the worst transport links in London to this day. No one had yet made a distinction between urban transport problems and rural ones.

But it was always asking a bit much to imagine that urban planners and transport planners might talk to one another. The different offspring of the British Transport Commission didn't talk to one another. The departments of British Railways didn't talk to one another. David St John Thomas noted that some of the maddest acts of all came because the commercial and engineering departments failed to communicate. 'During the 1950s several branch lines were extensively relaid or resignalled shortly before closure. At one station – Clifton Mill [in Warwickshire] – the office was actually being enlarged to take a new stove, which had just arrived, two days before total closure.'

According to Thomas, the new trains arrived far too late for many lines that could have been viable. By the time the railcars or diesel multiple units appeared in any numbers, steam was being phased out, and so the main lines wanted them. And the five different types of lightweight railbus, precursors of the wretched Pacer, specially developed for branch lines, were all totally unreliable. The miracles they wrought could be

255

overstated, anyway: the Donegal lines all closed in 1959. You do reach a point in trying to run a train like a bus when you might as well run a bus.

The pace of closures quickened in the late 1950s, pushed by Boyd-Carpenter's successor at the Ministry, Harold Watkinson, who later groaned: 'Three years in charge of the Transport Ministry provided ... a useful corrective to any illusions that politics is about doing things in a businesslike fashion.' His most urgent task was to give Britain the beginnings of a modern road system: Hitler had been building *Autobahnen* in the 1930s; Britain did not have a mile of motorway until 1958. He also had to battle the railway unions. Watkinson did see off the Muddle & Go Nowhere; it is hard to imagine there could have been an alternative future for most of that extraordinary monument to late Victorian optimism. Finally, the Whitehall gardeners were beginning to snip away some of the most straggling stems of the rambling railroad.

And through all this, Richard Beeching PhD was rising through the managerial ranks to become the technical director of Imperial Chemical Industries. He had built up quite a good reputation within the company for improving the profitability of zip fasteners and Terylene. He had no known connection with railways.

No More Will I Go to Blandford Forum...

In early August 1963 a youth appeared before Linslade magistrates in Buckinghamshire, charged with stealing a loaf of bread. Asked why he had done it, he said he was bored. 'Nothing ever happens round here,' he said.

A few hours after that, the Glasgow to London travelling post office train was stopped by a red signal just outside Linslade. The light was actually green but that was covered by a glove, placed there by a group of thieves who had powered their own red light. They had rather more bread in mind than the boy in the courtroom.

Thus began the Great Train Robbery, probably the most famous non-fatal crime in British history, at least since Colonel Blood stole the Crown Jewels. Two and a half million pounds were stolen in old banknotes while being sent for shredding. Taking into account inflation, this was probably not surpassed in Britain until the £53m Securitas robbery of 2006.

But Securitas has not passed into folklore. The places associated with the Great Train Robbery impinged themselves on the national conscious-ness: the signal at Sears Crossing, the actual robbery site at Bridego Bridge, the hideout at Leatherslade Farm. The robbers became and re-mained famous: years later, Buster Edwards would be the florist at Waterloo Station, to be pointed out to tourists and become the subject of a biopic starring Phil Collins; Bruce Reynolds became a well-known media guru on crime; and the escape and adventures in Brazil of Ronnie Biggs were so entertaining that his fate (even after he returned to jail in Britain) was still a major story forty-five years later.

They were famous, note, not infamous. From

the start, the crime was tinged with a romantic glow. The plot was ingenious; the money was only going to be destroyed, so no one actually lost anything; and no one got hurt. Much. Or so it was believed, although the train driver, Jack Mills, was bashed about the head, never fully recovered and died before his time. Even the evidence that caught the gang members had a human touch: some of their fingerprints were on a Monopoly board at Leatherslade Farm, where they had been playing with real notes. One of the robbers, Roy James, was nabbed because he had given the farm cat some milk, and his fingerprints were on the bowl. (No good turn goes unpunished, as the saying goes.) The judge at the main trial imposed thirty-year sentences, way above the normal tariff. He appeared to be passing sentence on the public rather than the villains, punishing us for having the gall to glamourize them.

And why, above all else, was the crime so alluring? It was a TRAIN robbery. The Great Van Robbery? The Great Bus Robbery? The Great Charabanc Robbery? They wouldn't have had a fraction of the resonance. It was the magic of the tracks that made it so special.

And yet 1963 was also the year when Britain finally and officially fell out of love with the railways. Like Ronnie Biggs, the name Beeching still has instant recognition to generations unborn in the 1960s. In late 2008, the BBC, obsessed with commemorating anniversaries, put together a special TV night on his legacy, which appeared to mark the forty-fifth and a half anniversary of his report. And here the word 'infamous' might truly be applied. When I started telling people I was writing a book about Britain's railways, several just shrieked 'Oh, Beeching!' as though no one and nothing else had ever happened.

It is an extraordinary fate, given that, as chairman of British Railways, he was merely a functionary – answerable to politicians – and that he held the job for just four years, from 1961 to 1965. And for almost all that time, he was a far less controversial figure than his boss, Ernest Marples, the highest-profile transport minister of them all.

Marples was a grammar school boy from Manchester, the son of a foreman; he never went to university and trained as an accountant instead, before arriving in London to run a then novel one-man business converting terraced houses into flats. After the war he founded the civil engineering company Marples Ridgway. Marples was a flamboyant entrepreneur and already an up-and-coming Conservative MP; Reginald Ridgway was the workaholic details man. 'He had no discernible interests outside work,' said the *Daily Telegraph* obituary, when he died in 2002. His partner certainly did.

As a politician, Marples made his name as a junior housing minister, pushing through the big Tory home-building programme of the 1950s, cutting corners and getting things done. When Harold Macmillan became prime minister in 1957, he gave Marples the high-profile job of postmaster-general, in charge of both post and telecommunications: Marples made it higher profile still. He was 'Ernie', shiny-new and slightly risqué just like Ernie, the fancy computer that determined the monthly premium bonds draw. Two years later Ernie the human was elevated to the Cabinet, a self-made millionaire surrounded by Etonians, as Minister of Transport. He held the job for five years: only the undemonstrative Alfred Barnes lasted longer.

Marples was a very intriguing figure. Charles Loft, in his academic account of the era, found no evidence of corruption but noted, rivetingly, that 'he certainly showed a carelessness towards the rules' and that 'rumours of an exotic private life abounded among his colleagues'. And he certainly seemed dodgy, with his unBritish addiction to publicity and a look and manner rather like Hughie Green, the host of the TV show *Double Your Money*. Marples was rather good at doubling his own money. George Cole might have played the part, with just a few variations from his role as Arthur Daley. Marples was undoubtedly one of life's used car salesmen.

In the early 1960s he was one of the most reviled men in Britain. The slogan 'Marples Must Go' passed into the language and lingered on a bridge over the M1 for decades afterwards. Most of the hatred actually came from motorists, who blamed him for parking meters, traffic wardens and the totting-up system of penalties for speeding, all of which clouded life on the once carefree open road.

But Marples liked cars. And his appointment as minister after the Tories' thumping 1959 election win coincided with the general loss of patience within the government at the hopelessness of the railways. The situation was worsened in 1960 when a government-appointed commission handed the NUR a large pay rise. The prime minister was Harold Macmillan, former director of the Great Western, and an instinctive nostalgist. In 1952 he had complained about the lack of reverence for tradition on the nationalized railway: he said it would give great pleasure if the Western Region could be rechristened the Great Western, with its old colours restored. 'Our men used to be proud of their chocolate brown suits and all the rest ... the regimental system is a great one with the British and it is always a mistake to destroy tradition.'

Eight years on, when his complaints carried more weight, he told the Commons: 'If fair and reasonable wages are to be paid, which I think is right, in an industry which is losing as much money as this, everybody is under an obligation, in return, to play their part in any form of reorganization which may help it to do better.' He spoke, he said, 'with real affection for the railways'. Those charged with the task had altogether less affection.

Marples set up his own rather secretive advisory panel under the industrialist Sir Ivan Stedeford to try to sort out the mess. Someone in ICI recommended Beeching for the committee and he immediately established himself as a combative and clear-minded character who got up Stedeford's nose, and impressed Marples enough for him to offer Beeching the chairmanship of the BTC, which was about to mutate into a new British Railways Board.

There then came what was known at the time as 'the Beeching Bombshell'. This was nothing to do with his list of closures, which was still two years away. In March 1961 it was announced that he was to receive the salary he received at ICI; £24,000, more than double the going rate for chairmen of nationalized industries. Ministers then only got £5,000. There was a horrified reaction, not least from the chairmen of other nationalized industries. There had always been an understanding that public corporations had a different ethos to private ones, and that money was not the prime consideration. That was shattered by Beeching's salary. 'It was almost as if the Royal Navy had sold out to Shell,' wrote Anthony Sampson in *Anatomy of Britain*. 'The Beeching bombshell seemed to imply that public and private service were indivisible, that service was not its own reward.'

It is necessary to understand the spirit of the times, which might not be obvious from this distance. In the early 1960s there was far more tolerance of the economic ambitions/greed of the workers and far less of the economic ambitions/ greed of their bosses than would later become the case: Conservative politicians were still suffering residual guilt from the 1930s.

But there was also, far more briefly, a burst of almost Victorian faith in the future: in technology, in novelty, in youth. The British were uninterested in the past and the Arcadian idyll: old country houses and cottages were almost worthless. People wanted cars, televisions, washing machines and fridges (which were beyond the average pocket even a decade earlier). They embraced even the goriest aspects of the future: as the new Ml slashed through the fields, elderly ladies who now had to plant their hollyhocks amid the roar of traffic would shrug and say 'Well, you can't stand in the way of progress'. The Beatles and the satire boom were about to take over. Macmillan, with his elegaic understanding of the past, struggled to keep up. Marples and Beeching were far more in tune with it all. The railways represented the past; the car represented the future.

And Whitehall thinking was heading the same way. The new Transport Act shifted the onus on the railways much more towards profit, and made closures harder to fight. A month after Beeching's appointment a White Paper specifically insisted that nationalized industries were not 'social services absolved from economic and commercial justification'. The stage was set.

Beeching did not start the process of railway closures, as we have seen. It was gathering pace well before he arrived. In 1960 the fuddy-duddy BTC recommended scrapping the four-and-a-half-mile branch that ran off the main line north of Sevenoaks in Kent to the little town of Westerham in Kent, prime commuter territory. The commission said *only* two hundred people a day used the line. Both the regional and central consultative bodies then involved in this process said that *as many as* two hundred people used the line, and that it should stay open. Against precedent, Marples rejected their advice and insisted it must go.

So in 1961 it went, with the obsequies that were

263

becoming familiar, including the presence on the last train of an octogenarian (in this case Mrs Jane Graves) who had been on the first. But the opposition in Westerham was unusually spirited and clued-up. Local activists put together a very credible scheme to reopen the line, running diesel railcars instead of clanking and expensive tank engines to Dunton Green on the main line on weekdays, and vintage steam trains on summer weekends. They had the rolling stock already in place. And even after Beeching took over, the railway authorities were not unsympathetic – with good reason because, after the closure, they had to subsidise the replacement bus service.

But then things changed. Suddenly the re-opening plan began to run into obstructions from Kent County Council, which imposed impossible conditions. You may well have travelled over part of the railway today, but may not have noticed because it has a new name. It is called the M25.

On the web, it is easy to find allegations that Marples closed railways to make money out of road construction: that, although he had sold his shares on becoming transport minister, he had merely shuffled them around relatives. Colin Divall of the University of York follows Loft in rejecting the notion of corruption: 'a conspiracy theory too far'. But the county council knew where the London Orbital Motorway, as it was then known, was going; and quite obviously the minister did too.

Marples is long dead now (he died in Monte Carlo, and you can't get more exotic and dodgy than that), and the libel laws are beyond his grasp. He is largely forgotten as well. But at the time he was seen as the chief perpetrator of rail closures. When the Cirencester branch closed down in 1964, it was Marples who was burned in effigy, not his highly paid appointee.

Beeching was an improbable representative of the Swinging Sixties. He was neither mop-haired nor satirical. He was corpulent, with an unpleasant toothbrush moustache, and could easily have passed as a provincial Gestapo official or Hermann Gessler, the brutal enemy of William Tell, the eponymous hero of what was then a very popular children's TV series. He also had the most extraordinary hairstyle, combing what little hair he had over the back of his head, as if to persuade someone standing behind him that he wasn't really bald.

Many well-placed judges did find him convincing. 'He might be mistaken at first for one of those large phlegmatic men who tell long stories over a pint of beer in a country pub,' wrote Sampson, to whom his virtues seemed endless: 'fundamental niceness ... dispassionate expertise ... homely confidence ... striking intellectual honesty.' In the updated version of his book *Anatomy of Britain Today*, which came out three years after Beeching's Report, Sampson threw in 'brilliantly presented', 'ruthless analysis' and 'heroic'. Nor was he alone: the press response to the report – officially titled *The Reshaping of British Railways* – when it came out in March 1963 was close to adulatory.

'BEECHING'S BLOCKBUSTER', the *Daily*

Mirror, the biggest-selling paper of the day, squealed with delight. 'Unanswerable,' said *The Times.* 'Dr Beeching has shown brilliantly how the railways may be made to pay.'

Paul Ferris, in the *Observer,* sounded a note of caution: 'No one could be as perfect as some of his fans suggest.' But that was only a momentary pause in Ferris's argument: 'He's a business intellectual who thinks clearly, who also looks impressive... He has steamroller qualities – sometimes intimidating, but just what the railway needed.' Beeching's chief PR man, John Nunneley, had done his work well.

Reshaping had one fundamental, incontestable virtue. For the first, and last, time someone with the power to act sat down and asked: 'What are Britain's railways *for?*' No one, least of all in government, had done that in the 1830s when the network began, nor at any other time in the nineteenth century, nor after 1918 when the railways were consolidated, nor after 1945 when they were nationalized, nor after 1955 when the Modernization Plan emerged. And certainly no one ever did it before privatization. Beeching, a scientist and businessman with no special interest in railways as such, asked the questions.

He was rightly horrified by what he found: it was a filthy mess, especially on the goods side, almost invisible to the public. The railways' wagons spent only one-sixth of their time actually carrying anything, and the least-used one-third of the route mileage carried one per cent of the freight-ton mileage. Equally, the most deserted one-third of the 18,000 passenger route miles was responsible for only one per cent of the total passenger miles. Two thousand stations and 5,000 miles of track were to close, and the overwhelming majority duly did.

The case did indeed sound unanswerable. It is hard to avoid medical analogies with Beeching, even though his doctorate was in physics. He was inclined to talk about surgery himself. Someone had at long last diagnosed the railways' ailments; it followed that the operation must make things better. And its drastic nature was detailed in Sections 3, 4 and 5 of the report:

PASSENGER STATIONS AND HALTS
TO BE CLOSED

It is only a list of place names, but to my ears no more beautifully melancholy poem has ever been written, at least not since the list of failed schemes of 118 years earlier. No one mourns Pilbrow's Atmospheric Railway any more than they mourn the children that were never conceived. They do still mourn the railways closed by Beeching. Michael Flanders and Donald Swann, who were wonderfully precise observers of the early 1960s, famously turned the station names into their song, *Slow Train:*

No more will I go to Blandford Forum and
    Mortehoe
On the slow train from Midsomer Norton and
    Mumby Road...

But the list itself was like an elegy: the fifth name

267

in Section 3, the stations to be closed in England, was Adlestrop, which gave its name to one of the best-loved of all railway poems. And you just have to savour some of the names to conjure up the lost world of the country branch railway: Bassenthwaite Lake, Ben Rhydding, Bere Ferrers, Bishop's Nympton and Molland, Black Dog Halt, Blue Anchor, Cross Hands Halt, Evercreech Junction, Ham Green Halt, Luton Hoo for New Mill End, Marazion, Marishes Road and, ah, bless it, Melton Constable (what little was left of the once-bustling junction by 1963)...

...Moira, Morebath Halt, Morebath Junction Halt, Newton Poppleford, Newton St Cyres, Pampisford, Penda's Way, Pleasington, Point Pleasant, Shepton Mallet Charlton Road, Shoscombe and Single Hill Halt, Three Oaks and Guestling Halt, Tinker's Green Halt, Trouble House Halt.

(This one, which gets a mention in the Flanders and Swann, served a pub near Tetbury. Quite bizarrely, it had only opened in 1959.)

The names didn't even have to be rustic to produce the effect: Broadbottom, Castleford Cutsyke, Codnor Park and Ironville, Corkickle, Daimler Halt, Vulcan Halt. And some had the virtue of glorious simplicity: Cole, Drax, Drigg, Frant, Hole, Holt, Hope, Pant, Pill, Shap, Sleights, Swine.

Swine? That was north-east of Hull on the Hornsea line, closed on October 19, 1964. It was not a coded reference to the report's author.

England, our England. The proposed closures for Scotland and Wales were listed separately, and parts of those do not even have to be edited

268

for euphony.

...Kennethmont, Kennishead, Kentallen, Kershope Foot, Kilbarchan, Kilbirnie, Kilbowie, Kilconquhar, Kildonan, Kilkerran, Killiecrankie, Killin, Killin Junction, Kilmacolm, Kilmaurs, Kinaldie...

And one could keep going all the way through Kittybrewster (aye, what a lovely lassie she was) to Longmorn, Longside, Lonmay, Lossiemouth, Lugton, Luib, Lumphanan and Lundin Links. With connections perhaps to Maud Junction, Moy, Racks, Rumbling Bridge, Salzcraggie and Whifflet Upper.

Most of these stations must indeed be regarded as sweet but hopeless. Beeching was generally right to close the smaller stations on main lines, which complicated the signalling and clogged up the system. And how on earth had the Killin line stayed open this long? A branch off a branch of a branch, barely even a twiglet, heading towards the shores of Loch Tay, connected Killin (population: 640) with the Callendar and Oban line. Somehow, it had retained its independence until 1923 when the newly formed London, Midland & Scottish insisted on exercising its right to take the poor mite over. The Killin managed to bid up the LMS from £1 a share to £8, for which the giant was rewarded with a hand-written set of accounts. 'I am without a typist,' explained the company secretary. It didn't close until 1965.

Rural railways had had their day (most of them long since) and both the Big Four and the BTC before them should have imposed closures more quickly. Beeching's brief was to do something about the railways' galloping losses. If the government wanted to retain lines for non-commercial reasons, that was not a decision for him, though he made it clear he thought that was a bad idea. Soon after his appointment as chairman, he squashed an interviewer from the *Panorama* programme on this point. He had said the railways were fossilized. The interviewer protested that it was not necessarily fossilizing to keep a line open just because it wasn't strictly economic. 'No,' replied Beeching tartly, 'but you might still have stagecoaches if you did that.'

Given how late – 130 years late – the simple review of the railways' purpose was, it is perhaps unreasonable to expect Beeching to have glimpsed the future accurately as well as the present. But we can see now that he misread the future very badly. First, he believed that his cuts would take British Railways into profit, or very close to it, by 1970. They did nothing of the kind, and had no prospect of doing so. Second, he thought the future of the railways lay primarily in bulk freight, which it did not, rather than passenger traffic. Third, he failed to see the importance of urban railways, even though towns and cities were already starting to choke. Fourth, being neither a historian nor a rail enthusiast, Beeching never thought 'Well, you never know'. Obscure railways had helped save Britain in two wars; he never saw how some less obscure ones could provide options in the future. There was a fifth failure too, the most important of all, which we will come to shortly.

Most of the first four points tie in, as usual, to

the wider failure of government. The Conservative Party was not thinking of potential traffic problems in the twenty-first century; it was concentrating on getting through the distinctly unpromising 1964 election. It wanted to show the electorate that it was dynamic, unstuffy, forward thinking and possibly even cool, with-it and groovy by grasping the problems of the railways. But there was next to no liaison between the transport and housing ministries about how the plans might link with another government policy of moving people out of London. In 1962 it was decided to triple the population of Haverhill in Suffolk; in 1963 Haverhill station was listed for closure.

The initial enthusiasm for Beeching quickly faded as Tory backbenchers contemplated the possible consequences for their own majorities. The reshaping of the railways was a popular policy; the closure of a local station was not. So the government started making political decisions about which lines would go and which would stay. Beeching, remember, did not shut so much as a single deserted wayside halt: only the minister could do that.

Behind Beeching was Marples; and behind Marples was Macmillan, who praised Beeching's efforts as 'Herculean' but skilfully avoided any association with the whole messy business. The one decision where he did get involved and blamed was over the demolition of the Doric Arch at Euston, the high point – and perhaps the turning point – of 1960s cultural vandalism. The last massive volume of Macmillan's prime ministerial memoirs contains no mention at all of either Beeching or Marples, except in the context of one pay dispute. The book is filled with stuff about Aden, Nyasaland and Katanga, where British government policies by that time made not an iota of long-term difference. Prime ministers much prefer strutting round the world to the boring task of building Britain's infrastructure, where their decisions can actually have an effect.

Instead, Macmillan outsourced the job to someone who had no more of a long-term vision than the politicians did. For this is the fifth and most crucial indictment of Beeching. He had no sense whatever of a future in which fast, efficient long-distance railways could take on cars and planes and beat them. This became clear in an interview he gave in 1981, sixteen years after he had left the railways, for a BBC TV programme called *Hindsight*.

By then he was a far more relaxed figure, with his pension and his peerage: his accent had become less stilted, his hair less ludicrous, and he seemed altogether jollier. This must have been the kind of man Sampson had glimpsed. He didn't mind being remembered as a mad axeman, he said cheerfully. 'Most people aren't remembered at all.'

He did not have many regrets although, he said, 'some of the excellent planning in my day has not been pursued with the vigour I would like'. The interviewer, Eric Robson, asked what he meant. He regretted that more lines had not closed; about half the surviving trunk routes should go, he thought. Pressed to give examples, Beeching first demurred then gave in to temptation: it was quite unnecessary to have more than one route to Scotland, he said. 'The East Coast route beyond Newcastle could be closed without any hardship to anyone except people in Berwick-upon-Tweed.'

This was madness even in 1981, never mind from the standpoint of 2009. Electrification? He didn't care for it. Faster trains? They make no difference. Robson quoted British Rail's then slogan which for the first time was just beginning to acquire a little resonance: 'Is this "The Age of the Train"?' 'Well,' replied Beeching. 'I don't wish to say that it isn't because my successor is saying that it is, but judge for yourself.'

If Beeching had had a genuine modernizing purpose to sit alongside his removal of ancient relics, there could have been an age of the train: he had the clout to make it happen. But he didn't. The cartoons of the time, which showed him pruning so hard that in the end there was no tree left, came dangerously close to his true intentions.

The week after *Reshaping* was published, the papers were filled with letters, many of them over-sentimental or downright silly. This one, however, from Barbara Preston of Marple Bridge, near Stockport, was published in the *Guardian*. She was complaining about the planned closures of commuter routes into Manchester, and the effect on road congestion.

'Is this what is really necessary here and now?' she asked. 'Or shall we, in a few years, when traffic in Manchester has inevitably become denser, be bitterly regretting these closures and

273

at great expense be rebuilding commuter lines?'
In Manchester they now call them trams.

Who saw the future more clearly? Baron
Beeching of East Grinstead, or Barbara Preston
of Marple Bridge?

Last of the Cast-Iron Bastards

After the brief interregnum of Sir Alec Douglas-
Home, Labour, under Harold Wilson, won the
1964 election. Wilson was a straightforward
politician in the sense that everyone thought he
was slippery, and he was. The party's manifesto,
amid much talk of a New Britain and a Scientific
Revolution, said that Labour would halt major
rail closures pending the preparation of a
national transport plan. Of course, it depends
what you mean by 'major'.

In the month before the election, Marples had
actually stepped up the pace of closures, possibly
out of bloody-mindedness, possibly to stop his
successor reneging. Despite local fulminations –
including a near-riot involving the Labour
candidate on the closure of the Carlisle-Silloth
line – there was no sign that the issue swung any
votes either way. Transport has always been a
subsidiary issue at British elections: that is one
reason why it has been so neglected.

Beeching did not last long under Labour, but
not because he was seen as a liability, far from it.
Wilson actually wanted him to take charge of his
transport plan. 'He represented the breed of man
who could bring about Labour's Scientific

Revolution – the technocrat, the skilled manager, the thrusting, capable expert,' wrote the lobby correspondent Anthony Shrimsley. The gloss had not entirely worn off. But there were objections within the government because Beeching was seen as *anti-roads*.

Wilson gave way, which he regretted. Beeching, with some relief, returned to ICI, having first produced what was supposed to be *Reshaping*'s nicer younger brother, *The Development of the Major Railway Trunk Routes*. It still assumed that the emphasis was on freight, and that the railways could not compete with air travel for inter-city passengers over distances of more than 200 miles, i.e. from London to anywhere beyond Manchester. He also changed British Railways' lion symbols to the double-arrow logo, which has survived privatization, and shortened the name to British Rail. Perhaps that saved on ink.

The Labour government which lasted from 1964 to 1970 was splendidly riven by fear and loathing. Wilson got through four transport ministers – Tom Fraser, Barbara Castle, Richard Marsh and Fred Mulley. Castle thought Fraser was dominated by his civil servants and hated Marsh ('cynical, superficial and lazy ... disloyal lightweight'). Marsh hated Mulley ('our working relationships were appalling'). And doubtless Fraser and Mulley had their own opinions, but no one was interested in publishing their memoirs.

Fraser took over the transport plan without doing anything in the fourteen months before he was replaced by Castle, who couldn't drive a car (as all the papers immediately noted) but did

275

have considerable skill at driving a department. She turned up smiling, which civil servants said they had never ever seen a minister of transport do before. Castle quickly decided she could not force passengers back onto the railways, though she had a feint at doing just that with freight. However, she did establish the principle that there was such a thing as social need, and that the railways should be subsidized to meet it. This was a crucial breakthrough.

Castle held the job for less than two and a half years. It is said, I think falsely, that she actually axed more railways than any other minister (there is a similar counter-intuitive statistic bandied around about Margaret Thatcher and comprehensive schools); but she certainly did not halt the process. As the 1960s went on, the more regrettable the closures got. Most of Watkin's folly, the Great Central, disappeared in 1966, to little general regret until, years later, its usefulness as a freight artery was suddenly grasped.

At the start of 1967 the government announced that Bletchley and the other small towns of North Buckinghamshire would be subsumed into Britain's biggest ever new town, to be called Milton Keynes. At the end of 1967 the Varsity Line from Oxford to Cambridge via Bletchley was severed. Crazy.

In 1968 Ruskin had his revenge: the Midland line north of Matlock was closed. And now people flock to Monsal Dale, divine as the Vale of Tempe, gaze at the Headstone Viaduct and think how beautiful and convenient and lucrative it might be if miraculously a train suddenly appeared out of the tunnel. And every fool in Buxton can be in Bakewell in about twenty minutes – by road.

In 1969 Marsh took another chunk out of the network by shutting the Waverley Line between Edinburgh and Carlisle, rendering the Scottish Borders almost wholly train-free. The Scottish Government is now paying at least £115 million to reopen part of it.

These decisions became highly politicized. Labour did want to cut the railways' losses: and the longer, run-down lines offered useful savings – which the tiddly branches did not – whatever value they might have in a notional but distant future. But public opinion was starting to turn. Several urban lines were saved, and the setting-up of the passenger transport executives in the bigger provincial centres allowed more sensible local solutions to emerge.

Labour also refused to shut the beautiful but preposterous line – now known as the Heart of Wales – from Shrewsbury to Llanelli, which was earmarked for execution even before Beeching. Supposedly, it was saved after George Thomas, the Welsh Secretary, exclaimed in Cabinet: 'But you can't do that, prime minister! It goes through seven marginals!' This was an exaggeration: it hardly passed seven potential passengers. But Labour had just lost Carmarthen in a by-election, and this was no time to be taking any chances. The Scottish Highlands north of Inverness were also thick with marginals, so its lines also survived. Labour had no political interests to protect in the Borders, hence the loss of the Waverley Line.

Beeching's successor was his deputy Sir Stanley Raymond, a rather short-tempered man who had worked his way up the hierarchy and thus had much to be short-tempered about. 'In my twenty-one years in public transport,' he recalled, 'I calculate that at least half my time has been spent on organization, reorganization, acquisition, nationalization, centralization, decentralization, according to the requirements of the now regular political quinquennial revaluation of national transport policy.' He was succeeded by another longtime railwayman, Henry Johnson. He reorganized.

In spite of everything, the trains did keep running, not well, not reliably, not profitably. But slowly, they were getting more modern. Almost unnoticed outside the organization and the fan base, steam engines were disappearing from their last strongholds, partly because the strongholds themselves were being abandoned to the brambles and the birdsong.

Then, on 1 August 1968, British Rail's last steam train ran with great ceremony from Liverpool to Carlisle and back. It was a fifteen-guinea special (i.e. £15.75, or £200 at 2009 prices), cold luncheon, high tea and commemorative scroll included. There were large crowds at vantage points along the route including Rainhill, the scene of the 1829 locomotive trials, and by the Huskisson memorial at Parkside. 'In forty-nine years on the railways I've never seen anything like this,' said the chief steward Reg Maker. Yet it rated only marginal press attention.

This was not a sentimental time. This was a year

278

the world appeared to be on the brink of global revolution. No one was looking to the past, and certainly no one in British Rail had the wit or foresight to see how steam nostalgia could be turned to advantage. For some years after 1968, all steam locomotives were completely banned from the network, except on the Vale of Rheidol line in Wales, which BR continued running as a tourist attraction, though without much conviction.

That mood ran throughout the corporation. When the driver of one of the last steam trains got out of his cab, he gave the engine a sharp kick and announced to a startled group of passengers: 'Well, that's the last of those cast-iron bastards then.'

A Strange Enchantment

And then nothing happened. This is obviously not exactly true. But for the next quarter of a century the railways, to the naked eye, seemed to become frozen in time.

The British fell out of love with the notion of progress for its own sake, and the now-vanished steam engine assumed the glow in the national imagination that it has retained ever since: as the embodiment of a lost innocence, of unlocked front doors, cheery pubs and laughing policemen giving kids a clip round the ear for scrumping.

The generation so desperate to change the world in the 1960s started taking their offspring to the Santa Special or Thomas Day at the local heritage railway to show them a steam train. In the early 1970s the environmental movement was just gathering its first surge of momentum, and protesters saw off a grand plan for a 'London motorway box'. The new Euston was reviled; old St Pancras, down the road, was now thought beautiful. Beeching's public reputation plummeted; John Betjeman, credited with saving St Pancras, became the much-loved poet laureate.

British Rail gained no benefit from any of this. Having failed to anticipate the steam nostalgia, it clunked forward like one of its nastiest diesel railcars, a Pacer 142 perhaps. It became 'good old British Rail', always spoken with weary sarcasm, famous for being delayed by leaves on the line in autumn and 'the wrong kind of snow' in winter. Internal morale, particularly in the early 1970s, was terrible.

Governments, ministers, chairmen and organizational plans all came and went. Every step forward seemed to be followed by a crashing fall. The High Speed Train, introduced on the Paddington main line in 1976, was an immediate success; the tilting Advanced Passenger Train (1981), which made passengers sick, was a disaster. The Channel Tunnel was on! Then (1975) it was off again! There was talk of investment. Then came the 1976 financial crisis. The trade unions, then at the peak of their power, might agree to some new technical innovation. But then they would insist on having an unnecessary fireman or guard to preserve their members' jobs, thus preventing any savings.

Even the advertising reflected the constantly

changing moods. The success of the High Speed Train and the associated Inter-City brand (which was adopted across the world – even, without translation, in Germany) brought forth 'This is The Age of The Train' with Jimmy Savile, cigar in hand as I recall, leaning back in a first-class carriage. It was followed by the defensive, defeatist slogan 'We're Getting There'.

Relations with government were decidedly patchy, reaching a nadir in the mid-1970s when British Rail's chairman was Dick Marsh, the ex-Labour transport minister who had fallen out of love with his party. Marsh had been given the job by Heath's Conservative government but, when Labour came back, found himself having to work with his old enemy Fred Mulley. 'Sensible dialogue ... became practically nonexistent,' Marsh wrote later. 'The board's financial position continued to deteriorate on a massive scale and no one in Government, from the Prime Minister down, gave a damn.'

Even BR's official history accuses Marsh of 'whingeing'. He should have counted his blessings. No one now expected the railways to make a profit, not that there was any chance of them doing so. And closures virtually ceased after 1970, with Marsh himself saying that the mileage, which had now stabilized at about 11,000, was about right. Beeching, who was occasionally sniping (and mentally snipping) from the sidelines, was contemptuous: 'He doesn't have to build anything because he'd never be able to make a case for it and he doesn't have to close anything because it would be highly unpopular if he did. I think that's almost too miraculous to happen to anybody except an ex-politician.'

It was the easiest way out all round. With the exception of a handful of reopenings, new airport links and the Channel Tunnel line, the railway system in England in 2009 remains almost precisely what it was almost forty years ago, preserved as if under a strange enchantment. Government retreated from Beeching into total inertia.

How much of a shambles was British Rail? The economist Sir Christopher Foster, one of its sternest critics, believes it was a total shambles, and that Beeching was partly to blame for distracting attention from the real problems. 'By writing that chapter on closing branch lines he ensured that the enemy won,' he said, looking back. 'The railway accounts were appalling. No one realized until later that *all* the railway was unprofitable. Branch lines distracted attention from the main issue that the whole railway was badly run.'

It is certain that successive chairmen, especially those from outside, had severe trouble getting a grip on the realities of the railway. Right from the moment of nationalization, three alternative power bases emerged beyond the control of the nominal bosses. One was the unions. Another was the bloc of regional general managers who, well after Beeching's reign, still operated rather like Afghan warlords, treating instructions from the capital with disdain, knowing that they controlled the troops.

'I remember being taken to lunch by Bobby

Lawrence, manager of what had been the London, Midland and Scottish,' Foster recalled. 'Silver on the table. Port. It was like an officers' mess. Lots of people sitting round. Very long lunch. It was absolutely stunning.'

London often had very little idea what was going on its more remote possessions. Duncraig station, on the line to Kyle of Lochalsh, was closed in 1964 – except, it emerged eleven years later, that trains still stopped there if anyone wanted to get on or off. In a nice display of British pragmatism, BR then agreed to restore it to the timetable.

The third power base belonged to the engineers, who found it easy to bamboozle outsiders with technicalities, especially if the magic word 'safety' could be mentioned. The engineers had dominated the railways from the days of Stephenson and Brunel, and that appears to have been continuous right through the days of the great engine-builders like Gresley and Stanier until the very end of British Rail. In the 1990s a Herefordshire farmer got a visit from a BR official trying to cut out unnecessary farm crossings. 'This is a very large engineering concern,' the railwayman remarked during the conversation. 'The passengers and freight just get in the way, quite frankly.' He was joking. Sort of.

The notion that managers of the nationalized railways were a bunch of incompetents who would never survive the rigours of private enterprise was bitterly resented by the people involved. 'There was stricter cost control under BR than there is now,' one former manager, Richard Malins, told me. 'You had to work within budgets and you couldn't budget more than one or two years ahead because you didn't know what the Treasury was going to give you. A BR manager was as good as any manager in Britain. Because we operated in very public and difficult circumstances, probably better.'

However, the malign influence of government was beyond dispute. In the words of John Welsby, chief executive of British Rail in its closing days: 'There was a complete lack of clarity about the objectives of BR.' And political considerations constantly intruded. In the 1970s Marsh was desperate to close the Heysham-Belfast shipping service which he said was losing £800,000 a year; the government told him it would exacerbate the political crisis in Ulster.

In the 1980s a nasty invader called teredo worm started eating the Barmouth Bridge in mid-Wales and floods north of Inverness washed a bridge away. The Thatcher government was very sensitive to suggestions that it didn't care about these remote corners. 'Politically, these things had to be actioned immediately,' recalled Welsby. 'The fact that the money had been earmarked for the West Coast Main Line was irrelevant. The priorities were dictated by politics. You had an incompatible set of objectives.' Fare increases were also determined by the political timetable, he added. 'It was not unknown for the minister's private office to ring up and say "You do realize there's a by-election on?"'

Marsh's chief whinge was that whenever he did try to cut costs, ministers opposed him. 'In any debate in the House of Commons on the nationalized industries, the first half was concerned with how wicked and wasteful we were in losing public money, and the second half consisted of a long list of things they would like the nationalized industries to do, all of which cost more money.'

Sensible politicians tried to run away from the transport brief, even in opposition. Margaret Thatcher, elected Conservative leader in 1975, offered the job to Norman Fowler. 'I know nothing about transport,' he protested. 'Norman,' she replied, '*I* did transport. *You* can do transport.' Mrs Thatcher famously knew nothing at all about railways, reputedly travelling just once on a train (the Gatwick Express) in eleven years as prime minister. But she knew what she didn't like. In her early days as opposition leader, Fowler accompanied her to a getting-to-know-you lunch with British Rail's senior executives. One of them incautiously remarked that the government was not spending enough on the railways. 'She went airborne,' recalled Fowler, 'and was whizzing round the ceiling for the rest of the lunch. No one else got a word in edgeways, including me.'

The railway's management was understandably apprehensive when she swept into Downing Street in 1979. But for once they had a series of lucky breaks. Fowler, the first of her seven transport ministers, already knew and liked Sir Peter Parker, the entrepreneur-cum-Renaissance man who had succeeded the disgruntled Marsh three years earlier. Like Barbara Castle, Parker's first contribution had been to cheer everyone up. He

285

was an enthusiast and a charmer, if not a details man. 'He could charm the birds off the trees,' as one civil servant put it, 'but they would be albatrosses.'

Fowler, meanwhile, set to work, without much encouragement, on a prototype Thatcherite scheme to build the Channel Tunnel using private capital. 'My stroke of luck was that Mrs Thatcher had this meeting with President Mitterrand of France,' he recalled, 'and the list of things they were likely to agree on was very short. But there had to be a final communiqué. Then she had this brilliant idea: "Fowler's been banging on about the Channel Tunnel!" So it was decided to underline the importance of it. That made it a completely different project. It wasn't Transport banging on about it, it was No. 10.' Luckily, perhaps, no one had mentioned to her that it could have been a road tunnel instead.

The third bit of luck was perhaps more a piece of skill. If it ever thought about the railways, Downing Street under Thatcher was against them and had predictably rejected Parker's suggestions for electrification. Instead it set up an inquiry into the shape of the railways under a crusty retired civil servant called Sir David Serpell. The inquiry was planning to announce a range of half a dozen options for a slimmed-down railway, one of which (Option A) slashed it back to 1,600 miles, beyond Beeching's wildest fantasies, reducing the routes to a handful of spokes from London. This was the only one, the committee was about to say, that could possibly be profitable. Serpell seems to have had no intention of actually recommending this course of action.

It was 1982 and the next election was getting close; at that stage the Tories were far from certain to be re-elected. Option A was leaked to the *Sunday Times* – almost certainly by Will Camp, Parker's stylish public relations adviser – as though this was a genuine plan, implying that Thatcher was about to destroy Britain's railways. The backbenchers saddled up their high horses at once. David Howell, who had replaced Fowler as transport minister, ran a mile. And Serpell – berated by a guard on the way home to Devon – briefly became more notorious than Beeching. The report was quickly forgotten.

The former Liberal leader Jo Grimond compared Serpell's fate to that of Lord Franks, who at the same time was investigating the causes of the Falklands War and finding, in the usual Whitehall fashion, that no one in the British government could possibly be blamed for anything. 'How relaxing to examine anything as unemotive as a war,' mused Grimond.

Until around 1988, when she introduced the poll tax, Thatcher had perfectly attuned political antennae. For all her boldness, she could sense which rocks were best left unkicked. And the Serpell affair seemed to reinforce her view that the railways contained some powerful *muti*, a man thing, folk-magic she did not quite comprehend. After the Conservatives did win the 1983 election, handsomely, Howell was sacked, and replaced by Nicholas Ridley, a Thatcherite *avant la lettre* and a ferocious opponent of nationalized

287

industries. Yet he was also a practical man, with a background in engineering, and he now hit it off with Parker's successor, Sir Bob Reid.

This Reid was later to be succeeded by another Bob Reid, who also got the statutory knighthood. This oddity was to confuse outsiders but, within the business, both men were admired and there remains a widespread view that Reid I was the best chairman the railways ever had. He was a cool, patrician figure who had, nonetheless, grown up within the organization; all the while, the story goes, he was formulating his plan to reform it, but kept quiet, against the day when he might be in a position to do something. This suggests that here was a man who really did have the virtues of ruthlessness etc., that journalists so freely ascribed to Beeching.

It is also said that Ridley and Reid did a deal. Both men are dead now, and the exact nature of the deal remains unclear. One suggestion is that Ridley, more influential than the average transport minister, said he would secure investment if the railways could get rid of their losses. As practical men, they would have realized both halves of that were incredible. The more plausible version is that Ridley promised to keep out of Reid's hair if this chairman, unlike his most recent predecessors, didn't interfere in politics.

Politics were actually working to the management's advantage in that the government was busy breaking the power and spirit of the unions, tilting the balance towards the bosses in a manner the railways had not experienced since Edward VII was on the throne. And Reid took full advantage.

'He set about running it like a business, and not a great British institution like the opera,' said Welsby. 'The management hadn't understood the impact of what they were doing at a market level. They understood gross income and gross costs but not how they were related.' So Reid split the railways into five sectors: three for passengers and two for freight, which were each given their own bosses and clear objectives. Thanks to clear management and a little creative accountancy, the flagship, InterCity, became – according to Christian Wolmar – 'Europe's only profitable railway'. In boom years the London commuter lines, Network SouthEast, made money too. And the railways as a whole became 'the most efficient in Europe and the least subsidized'.

It was hardly Nirvana: this was British Railways. But BR was allowed to undertake a (cheapskate) electrification of the East Coast line to Edinburgh, which Beeching and Serpell's Option A would have abandoned. And there was a sense within the industry, if not yet among the public, that all would be well as long as *she* never went near the railways or its management and remembered how much she loathed them.

She was all-powerful in the mid-eighties when the great Thatcherite panacea, privatization, was at its peak. British Telecom, electricity and gas were all sold off, to great acclaim, partly because the new management did make them more efficient but mainly because the assets were grossly undervalued and, in a booming economy, a new army of small capitalists found themselves

289

richer every time they looked at the share prices in the paper.

By 1990 Margaret Thatcher, as prime ministers invariably do after ten years in power, had not merely lost her touch but gone – to use the medical technicality – a little bonkers. Which is perhaps why, in what turned out to be the closing weeks of her imperium, she allowed her seventh and last transport satrap, Cecil Parkinson, to tell the party conference at Bournemouth when he mentioned British Rail: 'The question now is not whether we should privatize it but about how and when.'

CHAPTER NINE

PENTONVILLE ROAD

Even in 2009, after one of those dire train journeys always referred to as 'nightmares', people would often put the blame on 'Good old British Rail' or even 'British Railways'. By this point, British Rail had not run a train in twelve years and the name British Railways had been abolished for public consumption for forty-five years. But in this industry the combination of inertia and nostalgia is always unstoppable.

They do still have a mysterious half-life, both of them, in an anonymous office block at the top end of Pentonville Road by the Angel station in London. I seem to remember a pawn shop on that corner.

There sit the offices of the British Railways Board, a nationalized industry that still holds regular board meetings, and – technically separate – the British Railways Board (Residuary), a limited company now wholly owned by the Department for Transport. And in command of it all sits the heir to Dr Beeching and the dynasty of Bob Reids, an amiable man called Peter Trewin.

There is no silver service, nor even any visible memorabilia or railwayana to distinguish this office from a typical Islington software house. There is no legion of flunkeys and public relations men. There is no legion at all, though you could think of this as Fort Zinderneuf, Beau Geste's desert outpost. Having had nearly 700,000 employees at the start and 130,000 at what appeared to be the end, the two British Railways are now down to just thirty stout defenders, split between here and an engineering office in York. Trewin is a career railwayman, who joined British Railways as a management trainee a few weeks after the end of steam in 1968. Now, like the last survivor of a massacre, it is his job to look after the ruins.

The organization, Trewin explains, still has three inescapable functions. One concerns the Channel Tunnel. The board was party to the original usage contract, which is subject to French law. Handing that over to anyone else would be extremely complex. There is also a great deal of non-operational property left over, especially from the pre-Beeching era: a few office blocks, old branch lines, goods yards, bridges and viaducts on the old lines, many of them listed as historic monuments or complicated by restrictive covenants. These are referred to, rather cruelly, as 'the burdensome estate'.

Some of the lines are being handed over to Sustrans, the charity that turns old railways into cycle paths, and some to local councils. But the estate is diminishing only slowly. In the brief period of railway optimism that followed Labour's victory in 1997, the deputy prime minister, John Prescott, froze sales of railway property in case anything might be required for reopening routes. And when Eurostar services were moved from Waterloo to St Pancras in 2007, the board acquired both the disused depot in West London, confusingly known as North Pole, and the mothballed platforms at Waterloo.

The third – and potentially very burdensome – function is dealing with claims by former employees against British Railways, particularly those involving industrial diseases and most particularly those involving exposure to asbestos – which are expected to reach a peak by 2013. In the early days of privatization, the board still had responsibility for the British Transport Police.

But when potential greatness beckoned once again, Pentonville Road was ignored. In 2003 the then Strategic Rail Authority stripped one franchisee, Connex South-Eastern, of its epaulettes and temporarily renationalized the service. But it took charge of the operation itself, instead of handing the job to the British Railways Board. Now the SRA has gone the way of so many other short-lived organizations and acronyms of the privatized railway – Railtrack and Thames Trains, OPRAF and GNER – while good old BR lingers on.

When I saw him, Trewin had just come back from the funeral of a former colleague. There had been a good turnout of the old brigade of management and he was enthusing about the camaraderie the job engendered: 'Working for the railways is a bit like being in the army. There is this tremendous loyalty and involvement. You join for life in a sense.'

'Don't you miss, well, railways?'

'Not really,' he said.

'There's a tremendous variety in what the railways do: property, law, industrial relations. Railway management isn't necessarily about running trains.'

Trewin was somewhat tickled by the retrospective popularity British Rail now enjoys. It was easy to forget, he said, the reputation it used to have. 'When you went to parties, it was like being a doctor. You didn't say what you did for a living.'

The Slim Controller

Only a few weeks after Cecil Parkinson's promise-cum-warning about privatization at the Conservative conference, Margaret Thatcher was overthrown as prime minister, and replaced by John Major, who introduced a fresher and, most felt, less doctrinaire style of government.

Naturally, there was a new transport minister,

in this case Malcolm Rifkind, who was supposed to come up with a viable privatization scheme. This proved difficult in the eighteen months that remained before the general election which – it was universally assumed – the Conservatives would lose. Rifkind, who may have been less than ultra-zealous about the whole idea in the first place, was particularly unenthused by the plan being urged on him by the Treasury to split the trains from the infrastructure. And his own civil servants had some difficulty taking any of this seriously because they assumed railway privatiz-ation would be strangled at birth by the incoming Labour government under Neil Kinnock.

There were at least five different ways in which British Rail could have been privatized:

1. As a whole, substituting a private monopoly for a public one.
2. In regions, recreating an updated version of the inter-war Big Four. This was Major's favoured solution.
3. In business sectors, following the lines of BR's revamp.
4. Separating the ownership of trains and tracks.
5. Throwing everything up in the air and hoping for the best.

What emerged in the end, of course, was a combination of options 4 and 5.

Rifkind did try to resist this: 'I became increas-ingly persuaded that the split between infra-structure and trains was a mistake, it was foolish,' he recalled later. 'Forty per cent of an operator's costs are infrastructure. And to remove an operator from influence on forty per cent of his activities is a very poor way of running any business. 'The argument was that unless you split infrastructure from operations you don't get competition. But the reality is that, except in a very few cases, the competition you're talking about is with road and air. We were locked in that argument with the Treasury when the election appeared. I was making a nuisance of myself. They thought they'd got beyond that stage.'

During the 1992 election the Labour transport spokesman John Prescott argued – as cogently as that great language-mangler ever has done – for using private funds to allow British Rail to invest: 'It is absurd that French Railways can raise funds for new investment in the City of London, when British Rail is not allowed to do so,' said the party's manifesto. After thirteen eventful years in power, the Conservatives did not have many fresh ideas, and railway privatization stood out in a rather thin set of proposals: 'We will increase the maximum penalties for making obscene or malicious phone calls,' was one particularly thrilling subsidiary promise. When the public shied away from Kinnock and voted the Tories back – with a majority cut from eighty-five to twenty-one – it was not entirely clear how they might pass the time.

Much of the time, they looked for non-political entertainment. Between 1992 and 1997, a more than normally high proportion of their ministers and MPs were caught out misunderstanding the significance of the word 'member'. Between extra-mural shags – and dubious schemes for personal enrichment – they privatized the railways. The sex, I would argue, was far less damaging.

Rifkind was replaced by John MacGregor, one of those ministers depressingly known as 'a safe pair of hands', which means they can competently execute and defend as required any policy, no matter how dire. In this case MacGregor had to do more than that: on his appointment after the election he went into his office, sat down, and asked to see the privatization plans. We can imagine the polite Sir Humphreyish cough that ensued. 'We weren't expecting to see you, minister.' There were no plans.

An extraordinary period followed. 'I had a very intensive six weeks,' said MacGregor in a masterly understatement. 'I realized that if we were going to get this through we had to get the bill in the first session of parliament. So I had six weeks to make up my mind what the structure would be, then get it through cabinet sub-committee, cabinet and then do a White Paper.' No wonder what emerged was a dog's breakfast.

While all this was going on, there was a little foretaste of the future. Barely a fortnight after the election Stagecoach, the energetic Scottish-based company which had made a fortune running privatized buses, stepped in when British Rail crassly announced it would do away with seating carriages on the Aberdeen sleeper, forcing everyone to pay for a bed. Stagecoach leased six coaches from British Rail, painted them in corporate livery, and launched them with a journey graced by the presence of Roger Freeman,

MacGregor's junior minister. Even before the election, Freeman had demonstrated a political tin ear by speculating that the revamped railway could have 'cheap and cheerful' trains for typists and more luxurious trains for civil servants and businessmen. And presumably junior ministers.

Freeman took the inaugural train from Aberdeen, and enthused about the project – 'I am used to late-night sittings in the House,' he boasted as the journey began. Not to the extent of sitting bolt upright all night in one of Stagecoach's privatized seats, however. South of Carlisle he was spotted skulking off to a nationalized sleeper carriage. 'I've got a full day's work in front of me,' he said. 'I am fifty years old and I didn't feel like sitting up all night.' The contract was skewed in favour of BR, and the experiment only lasted six months. But it was a marker.

Freeman did indeed have work to do. By July, just two months after the election, MacGregor was presenting his rather thin white paper, *New Opportunities for the Railways*, to the Commons. It was the sort of speed Whitehall normally only achieves in response to a national emergency. The emergency was that the prime minister had determined there was a political imperative to do the job.

There remain two fundamental mysteries about this entire saga. Why was the Major government so determined to privatize the railways? And why did it choose this particular model which, was seen at the time – and since – by most observers as wholly absurd?

The first answer goes straight to the top. John

Major is often remembered as a nice but rather ineffectual prime minister and, for that reason, it is widely assumed, can hardly have known what was being done in his name on the railways. Christian Wolmar subscribes to this theory. 'He apparently showed little direct interest in the issue,' Wolmar wrote in *Broken Rails*, 'as there is no significant mention of rail privatization in his autobiography.' As we have seen with Harold Macmillan, autobiographies are an unreliable guide; and this ex-PM was also far more interested in recalling his more glamorous exploits. My own private information at the time was that Major was utterly determined on this issue and was driving railway policy; this was reinforced by an interview conducted for this book. (He agreed to this despite being well aware of my own views on his policy, for which he ought to get some credit in heaven).

'I don't deny that British Railways was more efficient than it had been in the 1960s,' he said. 'But it was quite difficult to find an argument for it staying in the public sector. It was unreliable, there was no cost control, the freight growth was below what it should have been and it was pretty unfriendly to passengers. And yet it was vital to Great Britain plc that it should be vibrant, successful and taking freight off the roads.'

Major admitted that BR suffered badly from under-investment and always had. 'Would it ever have got enough from government? The answer is no. It would have had to compete with health, education, defence...

'The PSBR [Public Sector Borrowing Requirement] was such that it would have limped along for ever. It had to go into the private sector, so it had access to capital to make it successful, so that whenever there was a crisis in government it would not be in the position of having its budget cut. There is a difference between dispassionate regulation and government control. The railways shouldn't be subject to the day-to-day whims of government.'

'Are you saying the privatization was necessary because of the government's flaws rather than the railways?' I asked.

'A bit of both. In the undertow British Rail was inefficient.'

MacGregor had made a similar case in a Radio 4 discussion in 2006: BR could never be sure about its capital expenditure programme because of all the other pressures the government faced. It is, when you think about it, a damning self-indictment when made, not by outsiders, but by ministers representing a government that had been in power – so it sometimes seemed at the time – more or less for ever. We cannot be trusted. Stop us before we kill again.

And during the five years of that parliament, no one in government ever made a coherent and compelling case that replacing British Rail, for all its manifest imperfections, would produce an improvement. What one suspected, and still suspects, is that a fourth-term government, with no obvious agenda, needed this project. Whether the industry needed it was a secondary issue.

Privatization had been a surprise hit for Margaret Thatcher in the 1980s. Previous post-war Conservative governments had been very cautious in pushing back state control. In the early 1970s Edward Heath had confined himself to resolving anomalies, selling off the Thomas Cook travel agency and the pubs in Carlisle. Thatcher astonished everyone with the boldness of her policies: British Telecom and British Airways, most obviously, perked up considerably under private ownership.

But the essence of the policy was a piece of political trickery. State assets were sold off to great armies of private shareholders who, in the bull market of the time, were thrilled to be handed certificates which increased in value every day. This was not surprising since the state's assets were sold off cheap to increase their palatability, and the public never noticed they were buying stuff that had belonged to them in the first place. Thatcher had sold off the family silver, as the aged Harold Macmillan put it.

However, these schemes had all been perceived as successes, and there was now a deeply entrenched belief – to which even the Labour Party was having to adjust – that private owner-ship was a good thing and public ownership bad. Full stop. Just as the reverse had been accepted in the late 1940s. The belief also grew, in govern-ment particularly, that *anyone* could run a railway except a railwayman. But even the government realized it would have to continue subsidizing the railways, as well as exercising a large measure of control. How did this square with the principle of free enterprise? There was no time for philo-sophical speculation like that. The government had a train to catch.

One problem with this privatization is that the structure, as initially conceived, offered no scope to buy off public opinion by appealing to its avarice. Another was that the structure made very little sense. 'Our aim is simple,' MacGregor told the Commons, 'to improve the quality of railway services for the travelling public and the freight customer.' The route he chose to achieve that was unbelievably convoluted. Some enthusiasts for privatization have insisted that trains and infrastructure had to be separated to comply with European legislation. This is true but mad: other countries have dealt with this requirement by small accounting procedures, not by a multi-billion reorganization.

The surest sign of the failure of railway privatization is that it is difficult to identify precisely who came up with the scheme that emerged. Those close to the action pinpoint either Sir Christopher Foster, who by now was advising MacGregor, or Sir Steve Robson, head of the privatization unit at the Treasury. Foster, a defender of privatization, denies paternity. 'If it was Foster,' said someone who dealt with them both, 'he did it through love. If it was Robson, it was hate.' But it probably was never that simple. There seems to have been a convergence of opinion between the Treasury's privatization unit and the Department for Transport's civil servants, who were themselves reorganized wholesale after the 1992 election to weed out recalcitrants.

At the heart of it seems to have been the fantasy – which can only have come from the Treasury – that the railways offered serious opportunities for internal competition which would at the same time drive down the need for subsidy. Major was not involved in the details, but was then persuaded to drop his enthusiasm for a return to a regionally based system. He admits what he got was not what he wanted originally, and that his own idea was influenced by nostalgia.

...I do not deny it may have been part of my thinking, a legitimate part of my thinking. I am interested in history, and there is nothing wrong with nostalgia. We do have a nostalgia for steam trains. It was precisely because of that that I wished to make the railways what they could be.

We went the way we did with advice from within the industry, the Treasury and the Department for Transport. There were a lot of dire warnings that, if we had privatized it regionally, the companies would have spent their money on rolling stock and not enough on track and safety and infrastructure. For presentational purposes.

My idea was more glorious but maybe this was the more realistic. It is quite difficult to ignore the advice you are given about safety.

'Some think you were not all that enthusiastic about the policy,' I said to Major.

'They're quite right in thinking I was not an ideologue for privatization. They're quite wrong in thinking I wasn't in tune with this privatization.'

'You drove it?'

'Yes, I did. It didn't get in the manifesto by chance.'

'You were the Fat Controller?'
'I was the Slim Controller,' he replied.

Not Even a Choc-Ice

There was very little glory as MacGregor's white paper was transformed into a bill that limped its way through parliament over the next year and a half. Even in the moment of his victory at the polls Major had already been warned that no one was going to give him much credit: 'I remember sitting with Chris Patten the day after the election. And he said, "You do realize that you won when you should have lost and that no one will have any sympathy or tolerance for anything that you now do?".'

Less than six months after its election, the government descended into terminal unpopularity in the financial crisis of September 1992. On top of everything else, it was besieged by headlines about the bleak future of the privatized railway, many of them presumed to have been inspired (to the fury of ministers) by British Rail as it fought its desperate rearguard action.

FULL STAFF 'TO STAY AT ONLY
88 STATIONS'

RAIL PASSENGERS LIKELY TO FACE
RIVAL TICKET SNAG

GREEN LIGHT FOR RAIL FARES
FREE-FOR-ALL

RAIL SELL-OFF 'COULD STARVE INVESTMENT'

FEARS FOR ROUTES, FARES AND SAFETY

However, there was also one serious enemy within. In January 1993 the Commons Select Committee on Transport, chaired by the Tory backbencher Robert Adley, issued a highly critical report on the plan. Adley was a rail enthusiast and author who commanded considerable respect for his expertise on the industry; he had already christened the privatization plan 'the poll tax on wheels', and dissident MPs were starting to coalesce around him.

With such a tiny majority, MacGregor was forced to toss out all manner of bones. And one by one the headlines had to be rebutted by concessions. Franchisees would be forced to honour the various cheap-travel railcards introduced by BR. Season tickets and saver fares would be price-controlled, with rises limited to one per cent *below* inflation. Tickets had to be 'inter-available' between operators. Closures would be almost impossible. And so on. Eventually, he also had to concede that railways were not airports and that franchisees would have a virtual monopoly of their routes. It was becoming increasingly hard to see the object of the exercise, since train operators would have very little commercial freedom. But the bill had to get through: the government's credibility depended on it.

In May 1993 Robert Adley died suddenly, aged only fifty-eight. The potential rebels were left leaderless, and the bill was safe. Intellectually, the government had failed to make any argument in favour of its plans. I happened to be in the House of Lords the day the legislation was forced through. No one had a good word to say for it. Lords Marsh and Peyton, both former transport ministers, joined forces to amend it; the government rejected their amendments. The only debate was whether the unelected Lords had the right to persist in their objections against the elected Commons. Another former transport minister, Lord Boyd-Carpenter, by then eighty-five, thought that could have 'serious consequences'.

The Lords were supposed to be able to make the Commons rethink. But, protested Lord Simon of Glaisdale, eighty-two and sagacious with it, the Commons had not rethought. 'It is the government, with its whipped majority, that does the thinking.' Britain did not look a well-governed country that night. At 244 pages, the bill was at least quite chunky by now, but the detail of the new institutions was still sketchy. It would be simpler, said the Liberal Democrat Nick Harvey, if the bill had just one clause: 'The Secretary of State can do what he likes, how he likes, when he likes, and where he likes.'

Now, however, the game changed. The question was no longer whether privatization would happen, but how. But the need for speed was still overwhelming. The government had a maximum of three and a half years before facing an election it looked almost certain to lose. The aim now was to get the new railway not merely completed but so entrenched that the Labour Party could not dig it out.

To ensure this, the issue of open access was set aside, for fear that it would terminally jeopardize the award of franchises, which was already looking a particularly fraught aspect of a terrifying process. Unified British Rail was broken into dozens of different entities: twenty-five train operating companies (TOCs), six track renewal companies, six track maintenance companies, six rolling stock maintenance companies, three freight operators, three rolling stock leasing companies. And they all had to be flogged off before the closure date of the next election. Hurry! Hurry! Hurry! Everything must go. And, with the trivial exception of Railfreight Distribution, everything did go, although in the initial stages the fabric of the railways – the track and stations – was to remain public property. It was an awesome achievement, in its way: the nearest thing to a scorched-earth policy one is ever likely to see in British politics. Whether there was a cost in blood is a matter for genuine debate. The cost in treasure was staggering.

Hereabouts, the railway industry began to acquire the mass of acronyms that would govern it henceforth. The final volume of Terry Gourvish's three-part history of the railways since nationalization, covering 1997 to 2005, lists – by my reckoning – 148, the majority of these specific railway creations. Welcome to the world of ORR, OPRAF, ORCAT, ROSCOs, RIDDOR, TOCs and dozens more.

OPRAF was the Office of Passenger Rail

Franchising, presided over by Roger Salmon, a merchant banker. ORR, the Office of the Rail Regulator, was run by John Swift, a QC. Their chief qualifications were that they had no knowledge of the railways. Indeed, this became the major qualification for any involvement. This was partly because of a visceral Conservative belief that anyone brought up in the sloppy and slap-happy nationalized sector was completely unfitted for the thrusting, competitive, customer-friendly industry that was about to be born. This feeling was strongly reinforced by what the government saw as British Rail management's sulky obstructiveness to the excellent idea of their company being eviscerated. The second Sir Bob Reid, Reid II, was always careful not to oppose privatization as such, merely to argue that his own sectors provided a more obvious basis for it. Not all his underlings were as self-contained, and they paid a price.

Railwaymen were out; anyone else was in. This notion reached a peak in 1997 when the British Airports Authority, itself a railway novice, announced plans for the new Heathrow Express link including the recruitment of '120 special staff, skilled in customer care ... a third of whom will be trained as drivers'. It was considered easier for a well-mannered person to learn to drive a train than to teach a British Rail employee manners.

Two groups of people were highly fashionable: consultants and lawyers. According to a parliamentary answer, quoted by Wolmar, £450m were handed to consultancy firms during the privatization process by the government. 'Many of these consultants had no prior knowledge of the industry,' he noted. This addiction has never gone away. The saddest story I heard on my travels was the attempt by a local group of activists to brighten up Homerton station in East London by planting a garden. Frustrated by the sloping site, too urban to have the expertise themselves, they paid consultants to advise them what to plant. Time was when half the signalmen and crossing-keepers in Britain would have known.

But this was nothing. Virtually every top legal firm in Britain had its snout in the gold-plated champagne-filled trough that the government kept refilling through the mid-1990s. There was an endless supply of billable hours working for a client, the British government, which had no interest in the cost but just needed the job done fast. The job involved transforming the wisdom of the years handed down within a unified, hierarchical organization into myriad contractual relationships. A solicitor involved in the process (who must remain anonymous) explained:

While the contracts were being drawn up for the first franchises in the mid-1990s, a whole new language grew up. There were 'figleaf contracts', which I'd never heard of before or since; 'overarching agreements' (I'm not sure what that means but it means something) and 'retrofitting' documents.

Basically, these were the contracts between OPRAF and the TOCs. No one had finished due diligence or worked out the contractual matrix, but we just had to push on. All sorts of things hadn't been thought through, like who would make the announcement to say that the train was about to arrive at a short station. You had to work out the contractual arrangement for something even as trivial as that. Or who puts up the announcement that a train is delayed?

The TOCs were buying a pig in a poke. They knew they were buying a pig in a poke. Everyone knew it. The lawyers were sitting around saying 'What the fuck are we going to do?' 'Do it,' was the answer.

We joked that we knew the election timetable before anyone else. Even very experienced professionals on privatization said this knocked spots off everything else they had worked on, because of all the interlocking complexities. Other privatizations were based on two-dimensional models. This was three- or four-dimensional. And it had to be done to an ever-changing political timetable. It's impossible to work out what it all cost.

'A billion,' I suggested.

'Not an unreasonable guess.'

'Did anyone say the whole thing was completely mad?'

'All the time.'

Some learned the complexities quicker than others. Roger Salmon announced that he wanted to axe the little-used sleeper service between London and Fort William, which newspapers promptly christened the 'Deerstalker Express'. There was a huge outcry, and a substantial immediate upturn in business from the free publicity. Salmon had to back down. It was clear now that every route had to be sacrosanct because any closure would be seen as a sign of the perfidy that lay behind privatization.

But the process itself also seemed immutable unless the Conservatives were faced with enough by-elections to destroy their majority: but only eight of their MPs died in the eight-year parliament; their lively sex lives must have kept them fit.

For some strange reason, the British government likes to use April Fool's Day as the date for major administrative changes. And so on 1 April 1994 British Rail handed over its core infrastructure functions to the new operation known as Railtrack. They temporarily retained the trains but with the Reids' precious sectors split into twenty-five franchise-ready geographical areas.

Railtrack was still a government-owned company but its chairman, another oilman called Bob – this time Bob Horton, an abrasive ex-BP manager – was already agitating for it to be privatized. The first change was the introduction of new grey-and-green staff uniforms at the major stations which had passed to Railtrack, suggesting that the new company had already acquired the taste for pointless corporate self-assertion that would be characteristic of the new railway. Contrast that with the mouselike entry of British Railways in 1948.

Horton was kicking at an open door. What rail privatization had so far lacked was the kind of concession to popular capitalism that could give ordinary shareholders a stake in the railways' success. Here too was the prospect of a large inflow of funds to the Treasury. And it added yet another padlock on to the new set-up to make it harder for Labour to unpick. Why on earth didn't they think of it before?

Meantime, the less visible parts of BR were already being sold off including the ROSCOs (Rolling Stock Leasing Companies) and the BRISCOs (the British Rail Infrastructure Companies). The nation's 11,260 locomotives and coaches were sold off for a song to three groups of chancers including Porterbrook, a consortium set up by an obscure BR manager, Sandy Anderson, who was himself involved in arranging the privatization process. Without a whiff of illegality, Porterbrook bought one set of rolling stock for £526m, and sold it on seven months later to Stagecoach for £300m profit, more than £30m of which went straight to Anderson, whose initial investment had been £120,000.

On the one hand, the vendors were desperate. But potential bidders were also kept out by vague threats from the Labour Party to keep clear. Anderson gambled that Labour were just indulging in windbaggery and won. The newly established National Lottery could not compete with this. Anderson personally thanked the Labour Party whose opposition to the sale – and the fear that they were serious in threatening retribution – helped depress the price. The National Audit Office blamed the government's haste and said it had cost the country something like a billion pounds. That's *another* billion pounds.

The infrastructure companies were sold off in 1996 to major engineering firms who were then given guaranteed contracts with Railtrack. The hidden agenda seems to have been the need to break the unions. The clash of cultures between the old rule-bound, come-day-go-day union-dominated British Rail ways and the can-do-and-do-it-now attitude of private managers was brilliantly portrayed in Ken Loach's 2001 film *The Navigators*. Loach is hardly unbiased, but what he illustrated was the manner in which both sides, in their different ways, cut corners. And the 1990s was the heyday of corner-cutting on the railways.

Railtrack was sold off in 1996, for just under £2 billion. It was a last hurrah for privatization: over-subscribed, with shares leaping by fifteen per cent on day one, even though the company was already starting to build its reputation for laxness and ineptitude. Once again the National Audit Office said governmental haste had cost the taxpayer money: had the sale been conducted in stages, it could have raised an extra £1.5 billion.

Amidst all this came the sale of the franchises. In just over a year, under the comparatively emollient stewardship of the bicycling baronet Sir George Young, all the trains had been sold off. It began, amid farce, in February 1996, when South West Trains began operating into Waterloo and Great Western into Paddington. There should have been three companies operating. But the third sale, involving the lines into Fenchurch Street, had to be scrapped following allegations of ticket fraud. Then there was the question about which train was the first. The secretary of state was anxious to make it clear that the 0150 from Fishguard to Paddington belonged to the old era, especially as – under the familiar Sunday engineering arrangements – it had started out as a bus. Anyway, that was an even less enticing obligation than getting on the first South West train, the 0510 from Twickenham, which is what he did, along with various members of the media, seven fare-paying passengers and one non-fare-paying passenger, who was the first person off at Waterloo and somewhat surprised by the size of the welcoming party at that hour on a Sunday morning. He was fined £10.

The Fenchurch Street ticket fraud, explained Steve Norris, the junior transport minister, was 'not particularly large': about £30,000 a month. That was somewhat larger than a single evaded fare from Twickenham, but considerably smaller than the billions that the government was flinging at all-comers to preserve some semblance of respectability for the process. However, most of the other franchises did go without much difficulty. The South West franchise was owned by Stagecoach, undaunted by their pioneering failure on the Aberdeen sleeper. And Stagecoach's enthusiasm encouraged other bus companies to join in. When the last British Rail train ran, before the start of the ScotRail franchise in February 1997, it hardly registered.

It would be a mistake to imagine that the end of British Rail was universally unpopular. Nostalgia doesn't come that quickly. When one of the last BR evening trains from Euston before the takeover by Virgin went wrong in familiar fashion, passengers began a chant of 'Branson! Branson! Branson!' in honour of their presumed saviour.

313

'Surly ticket inspectors were taunted with predictions of their job prospects when the people's champion took over,' wrote the *Guardian* columnist Mark Lawson, having witnessed this outburst of popular delight. 'Metaphor became reality: these people really believed that Richard Branson would make the trains run on time.'

Virgin's airline had built a good reputation, which partly rested on the pleasing touch of giving cattle-class passengers a choc-ice during the film show. And Branson evidently believed in his own magic powers too. But arrogance was the defining characteristic of the train operators in the early days. The sensible approach would have been to keep his brand name off the trains until he was sure they would show some improvement on British Rail. In view of the foul-up of the West Coast Main Line upgrade that was to follow, this would have been at least ten years.

Instead, he rapidly had the word Virgin painted everywhere (what would the board of the London & North Western have made of that?) and took the blame for deep-seated problems that were not actually his company's fault. As I recall, the only immediate change on board was a switch in the buffet from Coca-Cola to Branson's ersatz Virgin Cola. Though Branson had been free with all sorts of baloney about providing on-board massages and the like, he never even bothered with the choc-ices.

And Virgin was not the only letdown. It soon became clear that improving customer service was not to be the mission of the new train operators. There were exceptions of course. In

314

case you have forgotten, let me remind you of Great Western's baked beans. The *Modern Railways* columnist Roger Ford noted that Great Western also had better litter bins, that ScotRail had improved provision for cyclists and that first-class passengers on Anglia Railways got a new free magazine.

In the opening months of 1997, there remained a widespread assumption that this was a brief interlude. After eighteen years, Labour government was imminent. The incoming prime minister, Tony Blair, had promised a 'publicly owned, publicly accountable railway'. Surely this was going to mean a return to something that looked a bit like British Rail.

For once, railways were an issue in the election in the sense that the whole pointless botch of privatization merged into the general air of decay that surrounded the government. The Labour landslide dwarfed even that of 1945. Surely Blair would use this remarkable opportunity to fulfil that promise and restore some sense to the railways. He would, wouldn't he? Wouldn't he? *Wouldn't he?*

Oh, no, he wouldn't

There wasn't even a pretence about it, not in the end. In opposition, Labour had been content to make whatever promises they thought the audience wanted to hear. 'It mattered what we said but not what we did,' explained Clare Short, recalling her stint as shadow transport secretary.

'That seat of the pants operating was very Blair.'

But as government neared, the leadership became more careful, and the 1997 manifesto was deliberately downbeat: 'Our task will be to improve the situation as we find it, not as we wish it to be.' Gordon Brown, the incoming chancellor, was implacably opposed to renationalization on grounds of expense. Tony Blair was not interested in railways, in keeping with a prime ministerial tradition that John Major would have done better to uphold. Indeed, though the threat of climate change became ever more obvious throughout his ten years in Downing Street, he displayed little interest in anything to do with the environment except as an occasional rhetorical device.

The railways did have a much louder and more influential voice in this government, perhaps louder than ever before. John Prescott, as deputy prime minister, was crowned as emperor of a new and sprawling department, Environment, Transport and the Regions, which lasted throughout Labour's first four-year term, with a shifting cast of understrappers taking turns as transport ministers. Prescott, the son of a railwayman, actually cared about the industry, which was a novelty. And he really preferred doing this job to strutting the world like Blair, starting wars here and there.

It was easy to believe that he would have renationalized the railways if only Brown had let him. He insists this was not the case. He remembered British Rail too well and was not enthusiastic. 'It was an old-boy network,' he told me in an interview. 'It was run by the military and still had military concepts. Even the canteen was still called the mess. The idea wasn't to run the railways more efficiently or more effectively – you just ran it.'

Had he become transport secretary five years earlier as he had been expected to do, he intended to introduce his own version of privatization.

If we'd kept the track public and owned by the state, I was quite prepared – and I remember saying this to Richard Branson – to let a private company come in for a period of time and see if they could run it any differently. You could have had a public East Coast line and a private West Coast line, maybe.

I wanted to see if there was any truth that a private sector management could be more efficient. I wasn't prepared to give over the railway system but I was prepared to consider if you can get a smartarse like Branson who thinks he can run everything, let him run it on a management basis, lease it for ten years or something and see if he could do it better. How can you shake up public sector management which in many cases was a dead hand?

I didn't want to renationalize. I knew the reality was there was so much money needed in the transport system, to spend all that money in compensation was sheer nonsense. For the first two years, we wouldn't get the legislation. We couldn't assume we would be in for three terms. So it was 'let's run it as it is and see how it goes'. The fact that the rail link to the Channel Tunnel was already in financial trouble and had to be rescued was another reason in favour of inaction.

There was another argument too, never stated publicly at the time and perhaps not even grasped by the new government until they were actually in office. The less Labour did to clear up what was perceived as a Tory mess, the less likely it was to get the blame.

Gavin Strang, transport minister for Labour's first year, put his finger on it: 'We would come in at Transport Questions and when someone attacked the railways, we would sympathize. It was easier to maintain this kind of distance from the fragmented network, and not accept responsibility for its failings, than to embark on a bold programme of nationalization.'

At party conferences, Prescott would excoriate the train operators for their obsession with re-painting trains rather than running them, and be loudly cheered, especially in 1998 at Blackpool, when the Virgin service had a bigger stinker than usual and shunted much of the parliamentary Labour Party into a siding at Crewe. Prescott called the train companies 'a national disgrace'.

But even within the party, the pressure to do something was slackening. The unions had implacably opposed the fragmentation, fearing the staff-cutting zeal of the new owners. And, sure enough, in early 1997 South West Trains began a 'driver restructuring initiative'. Everyone knew British Rail was overstaffed, didn't they? Let's start sacking people! However, the resulting shortage of drivers led to mass cancellations, the threat of a £1 million fine from the regulators and oodles of bad publicity. It also led to the realization that, for the drivers' union ASLEF in particular, the new set-up was more of an opportunity than a threat. Twenty-five franchises

318

meant twenty-five prospective employers. The old monopoly, whereby British Rail was the only railway employer, was dead, and this vastly improved the unions' bargaining position. In this way, as in several others, the effect of Major's reforms was the reverse of that intended.

For the passenger, not much changed for the first three years under Labour except that things got steadily worse. In 1998, at a time when Virgin and Connex were the most hated operators, I recorded seventeen late journeys out of nineteen on my regular Great Western run between Newport and London. We avoided eighteen out of twenty when a London-bound train suddenly gathered speed and went from eight minutes late to five minutes early between Swindon and Paddington, a stretch timed at less than an hour. This was my first inkling of a piece of railway roguery that was to become far more general.

That year, the management buyout team who had picked up Great Western sold it on to First Group, and duly collected their own millions for doing bugger-all, with Prescott fulminating helplessly. First Group repainted, stuck their own name everywhere (completely confusing passengers looking for first-class carriages) and squeezed harder at ancillary costs and charges not under regulatory control: they abolished the refreshment trolley, raised car-parking charges by thirty per cent and nipped away at the hours when cheap tickets were permitted.

One theory was that the groups now starting to dominate the industry – First, Stagecoach, National Express, Arriva – were bus companies for whom passenger comfort and satisfaction were not high priorities. They had not got big by bothering. But the nature of their contracts, the short-term franchises and their lack of control over rolling-stock meant none of the companies had much incentive to add any gracenotes to their service, especially as passenger numbers were now increasing rapidly.

Those desperate for justification claimed the rise was due to the popularity of privatization, which was palpable rubbish. Much more relevant were the clogged roads and expanding economy (and also the expanding higher education system, with many more railcard-bearing students taking their laundry home to mum). Prescott was desperate to be given a space on the legislative programme for a transport bill and he produced a white paper that hinted at encouraging people out of their cars and on to trains and buses. However, Downing Street – terrified of offending motorists – made sure this did not actually mean much.

His big idea was to establish the Strategic Rail Authority, though it was never wholly clear what its exact purpose would be. ('What's it actually going to do, Deputy Prime Minister?' one insider claims to have asked. 'Be strategic,' was the reply.) Sir Alastair Morton, the large and combative former head of Eurotunnel, was put in charge, although strategic thinking was arguably not his strength. The upshot was another failure: 'Not much strategy, not much authority and not much rail if they'd had their way,' as the railway writer Andy Roden put it. There was confusion between the roles of the SRA and the regulator, which at one summit – at Prescott's official country house, Dorneywood – led to a near punch-up between Morton and the regulator Tom Winsor, who is not large.

The last part of Roden's aphorism may be unfair: Morton did want to harness public and private money to improve the system. And he also wanted to give the train operators twenty-year contracts to give them some reason to care, though in the event only one was ever awarded – to Chiltern Railways. Once Prescott gave up transport in 2001, the Treasury reassumed total control, handcuffed his weaker successors, and put paid to any notion of major discretionary investment.

Before this happened, one problem had turned into a crisis. There were two major crashes outside Paddington, at Southall (seven dead) and Ladbroke Grove (thirty-one dead), both of them involving drivers going through red lights, both of which could perhaps to some extent be blamed on changes wrought by privatization, and both of which turned every newspaper reader in the country into instant experts on the technically complex problems of railway safety systems. Everyone had an opinion on the relative merits of such acronyms as ATP, AWS and TPWS until they got bored and forgot all about it.

But someone needed to have an opinion, because it was no longer possible to trust the people in charge of the railways. The stock market boom of the late 1990s was such that if Pilbrow's Atmospheric Railway and Canal Propulsion

Company had returned from the 1840s and added the suffix .com, its shares would have hurtled out of the atmosphere and into the stratosphere. Railtrack shares joined in the general euphoria. From £1.90 on flotation, they reached £17.68 by November 1998.

And yet the company's failings were common knowledge. Even Railtrack knew there were problems, telling the government that the set-up of the industry meant it had 'perverse incentives': there was no encouragement to invest because its income was largely fixed. It was widely derided by the public as the most obese of all the fat cats (most effectively by the *Guardian* cartoonist Steve Bell), far more interested in its property portfolios. And it absorbed regular kickings from Prescott, Winsor, the train operators and anyone else who passed by.

Its internal culture was discussed in shocked whispers among railwaymen. A senior executive told a manager at Euston who was trying to convey some difficult technical point: 'As far as I'm concerned you have no more status than the person running the branch of Sock Shop.' (This must be true: I heard it third-hand.) And in a strange way the executive was right. Under corporate law, the company's prime duty was to maximize value for its shareholders, not run a railway or guard the lives of the passengers.

However, on 17 October 2000, the separation of the trains and the track became all too literally true. A King's Cross to Leeds train came off the rails at Hatfield, killing four people. The death toll was miraculously low, but the consequences for the industry were greater than for any accident since Armagh 111 years earlier. A broken rail was identified as the cause, and now everyone became an instant expert on the previously arcane phenomenon of gauge-corner cracking. Except, again, for Railtrack's management, who had no idea what they were doing.

The company immediately went into headless-chicken mode, and staged a nationwide gauge-corner crack hunt, closing the West Coast line a week later and imposing a total of 1,286 20mph speed limits within the next seven months, the vast majority, according to experts, unnecessary. Six weeks later one train from Nottingham took nine hours to do the 126 miles to St Pancras. Morton said the railways were suffering from 'a nervous breakdown'. Tony Blair admitted that rail travel was 'absolute hell'.

Hatfield itself was caused by an accretion of normally minor misfortunes which is almost always the cause of crashes. But these misfortunes soon began to look more avoidable than usual. Winsor, it emerged, had been nagging Railtrack about broken rails for over a year; two sets of contractors, Balfour Beatty and Jarvis, knew there was a problem with this one particular rail, and made half-hearted and wrong-headed attempts to fix it; here a speed limit should have been imposed and it wasn't. It emerged that Railtrack had introduced a strategy known as 'Project Destiny' that involved replacing equipment when required rather than at set intervals. What emerged above all was the hopelessness of Railtrack's relations with its sub-contractors and its lack of engineering expertise.

Yet the most perceptive critic was Railtrack's own chief executive, Gerald Corbett, who even before the crash had become seen as a poster boy for the privatization fat cats. He knew where the blame really lay. Two days after the crash he told the BBC: 'The railways were ripped apart by privatization and the structure that was put in place was a structure designed, if we are honest, to maximize the proceeds to the Treasury. It was not a structure designed to optimize safety, optimize investment or, indeed, cope with the huge increase in the number of passengers the railway has seen.' Note the phrasing: 'If we are honest.'

Railtrack's destiny was to be oblivion, undone by its wretched reputation and the spiralling costs of its obligations to maintain the network and to renew the West Coast Main Line. However, everyone who went near Railtrack also seemed to vaporize, including Stephen Byers, Prescott's successor, who forced the company into administration in 2002. Instead of being given a ticker-tape parade and a dukedom, Byers was dragged into court by irate shareholders who accused him of 'misfeasance in public office'. He escaped that, but was forced to admit he had lied to the Commons.

His tenure will be best remembered for the email sent by his special adviser Jo Moore on 11 September 2001 (a date infamous in another context), telling the press office that this was the perfect moment to release any news it wanted buried. That, and the eloquent, erudite statement made by the department's permanent secretary,

Sir Richard Mottram, during the fallout from that incident: 'We're all fucked. I'm fucked. You're fucked. The whole department is fucked. It's the biggest cock-up ever. We're all completely fucked.' Byers never said anything as memorable himself.

Railtrack morphed into Network Rail, a nationalized industry in all but name but constructed in a peculiar arms-length way so as to keep its losses off the government's books and maintain ministers' posture of deniability. Some observers felt it was also constructed so as to avoid any semblance of sensible financial control.

Indeed, the whole industry was like that. Roger Ford, the most respected of all railway analysts, estimates that the government subsidy has quintupled *in real terms* since 1990 to approximately £4.8 billion in 2009–10. But, since there was no longer any headline figure for the media to grab hold of, hardly anyone noticed. You might argue that this was a kind of justification. British Rail would never have been allowed to eat so much money but, as Major said, in private hands the railway would have access to capital. He never mentioned it would be provided by taxpayers.

Where has all the money gone? 'Wages and salaries,' according to John Welsby, British Rail's former chief executive. 'Increasing infrastructure costs,' according to Matthew Elson and Stephen Fidler in a paper prepared for Tony Blair in 2003. '£800m a year in dividends to investors,' according to the Labour MP Jon Cruddas. And they all appear to be at least partially right.

'British Rail was living on borrowed time to a

huge extent,' says Adrian Shooter, chairman of Chiltern Railways. 'A lot of the structure – the bridges, the viaducts and all the boring stuff like embankments – hadn't been repaired properly, in some cases since the First World War. There had been long maintenance holidays. What was privatized was a clapped-out railway.

'Because it was privatized, government had to find the money to prop up the mess it had created. It wasn't enough to say to BR, as it would have done, your problem. It was clearly now the government's problem. It had to throw money at the railway, and eventually some landed on the tracks as well as in the laps of shareholders, managers, lawyers and consultants.'

By the start of 2009 trains were newer, more frequent, more punctual and probably safer than they had been ten or fifteen years earlier. In 2007 the fast route to the Channel Tunnel opened, a mere thirteen years behind the French and only 205 years since the original proposal. In December 2008 the new faster and more frequent West Coast Main Line timetable was in operation. There is no reason to attribute any of the improvements directly to privatization. Most could have come far more quickly if so much time had not been wasted on an irrelevance.

The trains were also very crowded, sometimes disgustingly so. The railways had been sold off on the assumption of continuing decline: instead by 2007 passengers travelled a total of thirty billion miles, up by fifty per cent in ten years, and more than in any previous peacetime year. And on many lines, trains were much slower: services between London and Bristol, for instance, took about twenty minutes longer than in 1980, under BR, a fact not mentioned in the punctuality statistics. Newspaper stories also usually omit the loose definition of 'on time': within five minutes for short distances and ten minutes for long.

The operators have also become rather obsessed, bullying the staff to ensure that trains leave to the second: it is considered bad form – or bad PR anyway – if anyone in a wheelchair is left on a platform glowering at a departing train, but everyone else has to take their chances. 'We've become totally heartless,' one railwayman told me sadly.

Nothing seems more important to the companies than ensuring a respectable place in the league table. 'Punctuality is the most important thing,' George Muir of the Association of Train Operating Companies told the BBC in 2007. It is nice to know that the companies take punctuality so seriously – but that is a remark of ineffable stupidity.

Quite obviously, safety not punctuality is the overriding objective. And as I write – touch wood – the record since 2000 has been remarkably good. Andrew Evans, professor of transport risk management at Imperial College, London, says that actually the privatized railways' record has always been good: 'Except in the matter of fatalities – and that was entirely due to Ladbroke Grove – the data shows that the other indicators were better than they were under British Rail and better than BR would have been on an extra-polated basis. When the data contradicts the anecdotes, you have to go with the data.' He found it hard to come up with an explanation, though.

And the cost of train travel is staggering. On the one hand, Britain offers frequent trains, some of them reasonably fast, which provide a theoretically excellent incentive for people to stay out of their cars. But, because the system is so inadequate, casual users are deliberately discouraged. You can get very cheap fares if you are bored enough and anal enough to know precisely where you will want to go in precisely twelve weeks' time, and can navigate both the web and the complexities of the fare structure.

What's the point of having four trains an hour from London to Manchester if passengers have to pay penal rates (£256 second-class return in peak hours) to use the wretched things without planning it well in advance or even if they travel a few minutes later than they originally thought? It would be more efficient to do it the French way and just run one long train now and again. In 2007 the Liberal Democrats worked out that £10 bought an average of thirty-five miles rail travel in Britain, compared to 663 miles in Latvia. These were the highest fares in Europe and presumably the highest in the world. And they have gone up at least twice since then.

There have been four post-Byers transport ministers, none of whom has so far left a single footprint (Alistair Darling did four years, possibly without waking up). They have had only two consistent policies. One is to encourage the train operators to raise fares as much as they dare to reduce the subsidy. The other is to accrete managerial power within the Department of Transport.

This has been an astonishing development, bearing in mind the weakness of the ministers involved. For the first time in the history of the railways, the precise details of service provision are determined by civil servants with no obvious training or expertise. Not much civility either, judging from the public performances of the head of the department's rail directorate, Mike Mitchell.

According to the former regulator Tom Winsor: 'The train operator nowadays has to ask permission to breathe in, and he may or may not get permission to breathe out again. Early franchising agreements just set minima. Now any change to the timetable, even additions, must be approved by the department. The operators are allowed to change the staff uniform, and whether there will be two sausages rather than one. That's about it.'

It is perhaps not so surprising then that they are so obsessed with uniforms and paint. East Midlands Trains, the new domestic operator from St Pancras, is being graciously allowed to take delivery of three new coaches between 2010 and 2014. 'Gee,' said a manager, 'I hope they don't come all at once.'

There is no need to cry too much for the operators. They claim they only make a return of three or four per cent per annum from their franchises, but since their role involves almost no capital investment or risk, it is not clear what this means. Three per cent of what? Most show minimal commitment to the railways. In practice, they seem able to wriggle out of their contractual obligations, or even vanish entirely. They come, they go, they can give up and put their money in an Icelandic bank. In early 2009, as the economic crisis worsened, there were signs that this proposition might be tested.

Government hypocrisy about all this is breathtaking. In December 2008 *The Times* reported that Geoff Hoon, the latest transport secretary, had criticized the operators for their latest fare increases. Hoon had urged the companies to bear in mind 'the difficult economic circumstances' and was disappointed that they had ignored him. Yet government policy is that regulated fares should go up every year by an average of one per cent *above* inflation, rather than the original one per cent *below*, to shift the burden from the taxpayer to the passenger. You have to admire the man's chutzpah. The main object of Labour railway policy has been to maintain plausible deniability; we are now moving to implausible deniability.

There is still a regulator charged with making sense of all this. His name is Bill Emery, but he is perhaps not quite as plain spoken as Winsor. Asked by *The Times* what he thought of the current railway set-up, he replied: 'There are lots of people who say that the current structure is not optimal. I would probably take a raincheck on whether it's ideal.' That is presumably the more normal Whitehall way of providing Sir Richard Mottram's summary of the situation: 'It's the biggest cock-up ever. We're all completely fucked.'

The scandal is that still no one in authority has emerged with any vision of what the railway is for, and of the role it could and should fulfil in twenty-first-century Britain. The inability to invest means it can only get worse. In 2007 (a mere seventy-six years after the recommendations of the Weir Report) the government rejected the idea of further electrification, partly on the grounds that electricity could be superseded as a means of traction by 'a truly renewable source of hydrogen, such as photosynthetic splitting of water using bioengineered algae'. Or indeed fairy dust.

In 2008 the minister *du jour*, Ruth Kelly, announced her conversion to the cause of electrification. This may have been connected to the discovery that, pending the arrival of green slime power, it will otherwise be outrageously expensive to get new trains for the lines out of St Pancras and Paddington because every other advanced country gave up on high-speed diesels years ago. This being Britain, this was not the prelude to action, merely a theoretical statement. She was gone within weeks anyway.

Since then, the new Minister of State, Lord Adonis, has been showing dangerous signs of being bright-eyed and bushy-tailed about new fast lines. All history suggests that his spirit will be broken even before he's reshuffled. And with the country moving into recession, there was even less chance than usual of anything being done. The nature of a long-term transport scheme is that there will always be a recession at some point in the process which means that in

Britain it will inevitably get axed.

John Major had a plan for the railways. It was a terrible plan, execrably executed. But looking back now on almost twelve years of Labour posturing and procrastinating, you can say this for him: at least he had a plan. At least he had a plan.

CHAPTER TEN

THURSO

You probably won't remember this, but the author of the book was last seen (in Chapter Two) at the northern extremity of Britain's railway network. I have been fine, honestly; and it was there in Thurso, the most northerly town on the British mainland, that I met the man who is probably Britain's most northerly railway expert.

Mike Lunan is a retired actuary, and convener of the Friends of the Far North Line, which fights for the interests of the ever-fragile route from Inverness under the splendid acronym of FoFNL. He is a sagacious observer of life in general and railway politics in particular. Perhaps being on top of the world gives one a certain perspective.

We were sitting in his kitchen discussing why it is so hard to do *anything* in Britain when it comes to improving infrastructure. And Mike explained to me his 'nine-year theory', taking as an example the Dornoch Bridge, the project so beloved of Highland rail campaigners to cut a huge curve off the Far North Line, a project only likely to happen if the Messiah fetches up in Scotland, and turns out to be really nuts about trains. Mike Lunan knows this better than anyone. So this is totally hypothetical. But anyway, he began:

Let's just say that the minister wakes up one morning and says 'Right, let's build it. Action this day.' First you go out and tender for the initial scoping, the investigation of the site. It takes about four months to publish the tender to get preliminary consultants in to prepare a report and costings that can be presented to the engineers. And it would probably require another tendering process to get the engineers in.

Then you have to go to detailed work. Is it good rock? Or are there environmental issues like a rare butterfly or newt? And so on. That's another year to eighteen months. Then the government's got to sit down and look at it. Can we afford it? Can we get round the business of the butterflies? Three months if they're trying. Normally more.

Build it. You can't just go to Bob McAlpine. Public work on this scale has to be tendered across Europe. Three months for that. Two to look at the answers. One month of delay. The minister can then appoint ABC Construction. Two to two and a half years so far, and that's very fast.

At Dornoch you need an access tunnel to get the railway to the bridge south of the town. That would go under at least two houses which would be rendered uninhabitable. Government has to go to court to get compulsory purchase. Dum-de-dum.

Building the thing can't take less than four years. It can but in practice it doesn't. Then there will be the other things to do. The railway has to get the rails down. Including that, I reckon five years for building even if everything goes well. But it doesn't...

And of course that assumes the project has not been politically controversial, that the minister is either still in office or been succeeded by someone equally enthusiastic, that there hasn't been a financial crisis forcing cancellation, which there usually has been. And that the weather is favourable, there isn't a strike, and that the components are delivered on time. So nine years seems to me pretty optimistic when all's said and done.

In any case we are talking about a decision that would be taken by the Scottish government, and Scotland tends to be politically more consensual than England when it comes to these kinds of projects. It has a good record, since devolution, of bringing railway projects to fruition. And this is the Highlands: anywhere else would have far more than two houses facing destruction for almost any project of this sort.

Look at it this way, and it is no wonder at all that the English railway network has remained almost precisely what it was when the Beeching closures petered out forty years ago, like a woolly mammoth preserved beneath the Arctic permafrost. The only thing more politically fraught than opening a new and vital route is closing an old and useless one. Either way, there are always thousands of reasons why it cannot be done. This problem is not unique to the railways.

The former transport minister Sir Malcolm Rifkind tells the story of the British minister complaining to his French counterpart about the impossibility of building anything: 'Whatever we propose in Britain, there are huge protests, it takes eight years of public enquiries, and it still never gets built.' 'In France,' replied the French minister, 'when we want to drain the swamps, we don't ask the frogs.' (This has ramifications in English which the Frenchman may not have understood, but you get his drift.)

And so, in Britain, almost nothing happens. Addition and subtraction both involve such complex calculations that it is best to leave well alone. Politically, economically and environmentally, this may be insane. Yet the sheer illogicality of the British railway network does have a certain gloriousness. It is living history.

Every few years throughout my adult life I have bought the great thick railway timetable and stared lovingly at its *Wisden*-like pages – I am particularly fond of the distance tables – and the faraway places with strange-sounding names. Did you know that it's twenty-one and three-quarter miles from Clitheroe to Hall i'th'Wood? I always stared most at the map that was tucked inside. They were probably still running steam trains when I first conceived the notion of taking the line to Kyle of Lochalsh, hitch-hiking down through Skye, and then catching another train from Mallaig to Glasgow...

For most of the year, there is only one train to Kyle of Lochalsh on a Sunday. I took no chances: I made my farewells to Mike Lunan on Thurso station on Saturday afternoon. Wearing his FoFNL hat, he was very proud of his station. It has left luggage lockers, a rare convenience these days in paranoid Britain. They cost £3 a day even though the station closes at 4.30pm, so the convenience is limited. But a visitor might be very pleased to see them.

The decoration was a bit random: a picture of a Union Pacific loco as well as *Mallard* and *Evening Star*, neither of them obviously associated with Thurso. And, to be honest, the whole place felt more like a garden shed than a trainshed. I didn't want to upset him, but did pluck up the courage to say it was not quite on the scale of Penzance. 'That's southern, this is northern,' he replied.

The junction for the Kyle line is at Dingwall, or Inbyirheofharain, as the station sign puts it. I formed the notion that this was an ancient Gaelic tourist slogan, meaning 'In here out of the rain'. Next time I'll opt to get wet. Dingwall is a sad-looking, run-down place. The hotel was dire, the staff surly and ugly, and the breakfast inedible. Through the long May evening, the streets were full of pre-adolescent children, feral yet obese, as though they were filming a twenty-first-century version of *Lord of the Flies*.

The Chinese restaurant was, to my surprise, less disgusting than normal in such towns, and I concluded that Dingwall could rank only third on my list of Britain's Vilest Towns, behind the malevolently inhospitable dump of Caldicot in South Wales and ... but, no, let me spare you the name of the winner until we get there.

On the map the Kyle line is the most enticing of them all. Just past Dingwall come the most euphonious grouping of stations on the entire system: Achanalt, Achnasheen, Achnashellach. Field by the stream, Field of storms, Field of willows. I think.

Can we just pause for a moment to savour the beauty of these names?

There are other groupings of similar power elsewhere. What about Llandovery, Llanwryth, Llangadog, Llandeilo on the Heart of Wales line? English place names cannot quite compete with this: you have to look at words in a different way. The stations between Sleaford and Boston in Lincolnshire include Heckington, Swineshead, Hubberts Bridge. Or you might prefer Penge West, Anerley, Norwood Junction.

The translation of Achanalt was announced to the carriage by a rather loud know-all, an Englishman of course, which rather spoiled the moment. Like everyone else on the train, he was travelling for the sake of it. It is important on a train like this, I always feel – well, it's important to *me*, anyway – to appear to be going somewhere ('I am a traveller; you are a tourist; they are grockles'). David St John Thomas, who went on the line through Morayshire from Elgin to Lossiemouth before it closed in 1964, described the withering contempt of the guard when he

337

discovered that all fifteen aboard were just *enthusiasts*. Everyone on this train had a guidebook and/or a rucksack. They were all either grockles or enthusiasts, except me because my enthusiasm was starting to diminish.

The Kyle line is a little less beautiful than its place names suggest. Overall, the scenery is just a bit Jimmy-Shand-White-Heather-Club, you know, rather than West Highland spectacular. In places it is even rather ugly: the power line is intrusive, the Forestry Commission conifers are intrusive, the cars are intrusive, the building rubble is intrusive.

Yet the railway does not feel intrusive. One of the miracles of trains is the way they can come to feel like part of the ecosystem. Just before Achnashellach, a herd of deer skittered away from us. But they seemed to understand this was a ritual rather than a threat. Their Sunday was not going to be disturbed again until the return journey in the late afternoon. And then not till Monday.

Just after the Field of Storms, the wind got up a little – not that it affected us, in our sealed train – and then the sun came out. We were early at Strathcarron and were allowed on to the platform for a while. The conductor and driver had a slight disagreement about the exact time. It was not a serious problem. 'Aye well, it's the Kyle line,' said Davey the conductor. 'Set your calendar, not your watch.'

'Do you get any real people on this line?' I asked Davey.

'Nooo, just plastic cones,' he replied.

'I mean people actually going anywhere, instead of us.'

'We may pick up a few at Plockton going into Kyle for a bit of shopping, but not many, no.'

The cloud sat high on the top behind Strathcarron. We went through a tunnel that had windows enabling us to keep the view of the loch. Loch Carron is quite built up, but all the houses are on the other side of the loch, the north side, rendering the railway even more irrelevant.

At Stromeferry, on the banks of Loch Carron, we had another wait and Davey encouraged us to get out and take pictures. The loch glinted in the spring sunshine. The know-all did not know, or did not mention, what had happened here in the summer of 1882. One of the few good reasons for building this railway was the fish traffic. But the Highland Line's business objectives, hard enough to achieve in these depopulated regions, were perpetually hampered by militant sabbatarians. And when the locals at Stromeferry realized that a fish train had been loaded there on a Sunday, they became incensed.

Aware of this, but anxious not to let the weekend catch linger until Monday, the railway company arranged to load the next weekend train in the early hours of Sunday morning. The workers unloading the fish were greeted by about fifty local men, who had brought clubs, bludgeons and a sense of divine wrath, a combination that enabled them to overpower the crew. And though that may sound quaint, the sabbatarians won the war as well as the battle. To this day, trying to catch a Sunday morning train anywhere in post-

Christian Britain often involves acquiring an understanding of what it means when God's grace has been withdrawn.

Kyle of Lochalsh would not be a major shopping destination if you lived further afield than Plockton, even on a weekday. On a Sunday the old rules apply. There was, surprisingly, a bus running, but it just went over the new road bridge to Skye, where there were no connecting buses available, forcing me to return to my ancient intent of hitch-hiking down to the ferry port at Armadale.

There also appears, however, to be a stern biblical injunction against cadging lifts on a Sunday. And my once reasonably effective hitching skills (involving strong eye contact and a pleading labrador-ish expression) may have gone somewhat rusty. I gave up and called a local taxi driver, who bored me rigid talking about his days as a butcher in Preston while the meter clicked upwards at a terrifying rate.

It was now one of those lovely, rare West Highland afternoons that occur in that brief interval between the last knockings of winter and the midge-invasion. At Armadale, I dozed in the sunshine while waiting for the ferry and arrived in Mallaig to find a nice clean B&B and a lovely fish restaurant that was actually open.

The Monday morning 0603 from Mallaig to Glasgow Queen Street (164¼ miles, four hours twenty-five minutes) is as bleary-eyed as the 0603 anywhere else. The late Victorians crashed their way through the landscape, blasted through the crags, imposed themselves on this scene, so that German students, with only the vaguest idea exactly where they were or why, could doze as best they could on the train with a headrest that stopped just below an average-sized male shoulder blade.

The electronic indicator in the carriage was set so that the same message was repeated every fifteen seconds for the eighty-two minutes from Mallaig to Fort William, 328 times in all: PLEASE KEEP HOLD OF YOUR TICKETS WHEN LEAVING THE TRAIN. BARRIER CHECKS MAY BE IN OPERATION AT THIS STATION. Barrier checks may indeed have been in operation to bring about the prosecution and downfall of the extremely occasional passenger alighting at Morar (0609), Arisaig (0619), Lochailort (0634, by request only), Locheilside (0701 and ditto) and Banavie (0717), I mused. It might not have been the most sensible use of ScotRail's resources.

Then a mobile rang, loudly.

Between Lochailort and Glenfinnan the most amazing scenery in the world was appearing before us. Sometimes we lost sight of the road on the far side of the loch and only the railway fences gave any indication that anyone had ever set foot here. We went over the twenty-one-span Glenfinnan viaduct (built by Sir Bob MacAlpine, without going through a European tendering process), as the *Hogwarts Express* does. (In three separate Harry Potter films, apparently. For muggles [and grockles], daily steam trains run between Fort William and Mallaig in summer). Lone birch trees stood sentinel on their own

341

hillocks, like bonsai. Wisps of cloud hung over the crags and then, beyond Glenfinnan station, poured through a cleft in the mountainside. The station clock there stood at ten to three.

Then the mobile rang again. There were seven people on the train: four were asleep, two were looking out of the window, one was on the phone until she shut it with a bang and it rang a third time.

At Locheilside Susan Weir got on. She lives in the Station House (tourists aside, the highland lines seem to depend largely on the patronage of the residents of the station houses) and was on her way to the gym in Fort William. She was already unnaturally perky for this hour and was trilling away to the second real passenger of the day: 'Morning, Eleanor. How are you doing?'

The mobile rang a fourth time.

There was a seventeen-minute stop at Fort William's hideous modern station, time enough to nip outside for a smoke and to take an instant dislike to the place. The station newsagent was particularly grumpy. Since the town was put here to subdue the natives and now exists to service tourists, it may have spent its entire history in a collective state of irritation. But then I met a driver called John Hynd, on his way to start his morning turn, who told me that Fort William–Mallaig was the best stretch he knew: 'Going in there in the evening light on a sunny September day. You couldn't get anything better than that.' I discovered later that John Hynd is a legend, and was chosen as Britain's train driver of the year in 2007. He has been known to trek miles across this remote country to repair trains on bitter mid-winter nights, give people eighty-mile lifts to Oban (in his car, not his train) to spare them paying £60 for a taxi, and give tourists his spare bedroom in Fort William if they have nowhere else to stay. Fort William might not be such a bad place.

And the journey onwards was still fabulous. At Corrour, 1,338ft above sea level, where there is no public road, the conductor delivered mail and a Tesco package. Nearby was a ruined croft. Otherwise, there was no sign of habitation: the moor was unimaginably lonely, bleak, treeless, unearthly, stunning. It had been like that for several miles, and I realized my mouth had been open the entire time, in gaping admiration.

At Rannoch we met the Fort William sleeper, the Deer-stalker Express, coming the other way. By now the 0603 felt more like a normal train: someone was studying the runners and riders for Redcar and Windsor, and a man wearing a tie was working at his laptop. He turned out to be an American (I had guessed that) who commuted weekly to Glasgow from Spean Bridge (which I had not guessed).

But the scenery was still not normal at all. The station buildings are described in Biddle's guide as Swiss chalets, but that doesn't do them justice. They are more like colonial bungalows. Bwana might emerge from one of the green doors puffing a fat cigar and contemplating the afternoon game-kill. At the Horseshoe Curve past Bridge of Orchy the train executes the most brilliant ... what would you call it – a pirouette? a glissando?

The world's more mountainous railways often have a piece of engineering trickery known as Horseshoe Curve, but it's a cliché that doesn't do this one justice.

At Crianlarich, the Crewe of the West Highlands, there is an arrangement involving complicated timings, permissions and positionings so that our train can sink itself into the rear of the 0811 from Oban. It is a manoeuvre not unlike the pre-sexual behaviour of dogs, which involves rituals so complex that is a wonder the species ever manages to reproduce at all, let alone do it every time one of them finds a way out of the back garden. The scene below was not like Crewe: it was agelessly beautiful and reminiscent of the George Inness painting, which was in the Liverpool exhibition, of an early steam train chugging across the almost pristine Lackawanna Valley in Pennsylvania. The Lackawanna is an industrial hellhole now, and has been called the armpit of America. They never found coal in the Trossachs.

Still there was more: we moved on to Glen Falloch before turning due south to run alongside Loch Lomond. I had been reading the account, by John Thomas, of the first passenger trip along this route, for invited guests only, in 1894:

Waterfalls large and small cascaded into the glen from the surrounding mountains. The passengers had a wonderful view for many minutes of the great Ben-y-Glas Fall, foaming over a precipice and plunging 120ft to the rocks below with a force that sent a

344

curtain of vapour to the tree tops. The rush and roar of water was the characteristic sound of Glen Falloch. William Wordsworth called it 'the vale of awful sound'. Even Wordsworth the railway hater would have been impressed by the new sound that invaded Glen Falloch that day – the bark and crackle of Matthew Holmes's little West Highland bogies as they struggled to lift their ten coaches up the glen.

This train was of course travelling in the other direction and, even with the addition of Oban's two carriages to our two, I don't suppose Wordsworth or anyone else would have been much impressed by it. But the landscape was something else. We hugged the hillside above Loch Lomond, then crossed the birch-clad valley leading to salt-water Loch Long. Here is Thomas again:

It wound along on a ledge stepped out of the mountain and just wide enough to hold the railway. A wall of freshly cut rock rose up outside the right-hand carriage windows; on the left side a precipice dropped more than 500ft to the water's edge. The guests were thrilled at one place to find themselves looking down the face of a perpendicular wall. Through the large windows of their saloons they could see the engines nosing cautiously in and out of the crevices as they negotiated a continuous series of reverse curves.

I was wondering how on earth they could have built this thing. Can you imagine such an enterprise? 'Oh my God,' said a young woman, possibly the 7am serial phone-caller. Was this a

345

kink in time? Had she responded the way the first passengers had in 1894? Actually, she was playing knock-out whist with her friend.

After Helensburgh Upper we were approaching the Glasgow suburbs but still it was beautiful. The final stretch of the line ran along the Firth of Clyde. Dumbarton Central had stained glass and old globe-lamps that must once have burned oil. The first clear indication that we were back in the real world was when the conductor began arguing with a woman about the precise regulations governing cheap-day returns.

When we got to Glasgow, I was a little lost. I had the freedom of the railways for fourteen days and, for the first four days, I had a clear plan with set objectives: places to go and people to meet. I had always intended to get straight from Penzance to Thurso and back down to Glasgow via the West Highland. Now there were choices.

I was standing at Glasgow Central station, my favourite station in Britain. It is full of rich old wood, and rounded corners, and an air of informality: the windows on the bridge over Argyle Street are almost Parisian in their jollity – gaiety, as we used to say. It was still, in 2008, an open station without the nasty automatic barriers that guard the platforms on English stations, those symbols of the distrust with which the privatized train operators regard their customers. Indeed, it could be anywhere in Europe, except England. Even the smell was enchanting: the flower stall is in the midst of the concourse, and the scent of lilies filled the air.

The whole place hinted at exotic travel, a

346

promise not entirely fulfilled by the 1250 to Mount Florida. I really ought to have learned by now that because a place has a cute name, that is not a sufficient reason to take a train there. The same goes for the 1447 for Jordanhill, changing at Partick. Jordanhill is a reasonably agreeable university suburb that has a railway station with a peculiar global claim to fame. As half the population of Silicon Valley could probably tell you, Jordanhill station became, in 2006, the subject of the millionth article in the English language Wikipedia. As the entire population of Silicon Valley would have guessed, that does not make it worth visiting. I was beginning to lose the plot. The weather was growing colder.

I couldn't resist Golf Street, though. This is one of a run of four stations near the golfing town of Carnoustie on the Angus coast that have almost no trains. They don't even rate a proper mention in the timetable, just a footnote. According to the Office of the Rail Regulator only thirty-eight people a year used Golf Street station in 2006–07. That's not thirty-eight different people, that's thirty-eight entrances and exits, i.e. it only gets used about once every ten days.

These figures are clearly absurd, due to inadequacies in the system of data collection. Nonetheless these are stations that would be closed down if anyone could be bothered to go through the process. A similar strategy is employed to keep other stations in a coma, like Buckenham in Norfolk (twenty-eight passengers a year, allegedly) and Teesside Airport (eighty-five a year), which sounds busy and useful but emphatically isn't. Of course, they could always try a bold experiment and stop more than one bloody train a week there.

Golf Street is a pretty hopeless case: it couldn't even come into its own when the Open Championship came to Carnoustie because the platform is too short for the carriages. These stations are always neatly maintained: never mind the trains, the signage has to be spot-on.

Still, it was a nice run on the 1714 from Edinburgh Waverley, Golf Street's only northbound train a day, once we got into Fife and the commuter-crush eased a bit. It's a train that connects the city to fairways and fair winds. It ought to have a jolly name, like *The Links Express:* naturally it doesn't. I was very taken with the station gardens, especially at Ladybank, and at Aberdour, which not merely had a garden but a greenhouse. I got talking to Ellen, a software engineer whose daily commute to one of the other ghost stations, Balmossie, must constitute about forty per cent of the station's official annual usage. In fact, a bloke in an anorak got out ahead of me at Golf Street. Thirty-eight all year, then two come along at once. These statistics are phony because they are based on the stations named on the ticket, not where people actually get on and off – there is no one to sell tickets to at Golf Street, never mind count passengers. Massaged figures are everywhere on the railways: since Carnoustie is the last stop, and the possibility of fines for lateness has to be addressed, it allegedly takes a modern Turbostar train five minutes to get there from Golf Street. I walked it in six, pulling a suitcase with broken wheels.

Next morning, I headed south of the border on the 0700 from Edinburgh to London, a train mainly chosen because of its appeal to my breakfast-fetish. A lot of Scots were heading south too because Rangers had reached the UEFA Cup final, being held at Old Trafford. All trains heading down the West Coast route had banned alcohol, but it had not been thought necessary to extend that to the East Coast. And certainly not at seven in the morning.

At Berwick a prim-looking woman sitting alone in the restaurant car, reading a complex document with small print and pie charts, was asked if three gentlemen might join her. 'Of course,' she said. She managed to look only slightly startled when the three gentlemen lurched forward: blue replica Rangers shirts, huge forearms, shaven heads, gold bling, tattoos, bottles of Carlsberg. They started their second bottles just before 8am.

I never did find out how this story developed. At Newcastle I caught the train across to Carlisle, an unexpected delight that reminded me of childhood and the individual pots of jam. The rolling stock was old enough for nostalgia, and a fresh westerly breeze came pleasingly through the open window; we maintained a gentle, loping speed through gentle loping country lightly interspersed with contented-looking villages and contented-looking ewes.

Leaving Newcastle, we passed another Golf Street-style ghost station, Dunston, though here the alleged passenger figures have leapt to six a day. Just past Dunston there was the most

349

extraordinary collection of homing pigeons. At Prudhoe I saw a carving in the hillside which looked like a giant rat. We passed buddleia in bloom at Bardon Mill and the old evocatively named junction of Haltwhistle, which has a coat of arms on what looks like a Victorian water tank. I was entranced by everything now, happy to zip wherever the trains would take me. I made my way to stone-built Lancaster, most amiable and unhurried of the mainline junctions and constructed like a medieval castle, and started to scribble a list of my favourite stations putting Lancaster near the top.

Then I got on a two-car train festooned with pictures of the Settle to Carlisle, 'England's Most Glorious Line'. The train was heading for Barrow but this was pretty glorious too. As we neared Morecambe Bay, where the tide comes in like thunder, a hundred black-and-white waders took wing at our approach. Then we set out over the dinky little viaduct at Arnside, scene of the annual mass trespass, towards mysterious tree-shrouded Holme Island, set amid the sands. Who would live in such a place? The answer used to be John Brogden, the man who built the railway.

There is another improbable run from Lancaster to Leeds. Northern Rail, the current operator, gave the early morning train a bottom-of-the-barrel Class 142 Pacer, borrowed from Merseyrail who favour a garish yellow livery. The colour might have been obnoxious at that time of the day had it not been mitigated by the dirt. Yet it is a beautiful journey on a surprisingly expansive line, which Beeching listed for closure but failed to kill. Perhaps someone in London panicked and thought the lonely station at Clapham was the same as Clapham Junction. We pierced the silence of these gorse-flecked hills and headed through deserted country to Hellifield, still a functioning junction with that middle-of-nowhere grandeur once so common on the railways.

But sometimes the modern railway can be evocative too. On the advice of Lord Berkeley, chairman of the Rail Freight Group, I headed next to Doncaster to stand at the northern edge of the platform. This is the hub of the nation for fans of what we used to call goods trains, largely because of the ceaseless appetite of the huge coal-fired power station at Drax, which depends on imports rather than the home-mined coal that saved the nation in wartime. (The weirdness of British energy policy had better be a subject for someone else's book.) Something came by every few minutes, culminating in the daily Freightliner from Wilton in Cleveland to Felixstowe, apparently full and offering living proof that Britain still does have exports and delivers some of them by rail. Chemicals, steel and maybe even perfume, apparently. All in containers carrying the colours of the shipping companies as distinctive as those of football teams, indeed, rather more imaginative: K Line was red, GE Seaco turquoise, CAI orange, Hanjin sky blue, MSC mustard. UCS was russet and Evergreen, inevitably, green. Faraway companies with strange-sounding names. Lorries never look this exotic.

Back north at Darlington, the duty announcer

was a Texan called Ronda Franks, the wife of a local doctor, whose drawl added a hint of mystery to the evening rush. I decided not to get cross about the idea of trains to Peter-borrow and Middles-borrow. Indeed, I added Darlington to my favourite-station list, its case helped by the arches of the trainshed and a subway with entrances that would grace a ducal town house.

The station has an old map showing the course of the original Stockton & Darlington, including the branch to Yarm, the first of all railway closures – it went before the rest of the network had even opened. But the sense of history does not extend to running trains to Stockton: there are a couple of direct trains on a Sunday, taking sixteen minutes, otherwise it takes the best part of an hour. It's not the original route anyway. For that, you have to head the other way towards the old rail-dominated town of Shildon, which used to be home of one of the largest wagon works in Europe. Now it is a branch of the National Railway Museum. So it goes.

It was down the line at Heighington that Stephenson constructed *Locomotion No. 1* and along this very route, so the museum director, George Muirhead, told me, that it pulled its very first passenger train. Possibly along these very rails, since they sound as though they date back to the 1820s. Clump, clump, clump, clump.

The ghosts of the past are everywhere on the railways once you start hunting. And there are ghost stations, and the odd ghost train. The best-known runs at 1128 every Saturday morning from Stockport to Stalybridge via Reddish South and Denton, two stations that have no other purpose in life, like little old ladies left entirely alone in the world except for the weekly visit from social services. This train which makes no return journey has now become a minor celebrity. For the half-hour before departure, there was a buzz on the platform reflecting the fact that most of the dozen passengers were (pause for contempt) *enthusiasts*. Not all of them, though. There was Lawrence Cody, an ex-signalman from Stockport, who insisted that he used this train regularly to go into the Pennines. 'It used to be every hour and it should be every hour,' he said.

It is not a pretty ride, indeed I can't recall an uglier one. But the line has an obvious function as an emergency diversion round the south-east corner of Manchester. You would imagine that, on the crowded rails of the north-west, it could perform a day-to-day function too. But in 1991, just before British Rail was dragged to the gallows, a manager decided otherwise, and this line was condemned to join the living dead, keeping the one train to avoid the palaver of the official closure procedure which, aside from the costs, tends to get people excited and sentimental and inclined to start using the trains. Neither of the intermediate stations offers any cover, though Denton rates a bench and, of course, up-to-date signs. The signs, the signs, they always do the signs. Reddish South offered something far more improbable. Passengers.

On came Alec and Joyce Moores, as they do almost every week. 'Oh yes,' said Joyce, 'Week after week after week.' It doesn't cost them anything, with their pensioners' passes. 'We have lunch in Stalybridge and then we go back to Piccadilly. Reddish South is right at the centre of Reddish. It's a good, handy little station. Reddish North, you're actually going out of Reddish.'

The buffet in Stalybridge is also quite famous, with eight real ales and a clientele that extends way beyond rail passengers. British Rail also tried to close that in the early 1990s. It is surprising they didn't agree to let it stay open on condition it only served one pint a week. The Moores sipped a pint and a half of lager; I opted for a hot Bovril. It was a cold, wet Mancunian morning.

After the weekend, the weather perked up again and I discovered the trains of East Anglia. In the early days of privatization, they were run by a small operator called Anglia Railways which was a bit quirky and very well-liked. So of course it had to go – dumped in 2004 in favour of the giant National Express. In keeping with the spirit of open government fostered by New Labour, the Strategic Rail Authority, which was then in charge of such decisions, refused to divulge its reasoning. Anglia said it was simply outbid by miles.

Even more than the others, National Express is insanely obsessed by its corporate identity. The night it took over the East Coast service from GNER, another operator that tried to preserve a sense of style, it spent its time childishly putting its own naff stickers over GNER's rather classy-looking emblems. Still, I thought, give this lot its due: the bosses are not wreckers nor the most wanton cost-cutters, and the East Anglian trains remained do-different, as they say around here, and served very decent food including, if you were lucky, afternoon tea. And the stations were now painted a rather pleasant shade of Cambridge blue, though doubtless another colour would be along in a minute.

The main-line trains had a certain eccentricity too: they creaked like old tea clippers heading out of east-coast ports, bound for the Indies with a brisk wind in the mainsail (even if they were only heading into Colchester for connections to Clacton). And there were these mysterious signs on the platforms: 'Platform staff are available to despatch trains.' And all this time I had assumed they were just there to stand around looking useless.

The weather had perked up again now, with Constable clouds sweeping over the trees and the square, solid church towers which peeked from behind them. My friend Simon Barnes had insisted I should take the line from Lowestoft to Norwich, and my gosh, he was right. East Anglia cannot compete with the mountains of Mallaig (though I definitely saw a hillock somewhere). But for sheer English-rose loveliness, this was my favourite journey. It was a springtime evening of limpid clarity, and we crossed the water meadows by the Waveney to reach Somerleyton.

Somerleyton! The very name has a dreamy quality. It also has a place in railway history because Somerleyton Hall was the home of Sir Samuel Peto, one of the great Victorian railway contractors until he went bust in the 1866 crash and had to flee to Budapest. The oaks of Norfolk stood out against a sky that began as sapphire (or at least National Express corporate blue) before slowly turning violet. I love the railways. Did I mention that?

And the next day, something even better happened. I timed my exit from Norwich to catch the National Express afternoon tea. Thin-cut sandwiches. A scone with very rich cream. And there it was on the table: An Individual Pot of Strawberry Jam.

Through Needham Market, with its mysterious chimneys and towers like a miniature Gormenghast, and Stowmarket, which itself does a nifty line in cherry Madeira cake. I added them both to my list of favourites. They joined Glasgow Central, Lancaster, Birmingham Moor Street, rebuilt like a film set, tarty Sheffield, Church Stretton in Shropshire, with its floral displays and its sign indicating latitude and longitude (just in case the driver is lost), classical Huddersfield, which could serve as the capitol of a small but pretentious American state (Britain perhaps?), Kents Bank on the Barrow line with its splendid awning and its heavenly view, and remote Dolau on the Heart of Wales, lovingly maintained by the handful of locals.

Splendour, splendour everywhere, as Betjeman wrote in a completely different context – after birdying the par-four thirteenth at St Enodoc. How he would have loved this journey, and the scones and jam. It all seemed too good to be true...

Reality Bites

And it was: far too good to be true. As late as 11 November 2008, the company public relations office was still churning out self-congratulatory press releases: 'National Express East Anglia has a great reputation for its restaurant service'. On 18 November it announced that the dining cars were being axed. 'Passengers wanted smaller meals and snacks served at their seats,' a spokesman told the *Guardian*.

Oh, sure. Two days after that, the company announced – in common with the other companies – its annual round of way-above-inflation price increases. 'Passengers wanted higher fares and worse treatment,' as the press office would put it.

It was said that the restaurant cars were losing £10 m per year, which is a totally absurd statistic: it also costs money to provide seats, roofs, walls and other post-1840 fripperies. It is impossible to measure how many people go on trains because they actually still provide the occasional smidgin of civilization not available on motorways.

One of the nasty surprises of privatization is just how dreadful firms like National Express have been in offering any sense of style or pride or even marketing – all the things that private enterprise is supposedly good at. The original Great Western had locomotives called *Pendennis Castle* and *Lord of the Isles*. First Great Western, to take one example, has *Environment Agency* and *Oxfordshire 2007*. These are people with no class.

If you think well of Britain's railway companies for a second, they will turn round and prove you wrong. Standing on Leeds station, I was struck by a big double TV screen showing that all the trains for the next hour or two – about fifty of them – were allegedly on time. I thought this was magnificent enough to be worth a picture and whipped out my camera.

Up strutted a junior jobsworth, full of institutional paranoia and his own importance, to denounce me as a potential terrorist. 'Show me those pictures!' 'Why?' 'You could be photographing the pipes!' The railway magazines regularly report how the handful of 1950s boys who still care enough, as pensioners, to spend their days on station platforms writing down train numbers are forever being tormented by these clodpoles.

After that, I added Leeds to my list of most loathsome stations along with the Sunderland dungeon, which (in contrast to Hudson's now redundant Athenaeum) makes even Birmingham New Street seem like the gardens of Arcadia. There is also Plymouth, which would be ugly enough in its own right were it not overshadowed by Inter-City House, a 1960s tower block so monstrous and run-down that it would disgrace the streets of Pyongyang. If ever you get into a telephone argument with a First Great Western call-centre employee, bear in mind that any wish that the roof might fall on their heads could come true at any moment.

You can even sense the decay of Britain's railways in its most hyped, most treasured, most Betjemanesque possession. Yeah, I quite like St Pancras too, though I think the whole rebuilding project was soused in its own self-regard. And it is not obvious who gets the benefit. Passengers for Paris and Brussels are confined to the grim undercroft, deprived of daylight and the architectural delights of W.H. Barlow's restored roof. And those wishing to travel on the old Midland Railway have to walk beyond the train-shed, about halfway to Luton it feels like, to catch a sluggish diesel to Derby or Sheffield. Low Speed 1.

Instead, I took a Virgin train back to Lancaster, and this time there was long enough to hear the calm wrecked by an endless whine of hortatory recorded announcements. I crossed it off my list of favourites, and with relief caught the train for the four-mile trip to Morecambe, which some-how takes up to thirteen very long minutes. This did not improve my mood.

It is a disgusting journey: Britain's vilest train, a Class 142 Pacer, travels the country's vilest line, making a noise like a pile driver as it creeps from one short length of rail to the next: Bang! Bang! Bang! Bang! It arrives at a new station the size of a bus stop, the old station having been trans-formed into an 'arts centre' (Coming up: Alvin Stardust) and a particularly nasty theme pub, from which the staff were largely absent, possibly to avoid complaints about the food.

I had fancied staying the night at the re-furbished art deco Midland Hotel but I was a month too early – or possibly not, judging by some reports I have subsequently seen of it. The hotel looked terrific, like the *Queen Mary* run aground on a savage shore. It is hard to imagine this enterprise being a success because, quite frankly, it's in Morecambe, the most horrible town I encountered.

The guest houses that were open were run by jailers who came to the door brandishing bunches of keys and an expression of extreme suspicion. It took me several attempts to find a place that would take me, in a room with no lock or hot water. The general store next door had security measures suitable for a jeweller's shop in the crack-dealing quarter of Detroit. This shop did not sell jewellery. Or anything much.

I retreated home to wash Morecambe out of my hair, travelling via Holyhead, which was not a convenient route. But I had wanted to pass this way ever since I read George S. Measom's 1867 publication:

The Official Illustrated Guide to the Midland Great Western, and Dublin and Drogheda Railways, via London and North-Western Railway, WITH A DESCRIPTION OF DUBLIN, AND AN AC-COUNT OF SOME OF THE MOST Important Manufactories in Dublin & in the Towns on the Lines.

Not only does this book have this most magnificently terse title, it also includes the following wonderful sentence: 'Ten miles from Caernarvon is the small, rude village of Llanberis, remarkable for the vast rocks beneath which it lies embosomed.' Embosomed! What a word! Surely only two books in railway history have ever managed to get that in.

Unfortunately, the old London & North Western main line to Holyhead goes nowhere near either Caernavon or Llanberis. And the 1635 back to Cardiff, now operated by Arriva Trains Wales, did its best to go nowhere near Holyhead either, starting out 300 yards away from the buffers and the ticket halls, as though holding its nose. Holyhead is almost as dingy as Morecambe, but not as snarly.

The service from Holyhead to Cardiff could be described as the national train of Wales, linking the towns of the north with the nation's capital. Every nation needs a crack express and this one took a mere four and three-quarter hours to cover the journey, not much longer than Edinburgh to London. That journey just happens to be 393 miles and Holyhead to Cardiff is 253, or 190 for a self-respecting crow. No one had yet given this a name to match the *Flying Scotsman*, so we had better try. Welcome aboard the *Limping Welshman*.

Lots of nations would be proud of such a train: Liberia, Somalia, Equatorial Guinea, the list goes on. However, the politicians of these countries would jib at the fact that the three major junctions on the service, Chester, Crewe and Shrewsbury, are all in another country. There was no dining car; I never even glimpsed a trolley which is always a regret on Arriva Trains Wales because there is a slim chance of meeting their star employee Paul, who flogs his limited range of sandwiches with a surreal spiel worthy of a grander setting: 'Anaconda! Thomson's gazelle! And ... um ... egg.'

Oddly, the dining problem was being addressed

at that very moment. Against the trend and against their own normal approach to investment (pardon?) and customer service (wassat?), Arriva Trains Wales had decided to institute one daily train that's a fraction faster, with a first-class-cum-dining car. Since the members of the Welsh Assembly are the group most likely to use this service regularly, one can only interpret this as an attempt to keep them onside pending the renewal of the franchise.

I could hardly complain about the pace myself since one of my main objectives was to clock the station sign as we passed through Llanfair-pwllgwyngyllgogerychwyrndrobwll-llantysiliogogogoch. I got distracted and missed it, which didn't offer me much chance of ever reading the signs at Ayr, Ash, Ely, Lee, Lye, Ore, Par, Rye, Wem or Wye.

There was not much else to see on this run in Wales. From Anglesey you can look across towards embosoming Llanberis. You can catch one of the Britannia Bridge lions if you're very quick. But the sea is largely invisible because the wall is just at view-blocking height.

South of Shrewsbury, a young man, evidently on his way to what he believed would be a pleasing weekend, was on his mobile to the object of his ardour. 'I'm sweating like a pig here,' he said, not very romantically. 'Are you happy I'm on the way down?' The answer to that must have been equivocal. 'I'm on the train now, aren't I?' he snapped. 'Wait for me when I get down. I don't want none of your boyfriends there.' He relapsed into an understandable silence. Next to him there was a group of teenagers, less angst-ridden. 'Did you fuck Matt Savage?' one said. 'No!' the girl cried indignantly. 'Oh,' came the knowing reply. 'It was Nick Daniels then.'

The Shropshire part of the run is quite attractive, and this part of the country is full of pretty, bad railways rather than just pretty bad ones. I love the slouching Severnside run from Newport to Gloucester, but it is best not to be in a hurry. Oxford to Worcester and Hereford has its charms, though the journey is frequently inter-minable, sometimes literally so: much of the route was single-tracked to save money and the slightest mishap leads to exponential delays to which First Great Western sometimes respond by dumping passengers at some wayside station.

Personally, I boycott the line; my friend Matthew Hancock and his brother Chris relieve their frustrations by keeping a special misery diary. '2 November 2007,' reads one Perrinesque entry. 'Four hours late: hit a pheasant, Charlbury. Compensation not given. They did offer two custard creams.'

As I Was Going to St Ives

Back in Cornwall I took the little line from Liskeard to Looe, which had the narrowest of all escapes from closure, being reprieved by Barbara Castle in 1966 with just a fortnight to go. Plat-form 3 at Liskeard is effectively a separate station from the one on the Cornish main line and seemingly a world away, restored to Great

Western chocolate-and-cream yet still with the same stream of announcements: 'Luggage left unattended may be destroyed by the security services,' boomed a voice, as though the Bomb Squad was on hand for just such an eventuality, although the only people around were both outside the station confines having a smoke.

It's a delicious journey. Rabbits scurried away from us, through bluebells and great willowherb. Then suddenly – at Coombe Junction – the train stops, and the driver walks the length of the train to take us in the other direction while the conductor gets out and changes the points so we can negotiate a hairpin bend of Alpine proportions. Between 1879, the line's opening, and 1901 passengers had to walk up this hill. Now the train does the nearest thing to a three-point turn. The conductor said he enjoyed the chance to take the air. Springtime filled the carriage, and Cornwall was alive with birdsong.

'I'm not going to fucking sit next to you,' said a boy loudly.

'Fuck off, then.' It was his big sister, I guessed, the dead spit of Vicki Pollard: pallid breasts pouring out of a pink T-shirt, fat arms, dangly earrings, sour face.

We went past a limpid stream – the East Looe River – past campion and wild garlic. The stream became a river and the river became an estuary. Then I spotted an egret, the west country's most visible symbol of global warming. But in most respects, this was how rural branch lines used to be: quiet, eccentric, gorgeous, marginal. We travelled over old short rails without the ghastly pounding of the Morecambe line: duddle-duh-duh, clackety-clack, duh-duh, clack-clack. Vicki and the boy were snogging now, to the rhythm of the rails. This did not, I thought, *necessarily* rule out the brother-sister theory.

That night I took Cornwall's other improbable branch, St Erth to St Ives. Beeching tried to close this too; indeed Flanders and Swann sang of it as though he had. Yet there is hardly a more environmentally essential line in the country, since St Ives is almost unreachable by road: in summer these trains can be jammed solid. The route from the exotic, almost tropical-looking station at St Erth to the coast was the last broad-gauge route to be opened, in 1877, more than thirty years after Brunel had lost the argument. Yet it travels over a rocky promontory where there hardly seems enough width for a standard-gauge track, never mind one of the Great Western's seven-footers; it is impossible to see how it was done.

The road, such as it is, lies to landward; the line hugs the coast, high above miles of sandy beaches. In our fragile single-carriage, smaller than a bendy bus, we seemed so insubstantial, as though we could be blown away by a single puff. The light was declining gently, and the sea was slowly fading to black; I reflected that this might actually be the loveliest line of all. 'It *is* lovely,' said the conductor, wistfully. 'Mind you, on one of the diagrams we have to do this trip, there and back, thirteen times in a day. You get a bit fed up with it then.'

It was in St Ives that I suddenly started to under-

365

stand all those phone conversations I had overheard and all those I normally suffer when trying to read in what are supposed to be no-mobile compartments (a restriction the otherwise cowed and bossed-around British habitually ignore). Away from the station, walking by the harbourside, I passed a man who was bawling into a mobile phone at a volume others reserve for the quiet carriage. He was about seventy, from Birmingham or thereabouts, and was talking, I surmised, to his son. 'Look, Broyan,' he yelled, 'Joost appreesee-ite it. She's doing well. She's feeling better.' It sounded as though his daughter-in-law had been ill, mentally rather than physically perhaps, and the relationship was under terrible strain.

It was a conversation of delicacy and family intimacy, which – I guessed – he had felt obliged to have away from the guest house and prying ears. Yet he had no concern at all about the presence of passers-by. On French trains one is never bothered by fellow-passengers' phone calls, because they conduct them in a discreet hush. And I realized that the use of mobile phones is just an extension of the old silence and hostility of British railway carriages. The British are oblivious to the people around them, as they always have been. They're just noisier now.

Umerji

Twelve years after Virgin brought their reputation for customer care and service to the railways, I took the 0646 from Euston to Glasgow, which is self-evidently one of Britain's most important trains. What used to be called a crack express.

First-class passengers (single fare: £199.50) are given breakfast. Everyone else (£135.50) is allowed to visit The Shop. I went along and stared at the strange array of goods. They seemed to have been chosen almost wholly at random: five assorted paperbacks, some Ibuprofen, *Hello* magazine, the *Daily Express*, some nasty-looking drinks. I was reminded of the kiosks in Calcutta that sell whatever they can scrounge: months-old copies of the *TV Times*, a Latin textbook, used chewing gum, whatever.

The Shop was otherwise empty except for mine host, a young man with a vaguely estuarial accent called Umerji. I was just staring, appalled, at this pile of cack, dumped contemptuously on the public by a company past bothering. Suddenly he spoke.

'Have a bacon roll, you cunt,' he said suddenly.

At least I thought that's what he said. There was a silence again. Nah, I must have been mistaken. Perhaps it was 'Have a bacon roll or a Coke'. I carried on trying to find something that might make a tasty breakfast, and was beginning to wonder about the culinary possibilities of Ibuprofen...

'...Or you'll be here all fucking day,' said Umerji. There was still no one else about. There was no venom in it: it was a sort of pleasantry. Perhaps this was now standard Virgin customer care and I'm out of touch. I asked him why he called me a cunt. He said he didn't call me a cunt. But he didn't say it indignantly: the denial was even, unblinking, as though this was an accusation that came up from daft passengers every day. That seemed like the final proof that I really hadn't imagined this.

If I had wanted to complain, it was my word against his. Anyway, I didn't want to complain: I thought it was hilarious really, and decided to celebrate, not with a bacon roll, but with a cinnamon and sultana Danish, which tasted like cardboard, and not even nice cardboard. But I thanked him profusely, nonetheless, and felt like warning him.

I mean, what if, one day, instead of a harmless bloke like me, he picked on someone who was writing a book about the railways, someone vindictive enough to stick this incident in his book, using his real name, to illustrate the sheer awfulness of Britain's railways.

Seems like he had a narrow escape.

Paddington

On a cold and misty January evening in 2009, after a day of London meetings, I arrived at Paddington to catch the train home: First Great Western's 1645 to Swansea. It was cancelled: mechanical failure. As an old hand with time to make plans before the next train, the 1715, I played guess-the-platform, got it right, boarded ahead of the crowds, and won a prize, precious enough under normal circumstances but doubly so when the previous service has been cancelled: a seat.

A troubled conscience impelled me to give it up at Didcot to a woman who thanked me so profusely I felt a complete swine, since I'd been ignoring her and all the other standers for the previous forty minutes while I read the papers. She was paying the full rush-hour fare for the 133 miles to Newport, which had gone up the previous week by 9%, from £155 to £169 second-class return. (First-class was up from £237 to £259). 'Nightmare,' said a man close by (seated).

Oh, come on, we ought to be giving these train companies some credit. The genuine nightmare of western governments that strange, cold and economically fearful January was of deflation – falling prices leading to out-and-out depression. No one was doing more to counteract that danger than Britain's rail operators.

And this journey was not really the stuff of nightmares, not by British railway standards. By Swindon, an hour out, just about everyone had a seat. It might then have been at least theoretically possible to accept the regular invitations to visit the buffet, or to ask for a copy of the safety leaflet in Braille.

The train did seem more than normally sluggish as well as crowded, but it got to Newport only a couple of minutes behind schedule. Rats! I had been hoping I might be able to end this book by living up to the title and arriving eleven minutes late. Subsequent study of the timetable showed that this train, though normally off-limits to most passengers holding less expensive tickets, is about the slowest of the day. It takes ten minutes longer to Swansea than usual, or roughly half an hour longer than would have been possible thirty years ago.

At the very start of the first Reggie Perrin book, David Nobbs' hero writes to the traffic manager of British Rail, Southern Region, to complain that his train always arrives eleven minutes late. 'Why don't you re-time your trains to arrive eleven minutes later? They would then be on time every morning.' As fans of the series will know, Reggie was cracking up at the time. But, as we have seen, this has now become standard railway policy. Genius. Not for nothing did he go on to make a fortune from a company called Grot. Thus does life imitate art.

Reggie did something unusual and unBritish: he complained. The train companies regularly report that some overwhelming percentage of their passengers in surveys think the service is all right: only commuters whinge much. I am not that surprised. I myself have only ever written once to First Great Western, which was to say how magnificent the staff were when the system seized up due to the London bombs of 7 July 2005. I could have written hundreds of angry letters. But I didn't – I'm British.

In 2008 the philosopher Julian Baggini produced a book called *Complaint*. He conducted a survey which showed that the British complained far more about corrupt politicians than the Americans did – although the corruption of British politicians is on a miniature scale compared to their US counterparts. But the Americans complained far more about public transport.

And the weather.

This seems counter-intuitive, but maybe not. The British are used to grot when travelling. They expect it. They almost revel in it. I know: I'm one of them. The typical British railway experience is not being sworn at by the likes of Umerji (most buffet attendants are delightful if you can fight through the crowds to reach them); nor does it consist of marvelling at the mountains of Mallaig or sapphire-blue skies at Somerleyton. It is the high-price, low-grade hopelessness of journeys like this.

Among the stories that engrossed me while I was ignoring the standers was a report in that day's *Financial Times* that there were further delays in the fraught process of finding a company to develop a new generation of high-speed diesels to operate on this route. One potential bidder, Alstom of France, had already pulled out, describing the specification set by the Department for Transport as 'unworkable'.

The year 2030 will be the bicentenary of the Liverpool & Manchester. They should postpone any jollifications until 2031, the centenary of the Weir Report recommending total electrification of the system. The new trains, should they ever happen, would be able to transport revellers to the celebrations to mark the fact that the main line from London to the west – Brunel's pride, God's Wonderful Railway – would even then still be using an outmoded, uneconomic and un-sustainable technology.

The previous day's *Guardian* had reported that the new 220mph trains from Madrid to Barcelona had led to a huge rise in rail usage and a twenty per cent drop in domestic air travel. The Spanish government has major plans to expand its high-speed network. That's backward old Spain, you know: mañana, Manuel, all of that. Britain that week was announcing a third runway at Heathrow instead. Yesterday's solution to tomorrow's transport problems. More noise, more filth, more pollution, more climate change, more hypocrisy, more pound-an-hour Stasi agents confiscating your toothpaste. There was talk that a major rail hub for Heathrow might be included as part of the plans. But the object of that was to placate the anti-runway protesters, not to build the rail hub. We know what will be chopped first as soon as the cost mounts.

A couple of weeks earlier, the editor of *Rail* magazine, Nigel Harris, had revealed that when he Googled the phrase 'stupendously incompetent', the first forty-one references that came up all concerned Britain's Department for Transport. No. 42 referred to Inspector Clouseau. The words were a quote from a report by the House of Commons Public Accounts Committee into a new departmental centre in Swansea that was supposed to save taxpayers £57 million but ended up costing them an extra £81 million instead. Perhaps a few of the staff had put the train fares on their expenses.

A mysterious love of the railways remains a peculiar and often secretive British affliction – *le vice anglais*, the love that dare not speak its name. It is wholly unrequited. The people who run the trains do not love us.

Britain's railways desperately need, as they have done since the First World War, a coherent and well-controlled programme of investment and development to enable the country to function in a very uncertain future. This is further away than ever because the irredeemable short-termism of British politics is now compounded by the fragmented nature of the railway system. None of the main actors – Network Rail, the train operators, the rail directorate of the Department for Stupendous Incompetence, the revolving-door secretaries of state, the prime ministers who would far rather be strutting the chandeliered chancelleries of the world – have any incentive to try to build a better system. 'Rail is pricing itself out of the new transport market because improvements are so complicated and expensive,' says Anthony Smith of Passenger Focus.

Yes, political life is full of complex choices. But nothing can excuse almost two centuries of on-going fiasco detailed in this book. I have placed most of the blame on the generations of politicians who have taken the decisions. But it is not the politicians, in the final analysis, who are responsible for the mess. It's us, because we let them do it.

The author regrets to announce...

...that there are errors in this book. The problem for a non-expert writing about the railways is that there is someone, somewhere, who knows more about every single sentence than the author does. The trouble is that it is never the same person twice.

The man who can correct a detail about the early days of the North Devon & Cornwall Junction Light Railway is most unlikely to be the person who can explain the complexities of the relationship between the Department for Transport and the Treasury. I have been fortunate to have had a great deal of help from people at both ends of the spectrum. The railway community is a warm and welcoming one, and many members of it have given generously of their expertise.

But the usual disclaimer applies. This is my book, and any errors and flaws are my responsibility (unless I can find a convenient scapegoat). Furthermore, I never wanted to become an expert. This is a lovelorn passenger's personal view of the railways and I didn't want my passion and anger and love and loathing about this weird industry over-diluted by listening to too many politicians or professionals defending entrenched positions.

On the other hand, I didn't want just to rant, I wanted to gain an understanding of how this mess was created – so I talked to a substantial cross-section of people from whom I believed I might learn something. And I did, in every case. A great many others made useful suggestions, checked facts for me, let me pick their brains, bucked me up, or offered hospitality and/or companionship on my travels.

Top of the list is Colin Divall, Professor of Railway Studies at the University of York, who not only gave me a number of terrific insights, but kindly agreed to read the manuscript, and saved me from falling in to a number of heffalump-traps. My special thanks to him.

And also to: Brian Abell, Fiona Barnes, Simon Barnes, Helen Beeckmans, Lord Berkeley, Steve and Sarah Bierley, David Bishop, David Blagrove, Professor Mark Casson, Hugh Chevalier, Rhodri Clark, Erlend Clouston, John Crane, Anne Dixey, Harold and Jill Drewry, Professor Andrew Evans, Roger Ford, Sir Christopher Foster, Stuart Foulds, Lord Fowler, Dr Terry Gourvish, Matthew Hancock, David Haydock, Murray Hedgcock, Professor David Howell, David and Pru Jeffrey, Stephen Joseph, Livius Kooy, Louisa Kuczinski, Steve Lancey, Christopher Lane, Graham Langer, Mike Lunan, Sir John Major, Richard Malins, Peter Miles, Harriet Monkhouse, Pamela Monkhouse, Gerald Mortimer, Stephen Moss, Dr George Muirhead, Martin Myrone, Andy Newbery, David Nobbs, Sue Phillips, Philip Powell, John Prescott, David Prest, Sir Malcolm Rifkind, Frank Roach, Andrew Roden, David

Sheers, Adrian Shooter, Clare Short, Anthony
Smith, Bill Smith, Dr Gavin Strang, Peter Trewin,
Marilyn Warnick, John Welsby, Tom Winsor and
Christian Wolmar.

A number of railway employees helped me
along the way, some wittingly, some not. Several
who spoke frankly have asked to remain anonymous, a request I have of course respected. I have
also changed the names of those who chatted to
me casually or popped up on my travels just in
case they were too honest, or in breach of some
obscure regulation. The brave driver John Hind is
real. So (according to his name tag) is the
wretched Umerji.

My thanks go also to Richard Milner, Georgina
Morley, Tania Adams, Wilf Dickie, Bruno Vin-
cent, Anthony Forbes Watson, Jacqui Graham,
Lisa Footitt and Kathie Gill at my publishers Pan
Macmillan, the jacket designer Neil Gower, my
agent Carol Heaton, my colleagues at the
Financial Times and the helpful staff at the British
Library, London Library and the nicely named
new research facility at the National Railway
Museum, Search Engine.

And, above all, to my beloved family: my wife
Hilary (not least for her editing skills), my
daughter Vika (who really likes trains) and, for
inspiration, my late son Laurie.

This leads me on to take this chance to say
thank you to the literally thousands of people
who have supported our charity, the Teenage
Cancer Trust Laurie Engel Fund. They ensured
that 2009, as well as seeing the publication of this
book, will also see something far more import-

ant: the opening of the teenage cancer unit at Birmingham for which the fund has been striving since Laurie died in 2005. All the royalties from my previous book, *Extracts from the Red Notebooks*, published in 2007 by Macmillan, go to the fund. See www.laurieengelfund.org.

Readers who wish to correct errors of fact, vent their spleen against the railways or me, pick up on new developments, check the sourcing for my assertions, or join in a discussion about the issues raised by this work are welcome to log on to www.matthewengel.co.uk.

Writing any book is (so I'm told) much like childbirth. There are moments when you think that, if you'd known how much pain was involved, you wouldn't have started. But, more than anything, this one has been enormous fun.

A note on abbreviations

From the earliest days, railways have been be-devilled by abbreviations. It was inevitable when Victorian companies gave themselves names like the York, Newcastle & Berwick Railway; the Lancashire, Derbyshire & East Coast; and the Glasgow, Paisley, Kilmarnock & Ayr.

Now the arcane workings of the business since privatization have produced a new golden age of acronyms. Some railway magazines sometimes seem to be written entirely in capital letters. My favourite new discovery is OLE (Overhead Line Equipment).

This book comes as near as is sensible to being an abbreviation-free zone. The odd LNWR (London & North Western Railway) and GWR (Great Western Railway) may have crept in to denote the early companies. The Big Four companies that ran the industry after 1923 are difficult to write about without their abbreviations: the GWR survived to be joined by the LMS (London, Midland and Scottish), the LNER (London and North Eastern Railway) and the SR (Southern Railway).

Nationalization in 1948 brought forth British Railways, later known as British Rail but, either way, commonly known as BR. In its early days it was run by the BTC (British Transport Commission). The two big railway unions were for many years the NUR (the National Union of Railwaymen) and, to this day, ASLEF (Associated Society of Locomotive Engineers and Firemen).

All these should be obvious from the context, likewise any abbreviations used for the modern train companies such as FGW (First Great Western). The now-defunct GNER was almost never known by its full title of Great North Eastern Railway.

I regret that until now it has not proved possible to slip in my favourite railway acronym YCSFSOYA, which hung in the Atlanta commercial offices of the (American) Southern Railway. It stood for You Can't Sell Freight Sitting On Your Ass.

A note on sources

Publishers these days believe that a large quantity of numbered footnotes or endnotes to denote sources only succeed in irritating the general reader. They do have the advantage of enabling scholarly and sceptical readers to assess the quality of the information on offer, and letting the author swank about the breadth of his research.

The research for *Eleven Minutes Late* has led me to such works as *The Standard Edition of the Complete Psychological Works of Sigmund Freud* (Volume VII) (1953), *The New Annotated Sherlock Holmes: The Novels* edited by Leslie S. Klinger (2006), and *More Leaves from The Journal of A Life In the Highlands from 1862 to 1882* by Victoria R.I. And almost two hundred railway books.

Since this book is primarily intended for the general reader, I have decided not to list every reference, but anyone raising their eyebrow enough to want a source for a particular point should find the answer on www.matthewengel.co.uk.

The general books I have consulted that readers might find most enjoyable and/or useful would include *Fire & Steam* by Christian Wolmar (2007), the only modern general history of Britain's railways, *The Railway Age* by Michael Robbins (1962), *The World the Railways Made* by Nicholas Faith (1990), *The Railway In Town and Country* by Jack Simmons (1986), *The Railway*

Journey by Wolfgang Schivelbusch (1977), *British Railway Enthusiasm* by Ian Carter (2008) and *The Life and Decline of the American Railroad* by John F. Stover (1970).

On more specific subject areas it is invidious to single out books. But I'll attempt a top ten. Numbers two to ten in no particular order might be:

The Last Journey of William Huskisson by Simon
    Garfield (2002)
The Railway Navvies by Terry Coleman (1965)
The Railway Workers by Frank McKenna (1980)
Travelling by Train in the Edwardian Age by Philip
    Unwin (1979)
The Country Railway by David St John Thomas
    (1976)
The Crash that Stopped Britain [Hatfield] by Ian
    Jack (2001)
Britain's Historic Railway Buildings by Gordon
    Biddle (2003)
Government, the Railways and the Modernization of
    Britain: Beeching's Last Trains by Charles Loft
    (2006)
and *The Railway Clearing House in the British*
    Economy 1842–1922 by Philip S. Bagwell
    (1968)

But top of any list must come *The Oxford Companion to British Railway History*, edited by Jack Simmons and Gordon Biddle (1997); a wonderful reference book and a great bog-read too. Or indeed train-read.

The publishers hope that this book has given you enjoyable reading. Large Print Books are especially designed to be as easy to see and hold as possible. If you wish a complete list of our books please ask at your local library or write directly to:

Magna Large Print Books
Magna House, Long Preston,
Skipton, North Yorkshire.
BD23 4ND

This Large Print Book for the partially sighted, who cannot read normal print, is published under the auspices of

THE ULVERSCROFT FOUNDATION

THE ULVERSCROFT FOUNDATION

... we hope that you have enjoyed this Large Print Book. Please think for a moment about those people who have worse eyesight problems than you ... and are unable to even read or enjoy Large Print, without great difficulty.

You can help them by sending a donation, large or small to:

The Ulverscroft Foundation, 1, The Green, Bradgate Road, Anstey, Leicestershire, LE7 7FU, England.
or request a copy of our brochure for more details.

The Foundation will use all your help to assist those people who are handicapped by various sight problems and need special attention.

Thank you very much for your help.